Running Towards the Light

(Postcards from Alaska)

Safe travels -

Nathan o Dorothy.

16/4/16

NATHAN MILLWARD

ISBN 978-0-9572297-1-6

This book follows on from The Long Ride Home (Going Postal as it was known in Australia), about the initial trip from Sydney to London...

New York - Equinunk - Polk - Brighton - Ann Arbor - Detroit - Gary - Chicago - Carlinville - St. Louis - Wichita - Dodge City - Colorado Springs - Salida - Lake City - Silverton - Durango - Cortez - Bluff - Monument Valley - Pahrump - Zion - Grand Canyon - Seligman - Las Vegas - Bakersfield

TORONTO

EQUINUNK

DETROIT

POLK

NEW YORK

CHICAGO

St. LOUIS

UNITED STATES
OF AMERICA

Contents

"If you're going through hell, keep going."

Winston Churchill

Prologue
England

I don't fear many things these days – except perhaps flying still, and writing books – but I do worry about where all this ends.

I mean, all my life I feel like I've been running. Running away from things, running towards things, but always, in every case, running. And I think finally I've realised that all I've actually been running from is myself.

It took my journey across the world by motorcycle to realise this. From Sydney to London I rode for a total of 264 days, covering 23,000 miles and passing through eighteen countries along the way, and yet despite all that, I never did quite manage to leave myself behind.

Certainly, there were times when I was running so fast that I got lost in the moment and allowed momentum to really make me sing and dance. But whenever I stopped, or was forced to stop, by hold-ups at borders and what not, I was always quickly surrounded by all those dark and destructive thoughts I'd been hoping to leave behind.

This was especially the case when I returned home and spent a year locked away in a room writing a book about this journey across the world. All of a sudden there was nowhere to run to and nowhere to hide. For the first time in my life I really had to turn and face myself and figure out who

I was and who I wasn't. And I didn't enjoy this very much, mainly because I didn't always like the person that I found.

The publication of the book didn't help matters either, as the need to publicise it only served to chain me to the events of the past. Then when the Australian publisher decided not to publish it in England I began the long and difficult task of publishing it myself. This was hard and had I been less stubborn I would have walked away from it all and done something else with my life. But I stuck at it, and thus began a long and slow walk along the path of self-destruction, something I soon learnt can prove quite addictive at times.

I hit the bottom when severe burning sensations in all of my bones took me to the doctors, and the MRI scan said nothing was physically wrong, which made the doctor ask: 'how do you feel in yourself?' To which I cried and told her at times I just wanted to die.

'Do I need to worry?' she asked.

'No,' I said, 'I'm too indecisive for that.'

We both laughed. We laughed because what else can you do but laugh. Though I really did feel rotten that day and quite angry with myself. I say angry because at such times you can see yourself, and how you're acting, and how you're behaving, and all you want to do is shake yourself, or equally harm yourself, but you just can't. Instead you feel useless, and pathetic, and weak, and indecisive, and all of the other names you've been called by the people you love in the past. And they only hurt because you know that they had a point.

The doctor prescribed me antidepressants and a stint with a counsellor. I took the pills home and stared at them on my desk for a week before tipping them down the sink. As bad as things had become I felt that to take them would be cheating, and possibly make things worse. After all, I'd got myself into this mess, and it was up to me to get myself out of it. It had to be this way. That was just how I felt.

It certainly wasn't meant to have been like this. That journey across the world was supposed to have been my answer to everything; that one big trip, that lottery win, the thing that I hoped would take me to a place where I could at last be content with what I've done and what I've achieved in life. Instead, that trip opened up Pandora's box, and across the floor my mind tippled, and it felt as though a whole herd of elephants had trampled across it.

I was broken and lost. I didn't know what to do, where to go. I wasn't even sure who I was. It felt as though my whole world was on fire and that I had to keep moving in order to stop myself from burning up. Maybe I should have taken the tablets, numbed the pain for a while and hopefully got my life back on track. But for whatever reason that just didn't feel right. I didn't know what felt right, but it certainly wasn't that.

My fight back finally began with the rebuilding of the bike that had brought me all that way across the world. Dorothy – as goes her name – is a retired Australian Post bike, only 105cc, and a bike that had travelled all that distance needing nothing more than a few spare parts and a regular check-up and service along the way, only then to be abandoned in a shed at the bottom of the garden for the two years that followed.

For a while I hated the sight of her, reminding me most of the person I'd once been: riding through Pakistan, catching boats from Indonesia to Malaysia, dodging traffic in India, climbing the second highest road in the world in the Himalayas, riding through the night across Kazakhstan, Russia and Ukraine. Fearless almost of everything. Two years later I was sat in the doctor's surgery, crying.

Despite covering all that distance, when me and my dad took her apart in the garage at the bottom of the garden we found she needed nothing more than new piston rings, clutch plates and a cam chain, which she didn't really need, but we put one in anyway, just to be sure. I had the mechanic in the local village repair the engine bolt that had been bodged up all the way from Kyrgyzstan. He couldn't believe the bike had come this far, and still looked fit enough to be turned around and ridden all the way back again.

She fired into life the very first kick. What a moment that was. The first step to getting back on the road.

The next step was to retrace my steps. I did this by flying back to Australia, spending a few weeks in Sydney, simply saying goodbye to the place and catching up with old friends. This might sound extreme – a flight all the way to Australia just to do this – but Australia still felt like home to me. It felt like I'd left half of my life and half of my heart there and I needed to go back and retrieve them. And no, Mandy didn't live there anymore; she'd long since moved back home to Canada.

While in Australia, I visited Joe and the rest of the gang at One Ten Motorcycles up in Caboolture. It was great to see them again. Joe, Katrina, Dan – they were like family in a way, the lot of us all going over to some big postie bike gathering down the coast in Coffs Harbour. After that it was just great to hang out back at the shop; Joe setting me up with all sorts of bits to make the bike run that little better, and hopefully faster.

It was actually Joe's mechanic, Mike, who said that sometimes in life you need to retrace your steps in order to make sense of things. It was this that helped me understand what it was that I was doing back in Australia, because up until that point I wasn't entirely sure.

After a week or so in Caboolture, I caught the bus back down to Sydney, spending a few more days there, wandering the streets, trying to make sense of it all, before finally flying home to England. Another step closer to getting back on the road.

In England I went to a few bike festivals, even took Dorothy for a run to the coast. But even with all that, I just couldn't seem to muster the conviction to get back on my feet again. I was lost, and at one point lit a fire and torched so many of my things.

I attacked the shed with a pitchfork, I punched myself in the face until it ached. I think I was trying to kill the past, and me in it. The worst moment was measuring up the rope hanging on the wall in the garage and staring at the beam and wondering if it would support it. But I'd be useless at suicide. I'd kick away the stool and immediately regret it. I can't begin to imagine the bravery such a thing must take.

In a way I don't think I would ever have got myself right again had it not been for two New Zealanders – Rob and Greg – who turned up completely out of the blue one day, arriving on the doorstep of my parents' house near Scarborough, the place I was living at the time.

It turned out that a few years prior they'd read in a magazine of an Englishman who'd ridden his Australian Post bike all the way home from Australia and, both on the cusp of forty, both with wives and children, decided they'd like to give it a try themselves; before they grew too old and developed too many excuses.

They bought a couple of postie bikes, and after a fair bit of planning, shipped them from New Zealand to Singapore, and then proceeded to ride them all the way to England, on a route a little more direct than the one I took, having been fortunate in acquiring visas for Iran.

Their journey took them three months (that's all the time they had due to work and family commitments), and having arrived in England they rode north, to Scarborough, to meet the guy they'd read about in the magazine all that time ago. Instead, they met me.

Rob and Greg stayed at our place for a few nights. Mum and dad put them up in the spare room and loved having a couple of guests to fuss over for a while. We sat and talked about our trips, comparing notes and stories from the road (I was curious to hear what Iran had been like). I think it was good for my parents to see that it wasn't just me that does stupid things; there are plenty of others out there as well.

Finally came time for Rob and Greg to ride back down to London, where they would be handing their bikes over to a shipping agent that was going to send them back to New Zealand, before flying home themselves. They asked if I wanted to join them on the 250-mile ride down to the capital, and with nothing else to do, and the bike now rebuilt, I said 'why not.' I loaded my old panniers with all my old gear, and enough equipment to last on the road for a few days, before following the convoy on its journey south.

We camped wild those few days it took us, sleeping in a bus shelter one night outside the town of Holmfirth, where they filmed *Last of the*

Summer Wine. We passed through Mansfield, the town in which I was raised, as well as Oxford, a place they were both keen to see. It rained pretty much the whole way, but I was on the road again, after almost three years of not being able to find it. I remember feeling completely out of my depth, almost as though the journey from Sydney to London had counted for nothing and I had it all to learn again.

We arrived in London and handed over their bikes to the shipping agent. Rob and Greg caught their flight home whilst I rode back north a hundred miles or so, to stay at the home of Dave and Michelle, good friends who were on holiday and said I could use their place in Hinckley as a base to get back on my feet again. The plan was to settle down and get a job in the area; do the thing that people wanted and expected me to do. But I got to their house, and I sat on their couch, and I looked at myself, and I thought, 'This isn't you, this isn't what you want to do. You know what you need to do.'

I went online and booked a ticket to New York to fly the following week. I called the same shipping company that had sent Rob and Greg's bikes to New Zealand and asked Giles, a good friend and the man in charge there, if he could send my bike to New York by aeroplane, asking him how much as well. 'Bring her next week. Bring her on Tuesday, and she'll be there by Thursday,' he said.

It would cost £600, which I didn't think was so bad.

I spent the next few days processing what I was about to do: fly me and the old bike to America, with the intention of riding it all the way across to the Pacific Coast, and hopefully up to Alaska as well.

Why America? Because it was the nearest place west of England, and deep inside I always felt most comfortable when travelling west. Maybe it's something to do with the sun, and chasing it at the end of the day. I guess it's a simple case of *Running Towards the Light*, and the start of a brand new day.

I just knew that I needed to do something; something big, something desperate, to get myself out of the situation that I'd found myself in, because it couldn't go on for much longer, not like this. I felt so raw and angry; frustrated, desperate and lonely in the world. I suppose at such times some people turn to the bottle, whilst others turn to the road.

I didn't tell anyone of my plan, not even my parents. I couldn't, because I was struggling to convince myself that it was the right thing to do, let alone convince someone else. After all, I did fear getting back on the bike, and back on the road again. The first trip had in many ways been so destructive and taken me to such a dark place. Would going on another adventure improve or worsen that situation? I just didn't know. But as before I knew I had to try. And so once more, I cut the rope and fell.

That following week, completely in silence, I packed up my things, rolled the bike out of Dave and Michelle's shed, and at 5 in the morning began my descent to the shipping agent just outside of Heathrow. My heart was beating like a drum. I looked only forward, not back. I was excited. I was nervous. I was numb. Tell yourself: 'You're about to ship your 105cc motorbike to America and ride it across.' Now shit yourself, because today it's going to be done.

Looking back it was an act of complete madness. I had no plan, no money, no maps, no knowledge of where or how it might end up. It was just a case of taking an almighty leap into the unknown. Besides, by this stage I'd realised that if you happen to find yourself on the path of self-destruction then all you can do is see it through, and hope you come out the other side. There is no turning back.

The process of getting a bike ready for air transit was quite straight forward. I only had to take the front wheel off; the panniers I could leave on the bike complete with all my gear inside. The bike is then put on a wooden pallet, with a box built around it, and that's it, you walk away, or in this case, get a lift to the airport, catch your plane, and in two days' time you meet your bike in New York City.

And that's where this story begins.

Chapter One
New York

I landed in America on the 12th August 2012. Dorothy landed a few days later on the 15th. In the time between landing in America and the bike showing up, I took a Greyhound bus up to a town just outside of Toronto, Canada, as this is where Mandy now lived. I hadn't seen her for two long years, not since I'd written that first book and jumped straight on a plane with the certainty that she was all I wanted out of life, only to learn I was too late; there'd been too much water pass beneath the bridge.

This had left me with a gaping hole in my heart, and I think that was half my problem. It served me right though, as I'd messed her around far too much over the years, and she'd had the good sense to see there'd probably only be more of the same.

This time – two years on – I was only going back to say hello, as the pair of us were still good friends and had kept in touch. For the day I was there we drank coffee, played tennis, went around the shops picking up the things I thought I'd need for my journey across America. I guess you could call it déjà vu, because we did the exact same thing in Australia as I prepared for that long ride home to England.

It was just great to see her again and if nothing else to be reminded of the reason behind all this. I had travelled a lot of miles in the last few years. I'd walked a lot as well. But seeing her again I had no regrets. I'd do it all again, tomorrow, in a heartbeat, though perhaps hoping for a different outcome next time round.

Then came the time for me to get back on the bus to New York and say goodbye again, which was harder now than ever; knowing that there's someone out there who you want to see every single day of your life, but knowing that it might be a few more years until you see them again, that's if you ever see them again at all. I certainly didn't want to go. But I had to go. People move on. And if you love them, I guess you just have to let them.

***

I returned to New York on the Greyhound, checking into a hostel right at the end of the tracks in Brooklyn. It was run by a man named David, who had converted his two bed apartment into a place with ten bunk beds and a constant stream of travellers passing through. It was in a suburb deep in the heart of Brooklyn – the last stop on the subway – in a predominately black neighbourhood, which was unnerving at first, simply because I'd never stayed in such a place before. Yet no one even seemed to notice or care. We were invisible really, and I never felt unsafe. There was probably no reason to, much like the Aboriginals back in the Australian Outback, where I'd been scared to talk to them during the early days of that first trip, only to learn that it was only my own fears that was holding me back.

Now in New York, I caught the subway and paced the streets of Manhattan, walking through Central Park, past the Empire State Building, along Fifth Avenue, then sitting in Times Square on the steps, blown away by the scale and size of it all; the noise, the commotion, the traffic, the massive billboards and flashing neon lights. I'd been to New York before, but it felt different this time, like the start of something massive, which I guess it was; the second half of my journey across the world.

I walked along Broadway, picked up a slice of dollar pizza, then back to pacing the streets, still not feeling too good. I think it was just the reality setting in, that I was here now, and that I was going to have to somehow get to the other side of the country on the meagre resources that I had; around £500 by the time everything else had been paid for.

In the end, the shipping company had to contact me and ask if everything was alright, as I'd not been to the airport to pick up my bike yet, and if I didn't come for it soon then they would start charging me storage costs. The reality was that I was scared. I knew what picking up my bike would mean; that the journey would be underway and I'd have no choice but to hit the road and be alone again out there, this time knowing exactly what to expect.

The day I rode out of Sydney – after those few short days of planning – I had the benefit of naivety and ignorance. I set off oblivious and discovered what a trip like this would entail as I went along. This time I knew exactly what to expect; those times of loneliness and worry, of breakdowns and struggling at night to find suitable places to sleep. I imagine it's a bit like getting married and then divorced, and wondering if you should get married again. Second time around you know what to expect and so you might be reluctant to give it another try. But what do you do; get on with life, or put your life on hold forever?

The difference this time was that I knew there was no happy ending to be found at the end of this trip, as I'd mistakenly thought there would be at the end of the first. Naively I'd seen that first trip as the solution to all my problems; the cure of all my faults. Instead I found nothing at the end of it. No sense of satisfaction or contentment. I just found England, and nothing in it to necessarily hold me there.

This seems to be one of the biggest deceits of life; that somehow you conquer it by achieving that one thing you dream of. Sadly it doesn't seem to work like that. Once you achieve that dream, you soon move on to the next one. Perhaps it's what makes us human; the endless desire for something better, or something else. That's why I sometimes think the concept of contentment is just an illusion; another dream to chase.

Finally, I went and collected the bike from JFK airport. It wasn't as difficult a process as I thought it might be. I simply caught the free shuttle bus to the Virgin Atlantic cargo department, paid a $40 documentation fee, had my documentation stamped, then took another free shuttle bus to the other side of the airport, to the customs office.

Here I had to explain that I was only bringing in the bike for a short length of time and how it was just for personal use and that I would be exporting it back to England at the end. The process of shipping a bike to America is actually easier than to most other countries, as you don't need an expensive Carnet de Passage, and the shared language definitely helps.

Back at the Virgin Atlantic cargo depot I was directed through to the main warehouse and told to sit and wait. A short while later, a forklift truck brought a large wooden box and placed it on the ground in front of me. It felt like Kathmandu all over again, only on this occasion, rather than a team of eager helpers to assist me crack open the crate, I was given a crowbar and left to get on with it myself.

As I ripped the crate apart, a man named Vince approached and asked if the bike emerging from the crate was Dorothy. I was puzzled for a moment until he explained that he had just read my first book on Kindle and recognised the bike from the pictures on the internet. He said he'd enjoyed the book, which was kind of him. It was surreal to meet someone who knows so much about you, yet you know absolutely nothing about them.

We stood and talked for a while, just about life and stuff. He was a long-distance truck driver, picking up his next load from the airport and taking it to a destination far away. Vince took some photos of me and the bike and emailed them to me a few months later. I looked happy that day, though it wasn't to last, as that fifteen mile ride from the airport to the centre of Manhattan was one of the most terrifying of this entire endeavour...

The front brake didn't work properly after I snapped the lever unloading the bike from the crate. The front wheel also had a slow puncture having snagged the tube changing the tyres over. It was drizzling with rain,

21

making the road incredibly greasy, and with no maps or route planned for getting to downtown Manhattan all I could do was aim for the cluster of tall buildings in the distance.

Worst of all I had to take the interstate: six lanes of high-speed traffic, doing 40mph, head on the tank, flogging the bike and hoping that no one rear ended me in the process. That's when I realised I'd not tightened the back wheel nut, and so that sloppiness at the back end I was feeling was caused by the wheel wobbling around, and all I could do was hope it didn't fall out between the airport and downtown Manhattan. Thankfully it didn't and I spent the afternoon riding around Manhattan, waiting for it all to sink in.

To think I'd ridden that same bike around Darwin, Bangkok, Delhi, Islamabad, as well as London; it just didn't make any sense. Now I was here in New York and everything seemed so big and I felt so small. It was intimidating, especially the traffic, and I didn't want to think about which route I would take out of here. Instead I went back to David's apartment and spent a few days getting prepared for the journey ahead.

I bought a cheap compact camera, a couple of maps from a bookstore, and also spent an age trying to source a replacement brake lever as no where in New York seemed to have one for an Australian Post bike; with no surprise by that. A custom bike shop in Brooklyn was able to order me one, whilst from a nearby scooter shop – owned by a man originally from England – I was able to stock up on replacement inner tubes, as I always liked to travel with a few spare. It was all just a very strange and surreal time. It was almost like being on auto-pilot, just doing what I needed to do, one step at a time.

***

The day I came to finally leave New York I packed up my things, said goodbye to David and his temporary clan of travellers, and made my way through the streets of Brooklyn. As I rode beneath the subway on Broadway

– the road that leads into Manhattan – I was pulled over by the police. I jumped off the bike and asked the policeman what the matter was. He said that I couldn't ride here with a foreign number plate.

I explained that many people do this – bring bikes from abroad to ride here – but he didn't believe me and said that I would have to go and speak to the DMV (the Department of Motor Vehicles), which had a big office on the other side of Brooklyn. He gave me directions to get there and sent me on my way.

I was tempted to just ignore him and carry on going. Get the hell out of the city and not look back. But I thought, 'if I'm going to get pulled over here, then where else am I going to get pulled over, and how often, and how long before someone impounds my bike?' So I followed his directions to the DMV, parking outside on the pavement with permission from the security guard patrolling the area, before heading upstairs to join a queue of people, waiting in line to see an attendant.

When finally called to the desk I explained my situation to a lady who consulted with her colleague and left me stood anxiously hoping for good news. But it wasn't good news. 'You're either going to have to ship the bike home to England, or ship it across to San Francisco if that's where you're heading, but there's no way you can ride it here.' I didn't argue. There was no point, though I knew that this lady, and the policeman, were wrong. I walked outside and buried my head in my hands, wondering just what I was going to do. I didn't know what I was going to do.

In the end I rode up to a Starbucks on the corner as I knew I could get free Wi-Fi there and had with me a small laptop on which to do so. I began by sending an email to the company that had issued my liability insurance for the bike, as surely if you can get insurance cover for a foreign bike here in America, from an American company, then you can in fact ride it here. But the company was closed for the day as it was a public holiday.

I tried Googling for answers, before finally posting on ADVRider. com, an America-based adventure motorcycle site with members who've done this sort of thing before.

Several responded to say I should be okay; one of them contacting DMV directly and having head office in Washington confirm that as long as my bike was taxed and tested in my own country, and that I was the registered owner, then I was okay to ride it in America for the maximum period of a year. It was the confirmation I needed that the policeman and the DMV here in New York were both wrong, though I still remained incredibly nervous of being pulled over again in the future.

By this time it was too late to hit the road out of the city, deciding to check back into David's hostel and leave the following morning. Unfortunately the hostel was fully booked, as were most of the other hostels in New York that evening, what with it being a public holiday and all. Instead, I parked up in the centre of Manhattan, just off Fifth Avenue.

It was raining so I put a cover over the bike, as the panniers weren't waterproof, before going for a wander around the shops, just trying to get a grip of myself. It wasn't a good time. I was barely hanging on by a thread and felt quite vulnerable and alone.

I walked the streets of Manhattan, pacing myself out. I came to the conclusion while doing this that I really did need some help getting out of the city as I couldn't do it alone. I went into an electronics shop and bought a hundred dollar satellite navigation unit, as the bike now had a cigarette lighter that I'd be able to charge it from.

Sadly, when I returned back to the bike, I discovered that the charger was broken and that I wasn't able to make it work. The satnav only had a quarter of its battery life in it, I wouldn't be able to charge it, and I didn't know how long the charge would last.

I paced the streets some more. It wasn't long before it was midnight. I hurt right now. I hurt from the situation that I found myself in. Alone in this city, with an old motorbike, that couldn't go very fast, and the intention of riding it all the way across America. And still the rain would fall.

I wheeled the bike beneath the canopy of a loading bay. By this time there was hardly anyone else about. Between the wall of the loading bay and Dot's front tyre I squeezed myself, sitting in a nest of cigarette butts, trying to hide from the world.

A short while later a police car pulled up no more than five metres away. I hid behind the bike's front wheel, trying not to be seen. The lights of the police car were flashing red and blue. The occupants were getting out and looking around. There was commotion. I didn't know what to do. I sat there and didn't make a sound. They were there for almost an hour, and I still didn't know what to do. By now it was 2am. I was cold and wet. I didn't think they were looking for me.

At 4am I finally snapped, stood up, took the cover off the bike, put my waterproof jacket on, my helmet, and my gloves. I plugged in the new satnav system, keyed in a destination to the north west of the city, and set off. I couldn't sit there forever in that pile of cigarette butts; I had to move on.

The streets were full of puddles. There wasn't much other traffic about. I cruised through Times Square, half expecting to be pulled by another police car at any moment. I was scared.

With the rain falling heavier and my jeans getting wet, I hastily pulled into the driveway of an amusement park on the west shore of Manhattan, alongside the Hudson River. As I was putting on my waterproof trousers the security guard came out of his booth and asked if I was alright. I told him that I was, making small talk about the rain and about life in general. He had a whole family to feed and I felt for him, sat in his booth, alone through the night. I said 'Goodbye,' and this time properly hit the road.

***

The satellite navigation unit was nestled in the pouch of the tank bag that James and Nancy had given me all the way back in India, back when we rode over the Himalayas together. I followed the arrows of the flickering unit, holding so much hope in that little device and its quarter battery charge that it felt as though my whole life depended on it. I was certainly obedient to its directions as it took me from one dual lane highway to the next, hitting junctions I never would have made had I been on my own.

The battery ran out just as I hit New Jersey. I didn't have a clue where to go now. It was perhaps 6am, just light, raining heavily. I pulled into the car park of a bank that had a canopy under which I could shelter from the rain. I was cold, wet, and hungry; tired also from having had no sleep that night.

There was a supermarket on the other side of the road that had just opened for the day. I went in there and bought bananas, some bread rolls, a few other bits and pieces, and a coffee from the machine. Paying at the self-service checkout I knocked the coffee flying, spilling it all over the floor. As I did my best to mop it up, the woman using the machine beside me made some pleasant remark about the incident and from that we got chattering. She asked where I was going. 'I don't know, I'm lost,' I said.

This lady couldn't help me as she didn't know her way very well either. But she asked another man; a big stout man, with a kind face, who knew the area well, guiding me outside and beginning to point in all sorts of directions, instructing me how to get out into some clear open road.

'Take this road, take that road, left here, right there,' he said. I took little of it in, but was just grateful for the care that these two people showed me that day. Denise back in Mount Isa would have been proud; the fairies and angels of America were alive and well.

It wasn't long before I was completely lost again. I went round and around in circles. I ended up in an out of town shopping precinct which I just couldn't get out of. I could see the road I wanted, but I just couldn't figure out which slip road to take. Eventually I found it, and then I found myself on the busiest highway in the world, or that's what it felt like, waiting for the moment I got rammed from behind and pushed right through into the afterlife.

I pulled into a gas station to escape the heat, asking a woman filling her car with fuel if she knew exactly where we were. She didn't really know either, but she had a map in her car and together we studied it and tried to figure out where I should head. The conclusion was north-west, though which road, and to where, was anyone's guess. This really was quite stupid; riding across America with no real clue as to what I was doing, or how I was going to do it. I was just riding, because that's all at this time I knew how to do.

I returned to the highway of death, riding it for five minutes before realising I'm going to die if I don't get off it, taking a gamble on an exit, any exit, and following it around. And before I knew it, I was in peaceful suburbia; big old white-washed houses, perfectly manicured lawns, the American flag flapping on flag poles and the world suddenly appearing a whole lot quieter and calmer. It now about 2 o'clock on a warm Saturday afternoon, somewhere in New Jersey.

I passed a small car repair shop by the side of the road. A man stood outside sanding an old door on a workbench. I turned around and pulled into the yard in front of him. The man stopped sanding the door and asked if he could help. I told him about the power socket not working and wondered if he knew of a good auto electrician in town. The man said he was a good one himself, instructing me to unload all of my gear from the bike, while he went and got some tools from his workshop.

The man's name was John, in his sixties and a biker himself. He had a big Harley Davidson and planned on riding it across to San Francisco one day in the distant future. When I told him that was where I was heading, he just kind of scratched his head, looked at the bike and said 'Okay,' to suggest he didn't quite believe me, though I couldn't blame him for that.

John worked out that it was just a bad connection and that the wires had come loose from where the charger connects to the battery. He replaced the connectors, plugged it all back in and when we tried the satnav it was with great relief that it fired back into life and started charging again. I was so relieved, because now I had a vague idea of which direction I was going in. West; in the direction of the setting sun.

I reloaded all my gear, thanked John (who wouldn't take a dime), and returned to the road. For a destination I punched in Equinunk, the name of a small town in Pennsylvania where ten years previously I'd worked as a tennis instructor at a summer camp for kids from Manhattan as part of the Camp America programme. By chance, on that same ADVRider forum that had helped me with the DMV, I came across a man going by the name of Johnny Equinunk, and a few years back I'd emailed him and said: 'Is that the same place?' And he said: 'Yes, and if you're ever around this way then please drop by.' He knew I was in America. I'd emailed to tell him. So that's where I was heading now.

By this stage the road was single carriageway. The scenery to the side was quite pleasant. Green and rolling hills, home-made wooden white fences and huge red barns with tractors parked outside. This being a Saturday there were also a variety of local festivals taking place in the small villages I passed through. It was definitely a pleasant world out here, now in rural Pennsylvania.

There was however one moment that afternoon I'll never forget. I'd pulled over at a gas station that had a picnic table way off to the side of the forecourt, on which I sat and drank a coffee and ate a bag of crisps. The sun was hot and I was really tired, putting my head on the table and the next thing I knew waking up half an hour later with a jolt.

To suddenly find myself in this situation; to wake up in it – a random gas station somewhere in America, alone and scared and not really sure where I was heading – was a horrible moment. I thought: 'What the hell am I doing here, why am I doing this? I can't do this. I'm scared.'

The only answer I had to all of that was the harsh reality that I'd chosen to be there, because for whatever reason, for whatever purpose, I'd deemed this journey across America as the most important thing I had to do in my life, and I was doing it, whether I really wanted to or not. I know that sounds stupid. Surely you only do the things in life you want to do. But I don't really think it's as simple as that, otherwise we'd all be happy, and from my experience, many of us are not.

Finally, I peeled myself off that bench, slumped back into the saddle, kicked the old bitch into life and pounded her back on to the highway, adopting my regular spot riding right into the gutter, with one eye to the front, one eye on the mirror to see what was coming up behind.

You never relax travelling at these speeds on these kinds of roads. You're permanently alert, guarding yourself against the people that might not have seen you yet. I rode through the afternoon and into the evening, until I was perhaps five miles from Equinunk, when a motorbike shot past in the opposite direction.

It was a trail bike, a big KLR 650, which I thought was a bit odd as all I'd seen so far were Harley Davidsons. The next thing I knew the bike was right behind me, flashing me to pull over. I did so, putting the bike on the stand and going to enquire what the man might want. By chance it turned out to be Johnny Equinunk, on his way to fetch some food!

'Nate,' he said, 'I thought you might be heading this way. Come on, let's have dinner.'

And that's exactly what I did.

It was certainly good fortune that John had been travelling along the same road that evening, as while I knew he lived in Equinunk, I didn't know where exactly, as I'd forgotten to write down his address. I would have had to find somewhere to get online to retrieve it from the email conversation we'd had in the past. The reality, if our paths hadn't crossed that evening, would have been me sleeping in a tent somewhere out of sight by the side of the road, something I wouldn't have enjoyed very much at all, so to have met John that night was a godsend.

Chapter Two
Equinunk

John lived in a house in the woods. You took a long gravel drive from the main road to get there. In fact, it was a community of houses in the woods, all built haphazardly amongst the trees. To get to John's house we took a left off the main gravel road and then further along on the right it was there, built quite strangely in a basin in the earth as it rolled down and away from the road.

It would make a great Hobbit's house, the way you walked across a short wooden gangway to get to the main door, the first floor like a bungalow, with all the living quarters, then steps down into the basement which, because the house was built in a hole, had a door that opened out into the world, green and peaceful as it was.

John lived here alone after his mother passed away a few years before. He wasn't married, had no kids, and I imagined life out here could be quite lonely. He was a tall, stout man, with a thick bushy black moustache and a gentle demeanour. I believe he was in his fifties, working as a long-distance lorry driver and probably the kindest man you could ever hope to meet.

He said I could stay as long as I wanted, and so could Dorothy, who he doted on having read all about her on the internet. As well as the KLR he was riding when I met him that first night, John also had an old Yamaha sportsbike from the eighties, which he was slowly restoring in the basement, a handsome thing that John sat on and talked about with great fondness. He was going to ride it far some day. And I hoped that he would.

My bed was also in the basement, in the corner behind the stairs. I slept like a log that first night at John's, waking the next morning feeling a whole lot better than I did after the previous night, sat up amongst the cigarette butts of Manhattan. I was just relieved to have made it out of the city and out here to where there was a little more space to think and to breathe. After the chaos of getting from England to here it was just what I needed; a floating island of sanctuary to rest upon, in a sea of disarray.

The following morning we went for a ride on our motorbikes, taking a back road all the way into the main town of Hancock, some twenty miles away. It was gravel road for the most part, through this rural landscape of Pennsylvania; partly woodland, sometimes flat and agricultural, often with pretty lakes that you could ride right alongside, homes built on the shore, campsites nestled in the trees and wild deer darting amongst them. To say we were only perhaps 200 miles from New York, it felt like we were in another world entirely.

I followed John's shadow as he took it steady on his much bigger machine. My bike could only cruise at around 40mph, but on this terrain that was perhaps fast enough.

We stopped at a small festival taking place on the green outside an old wooden church. I bought a postcard from a man who took pictures of local wildlife and made them into cards. We were well away from the main road, passing through communities that felt as though they never wished to be found. It was a great way of spending a day, and John the perfect guide.

A little further along we swung off the road and into a clearing in the forest where we found a rifle range. When I say a rifle range, I simply mean a line of five targets built in a clearing at which anyone could turn up at their leisure and shoot. There were no marshals, no books to sign or fees to pay. If you have a gun you come here in the warm summer sun and shoot with it.

Practising were grandfather and grandson Frank and Thomas. Frank must have been in his eighties; Thomas was eleven or twelve, up from suburban New Jersey to visit his grandparents, who today were teaching him how to shoot. John and I introduced ourselves and stood around talking. Thomas couldn't believe it, he'd never met someone from England before. He wanted to take photos of me and text all of his friends to tell them about the weird hairy hobo he'd just met at the shooting range.

John told them all about my exploits on the old red bike parked across the way. I never talked about my trip unless I had to. It always made me feel a little uncomfortable, mainly because I knew the truth of it (the truth being how these big adventures are never the heroic acts they are perceived and often presented to be, and that in fact they are often born out of a certain sense of despair), and I'd rather John not have said a word. But he was more proud of it than I was and so all I could do was stand there blushing, hoping that soon the story would end.

When Frank asked if I wanted a go with the rifle I told him I'd never fired a real gun before, but that I would give it a go. Carefully, I took a hold of the rifle; long, metal and wood, striding up to the shooting plate that had a plinth on which you could rest the barrel. Frank loaded five bullets, the most the gun would hold. He told me to look through here, and line it up with that, then squeeze the trigger, and watch it doesn't kick back and black your eye. I held the gun firm. I lined it up as best I could, then, 'whack.' I fired my first bullet. And cracked a massive smile. 'Whack, whack, whack, whack,' went four more bullets as I sent them down the range.

I half expected the man in the next village to drop down dead from my aim which had gone astray, yet when me and Thomas bounded over to the target and looked at where the paper had been penetrated we both stood there in silence, because I'd hit the bull, and the four other bullets were all within a two-centimetre range. Beginner's luck!

We loped back down to where John and Frank were stood and examined the target, to which they both said: 'Well I'll be darned!' I was a sharp shooter with a gun.

I have to admit to quite enjoying it; something I didn't think I would. I think it was the sense of power, or the release of power, almost as though the gunpowder is made up of grains of your stress and worry, and when you fire it down the range you let go of some of the stuff that's been on your mind. Perhaps that's the core of its appeal, and on this day I could well understand it

After a while we said our farewells to Frank and Thomas before carrying on our way into town. I needed some things from Kmart: a roll mat, some plastic storage containers and gas canisters for my stove. John explained how the superstore was the main employer in town now that main industry of mining had fallen by the wayside. He corrected me for taking my own trolley back to the rack, insisting it would do a man out of a job. This part of the world was struggling just like so many others. Few jobs, dying industry, people struggling to earn a crust. John didn't earn much as a lorry driver, he just earned enough.

John had to go off driving the next day, planning on being out on the road for over a week. He told me to stay as long as I liked and gave me a key to his house. I shook his hand on the driveway and we gave each other a massive hug. I told him I'd see him again, though I wasn't sure when. He drove off in his truck, waving goodbye as he did so. I turned and walked back into the house, closed the door behind me, and spent the next three days getting my mind and gear together for the long journey ahead.

∗∗∗

In the basement I laid everything out on the floor: clothes, tools, electronic equipment, camping gear; all the stuff I threw together before riding down to Heathrow with the two New Zealanders, Rob and Greg. I'd not packed for America, only for those few days riding down from Scarborough to London. As before, I would simply have to manage with what I had and pick up the things I was missing along the way.

That may sound scary, but what you soon realise is that as long as you have access to money, the internet, and a reliable motorbike, you can pretty much go anywhere and do anything. The limitation is largely mental. The trick is learning not to worry about such things, and letting go of the desire for routine and security which tends to characterise a life in the real world. There is none of that out here. There are no walls to hide behind. If it rains, you feel it. If it's cold, you get cold. If you're scared and feeling lonely. Then you are scared. And you are lonely.

In terms of clothing I had a pair of old blue jeans, bought from a shop on the high street and not worn for several years, but they would suffice as a pair of riding trousers. I had an assortment of t-shirts, a warm blue jumper and to keep me dry an authentic Royal Mail postal jacket, kindly donated by a stranger named Simon, who I met at a bike festival earlier in the year. He previously worked for the Royal Mail and said I could have his old jacket; fluorescent orange, with reflective silver strips and the Royal Mail insignia on the left breast.

For much of the journey I would also wear the body warmer given to me by the Indonesian bike gang I met back in Sumatra. They were called the BigZoners, their motto; 'Keep Brotherhood Til Die', embroidered on the back of the jacket. The jacket was something I'd treasured ever since meeting them in the early stages of that initial trip from Sydney to London, the lot of us all keeping in touch via Facebook ever since.

Beneath the jacket I wore a red-check flannel shirt, one that I'd picked up cheap in the sale and just felt comfortable in, rolling up the sleeves to the elbow and eventually wearing it until the fabric wore thin. In the hot midday sun I would roll the sleeves down to keep my arms from burning.

In terms of footwear, I'd brought a pair of old flip-flops, some white Converse high-tops and a pair of sturdy Australian work boots. The latter were brown leather, with an elasticated panel in the ankle and a toggle on the back to help you pull them on. They were one size too big and so required an extra pair of socks.

My helmet was an interesting thing. It was bought from a shop in the town of Matlock, an old bikers' haunt right in the heart of Derbyshire, England. I'd taken my Nan there for a coffee, the same grandmother who had given me advice at the beginning of that first book. She saw me pick up the helmet and try it on, and so kindly offered to buy it for me. It cost £40, and was white, with red and blue targets on each side. A lady in the Starbucks back in New York thought it was a nod to the famous cover art by The Who. Others thought it would make a good target for rednecks and gangbangers. But I liked it, I thought it was cool.

The rest of my riding attire consisted of a red and white neckerchief that I tied around my face to keep the sun off, while in the Kmart I'd been to with John I'd bought a four-dollar pair of sunglasses with a diamanté encrusted 'J' on the left pane. They were aviator style, and all in all, what with the flannel shirt, neckerchief and a new pair of beige gardening gloves, I looked like an extra from *Brokeback Mountain*.

In terms of camping gear, my tent this time had come from an automotive supplies shop back where Mandy lived in Canada. It had cost $18 and despite claiming to be a two man tent, when I put it up for the first time I soon discovered that my head pushed against the fabric at one end, and my feet pushed against the fabric at the other. It was however incredibly light, easy to put up and take down, and those are the two key areas when camping on a motorbike.

My sleeping bag was fairly new, picked up from a camping store back in England. My stove, however, was one I'd bought in Kyrgyzstan; the sort you screw on to the top of small gas bottles. I'd used it to cook instant noodles and tea as I passed through Kazakhstan, Russia and Eastern Europe. On that occasion I'd cooked everything in a reused sweetcorn tin. This time around I'd bought a set of collapsible pans, as well as a folding cutlery set with vivid blue handles.

I carried with me a ten-inch laptop, for ease of uploading photos and getting online, as many places you go now have free Wi-Fi. To take pictures I had the same Canon 1100D digital SLR that I bought back in Bangkok after the original camera had packed up there. After years of abuse, the auto-focus and built-in flash didn't work on this one either, but I would just have to make do as I couldn't afford a new one. I had a mobile phone but no local sim and didn't plan on getting one as who would I call if I broke down anyway?

For sentiment, and for protection, I carried the six-inch hunting knife that I'd bought from a market stall in the town of Kashgar, on the western fringe of China. I'd bartered hard for the knife, the seller agreeing a price, then changing his mind, paying around ten dollars for it in the end. The blade was useless really; made from cheap metal that would rust and bend at the tip. I liked the handle though. It was black, and encrusted with red and white stones, with a copper grasp joining the blade to the handle. The sheath was tan leather and decorated with metal eyelets and engravings.

I kept the knife in the black fake-leather tank bag James and Nancy had given me in India, it bought for their tour of the country by Royal Enfield. Whenever camping wild, I would sleep with the knife beside me, even inside the sleeping bag, just in case anything happened in the night. Thankfully it never did. Also in the tank bag I carried a small black diary, which I would update, all the way until Death Valley, at which point I would lose it, and so this book is written from memory, not from notes, for better or for worse...

As for tools, apart from being one, I had the original assortment I'd carried with me on that first trip. A motley crew of spanners, screwdrivers and wrenches. Hardly any of them served much purpose, but I daren't throw them out in case one day they did. For storage I slung them all in a blue tie-top bag previously used for tent pegs. I also carried a handful of spare spokes, a spare front sprocket, a couple of spark plugs, not to mention three or four spare inner-tubes in case we picked up more punctures.

Finally, to hold all these things I had with me the black canvas throw over panniers that I'd bought from a back-street bike merchant in Delhi, back when I was preparing to go into Pakistan and felt I needed something more subtle than the bright orange ones I'd originally set off with. They cost around twenty pounds and in a way were completely useless. That first day I used them on the ride up to Manali the bottom and rear panels began to tear, and so in Manali I paid three local Indian boys to cut up an old leather jacket and stitch it in place in order to reinforce the vulnerable areas.

This worked to some extent, but for the rest of the trip I had to carry with me a needle and thread and almost on a daily basis repair any new tears, often at the seams which just kept on splitting. I later decorated the panniers with stitched flags of some of the countries I passed through. As terrible as the panniers were, somehow I felt attached to them and saw them as being a part of this experience.

As for Dorothy, the bike that now sat in John's basement, it was quite surreal to think that this was the same bike I'd come across that day in Joe's shop, back in the Queensland town of Caboolture. From there to here, a distance of almost 25,000 miles, which, if you include the down-time in England, spans almost three and a half years of my life.

At times I could have pushed her off a cliff, if only to be rid of the obligation I felt to get her back on the road again. Strange to think your fate can become so entwined with that of a motorbike, but no way could I have left her in that shed and come across America on anything else. *We* had to get back on the road, just as much as *I* did.

Would she make it across America, and in what state? It's fair to say that a 105cc motorbike capable of cruising at around 40mph isn't the most sensible choice of vehicle for travelling so far on, but I'd come to realise that no vehicle is perfect for a trip like this; all make compromises somewhere, be it their weight or complexity or even something simple as it being difficult to get tyres for them. Dorothy's only weakness was her speed, but if she could do a hundred miles an hour that's how fast I'd have ridden her across America, not seeing anything along the way, so at least she slowed me down, and forced me to engage with the world through which I was passing. She was then the perfect complement to my mind.

All I had to do now was plan a route out of here. That was a daunting task in itself, as when you look at a map of America you see nothing but a tangle of roads and directions in which to go off in. And not wanting to use the interstates – because of the speed of the traffic – meant that I was going to have to pick a route cross country, along the back roads, and so suddenly America seemed a lot bigger than its three thousand mile width would suggest.

After all, it had been 3,000 miles across Australia, but the miles in that country involved one road up the coast, one road across the Outback, and one road up to Darwin. Two turns in that entire distance, which definitely wasn't going to be the case here in America. I would have to take lots of turns and no doubt cover more miles than I originally thought it might be.

My original plan had been to drop down from New York to Philadelphia, on to Washington and then take Route 50 – the Lonely Highway – all the way across to the west coast. But with my fear of being pulled over again by the police I was keen to avoid the major cities, that decision pushing me much further north into Pennsylvania.

So from here to San Francisco I wasn't quite sure which way I would go; just head west I guess and figure it out as I went along. As for Alaska, I would give thought to that only once I'd made it across to the Pacific Coast, something I calculated would take around two to three weeks…

The reason for such haste was money. My budget to get myself across America was £500, that was simply all the money I had left after shipping the bike here, paying the £150 for mandatory third-party insurance and all the bits I'd needed to get myself back on the road. I didn't know if that was going to be enough money or not, especially as it had to cover food, fuel and accommodation. But sometimes, if you have the right time, and the right moment, you just have to go, and figure the rest out later.

***

Before leaving John's place I took a ride to Camp Equinunk, only a few miles down the road. I had worked there in the summer of 2001, for ten weeks between term times at college. For those ten weeks at camp I was a tennis instructor, though most of the kids were better than me, so my job really was to pick up balls after them. I also had a bunk of twelve kids to look after, my bed by the door to stop them from escaping and getting up to mischief at night.

They were around twelve years of age, all from privileged backgrounds in New York City, making them difficult to control. I really struggled and would often be woken in the night by sweets that had been thrown at my head. Or they would crawl under the bed and kick at the mattress, or set fire to aerosol cans and almost burn the place down. At the age of 21, with no experience of looking after children before, I didn't know how to keep on top of them, and so after a while I just stopped caring and let them get on with it.

Despite this, I had an amazing summer, mainly because of all the other international counsellors I was there with. At night we'd all sit outside the hobby centre or down by the lake, just talking and hanging out. Some nights we'd be taken in the yellow school bus to a town nearby for a drink in the Delaware Inn, a rough old place that I learnt has since been closed down. On the way back from the bar we'd all sing songs and put someone on 'deer watch,' as on these rural roads wild deer can and do jump out at any moment and cause real carnage.

Ten years on and I was now riding up the familiar driveway, past the nest of wooden huts to the left, up the hill, with the tennis courts to the right, and just before that the food hall where the kids would sing their songs and get up on tables and generally kid around. There were no kids here now; camp had just finished and they would all be back in New York, getting ready for the new school term, as by now it was midway through August.

At the top of the hill I parked outside the main office. Before taking a look around I thought I ought to ask the office staff if it would be okay, and having stepped inside I was stunned to see Caroline, the office clerk from the time when I was there, still there after all the time that had passed. I looked at her and said: 'Caroline?' And she said: 'yes,' and then I explained that I'd been there all those years ago and that I remembered her. She took a long look at me, before saying: 'Tennis, you taught tennis. Nathan isn't it?' It helped that I used to date her friend, Abi, who looked a bit like Isla Fisher. At least that's how I remember it.

Caroline was more than happy for me to have a walk around, leaving the bike at the top of the hill and taking a stroll down the bank to where the camp flattened out and the baseball pitch was found. Beyond that were the basketball courts, then the circle of benches with a camp fire often lit in the centre of them. I walked to the right, to where a new outdoor swimming pool had been built, then down into the square of bunk houses, almost thirty in total, with a giant lawn in the middle, and a lone tree planted in the centre of that.

The bunk houses had barely changed one bit, still red and white and made of wood. I had difficulty locating the one that I used to be in. Whether it was faded memory or that they'd remodelled the inside of them, I just couldn't fathom which of them it was. After wandering around a few and just reminiscing for a while, I walked down to the camp's lake, taking a wooden footbridge over the road to get there.

The lake itself is beautiful, surrounded by forest, with a jetty from which the kids would dive or just sit out in the summer sun. Despite the trouble they gave me, they were still great days and I would say that if you have the opportunity to do something like this you should do it, as the people you meet are what make it. I was just amazed to see that over a decade on and nothing much had changed, neither with me, nor the camp.

I found that interesting because in the time that had passed I'd been on all these journeys, I'd travelled so far and I'd chased internal change as much as the next man. But as I stood there and compared now and then I didn't really see that much difference. I'd certainly learnt a lot in that time, I'd grown and adapted, I was more aware of who I was and who I wasn't. Back then I still had all that to figure out. Yet fundamentally I was still the same person, with the same character traits, good and bad, which is why I still don't really believe in change, not in any conscious deliberate way in any case. Perhaps over time you just practice to be different. Which might mean all you do is learn how to act.

What I like about riding a motorcycle across the world, or on any big adventure for that matter, is that you have the opportunity to drop the act and be yourself for a while. That, to me, is the heart of its appeal. And what I missed most during those three years of not being on the road.

Chapter Three
Pennsylvania

I woke in John's basement at 5am. I went upstairs and made a pot of coffee. The house was silent and dark. I took my coffee down into the basement and began to load the last bits and pieces on to the bike. I wasn't sure where to store the tent and the sleeping mat; on the tent rack above the headlight or strapped to the postal rack at the rear? Strange as it sounds, I was bothered about how the bike looked and whether it appeared aesthetically balanced or not. I just couldn't make up my mind and had to concede it was nothing more than a delay tactic, designed to halt my departure from this place of relative sanctuary, not necessarily wishing to return to those seas of disarray.

Finally, with everything loaded and a last sweep of the house complete, I opened the back door and wheeled Dot out into pre-dawn sky. It was colder than I thought, and a slight film of drizzle wasn't doing anything to help glamorise the day I had ahead. It was going to be a case of simply riding as far as I could, hopefully around 500 kilometres, in approximately twelve hours, then finding somewhere to stay at the end of it. But I had no markers, no place to really aim for. I had nothing booked, just a rough idea of the route and that satnav to help guide me along it.

The sad thing about the satnav was that it had revealed my true cruising speed. All the way from Australia I'd believed the speedo needle when it read that I was maintaining a steady 75km/h, or around 45mph. Yet when I bought the GPS and plugged it in I was faced with the grim reality that the speedo was over-reading, and that in fact I was doing less than forty, an average perhaps of 37mph. This made America seem even bigger than it already did.

Having made one last check of the oil, and of the tyre pressures, there wasn't much left to do but turn the key, no longer watch the neutral light glow green as the bulb had long since blown, flick out the kickstart, then proceed to give her a firm long stroke with the right foot, while maintaining a gentle twist of the throttle with the right hand, and generally she'd fire in to life.

I tied the neckerchief around my face so that it completely covered my nose, slipped on my helmet, fastened it beneath the chin and pulled on the pair of beige gardening gloves. I also carried with me a second set of welding gloves, which were too big, but this was good because it allowed me to pull them over the top of the gardening gloves to give extra warmth on a cold morning such as this one. And that was that. Too dark for my sunglasses, and with no visor, I would just have to put up with the drizzle in my eyes.

I crept up the bank, between the trees and up on to the gravel road that would take me down to the main one. No one else was around. It was just me and this pre-breakfast world. Cold and wet. Mid-August, two-hundred miles north of New York, at least three-thousand from San Francisco, and another three-thousand up from there to Alaska, and nothing in between but miles of uncertainty.

It would be unwise to pretend you are confident at this point. More accurately you're a bag of nerves and apprehension, almost like going to school for the very first time. That sense of having to go, but not necessarily wanting to go; it all feeling a bit better once you've passed beyond the perimeter gate.

Having turned right at the town of Hancock I joined Route 6 and from that moment on I was heading west through rural Pennsylvania. It was certainly exciting to be riding through America. Something as simple as the road signs really hit home that you're in another world, and when you stop for 'gas' (petrol), the gas stations are often big, with lots of pumps, you having to pay in advance, like in Kazakhstan, and in the middle of the shop they have a huge selection of filter coffee in glass pots. Many different blends and flavours, then a vast array of flavoured creams and milks; vanilla, nutmeg, liquor... It became routine to buy coffee with petrol, if only to keep the pair of us going.

Despite the tension of leaving New York, it did now feel good to be back on the road again. The appeal is its simplicity. You get up, and you ride, and do that day after day, making it up as you go along. But suddenly you feel in control of yourself again. It's your world. Your schedule. Your time-keeping skills. At no time do you have to be somewhere, on other people's orders. It's freedom, or as close to it as you can get.

I think this sense of 'travelling' can be achieved when doing anything that makes you feel like you're getting somewhere. Like working towards a degree, or setting up a new business, starting a family, or learning to how to drive a car. It's that same sense of moving forward, not standing still, and that to me is all that 'travelling' represents; the simple act of progress.

Of course, as I pushed west there had been temptation to go up through Canada, past Toronto, and back down into America by way of Detroit, but I think for personal reasons that would have been going over old ground, and so I decided on this less confrontational route instead, though yes, a part of me could quite easily have ridden back up to see Mandy again. That's what my heart would have preferred to have done. But sometimes you just have to stop yourself.

***

After a few hours on the road I pulled into a Burger King for some breakfast. I asked if there was Wi-Fi as I would have liked to have updated

Facebook to let people know I was on my way, but this branch didn't have it yet, something that amused the counter clerk who called over to her boss, an older man, and informed him that I was another one, questioning the absence of Wi-Fi in this perpetually online world. It wasn't an annoyance, just a realisation that free Wi-Fi was my only connection to the outside world. At this stage, barely anyone knew I was out here. In fact, I'd only just told my parents where I was and what I was up to.

That sounds selfish, and perhaps it is. My mum in particular had sniffed that something was wrong, and so it came as no surprise to hear one day out of the blue that I was in America, planning on riding across it. I'd not told her I was going to do it – not 'til I'd landed in New York – because I was afraid she'd try and talk me out of it and point out all the reasons I shouldn't be doing it (age, money, get a job), and that would have set in motion an avalanche of doubt, which I just didn't need right now. I figured it was safer to just set off and tell them after it was too late to change my mind.

I think deep down mum wished I'd just get a normal job, one where she didn't have to worry or have the difficult task of explaining to her peers just what it was her son was doing with his life. Though I think secretly she was proud. At least I'd hope so, as everyone would like to think that their parents approve of what they're doing with their lives.

Without doubt though, had it not been for the support of my parents and my friends, I don't know what would have happened during those dark days back in England.

That's what bothered me about this trip. I would be leaving that safety net behind and once again stepping out alone into the world. I worried what would happen if I started having those dark and horrible thoughts again with nobody around to catch me if I fell. It was all a bit of a gamble really, putting my faith in the road and hoping that I was doing the right thing, for the right reasons.

What didn't help, was that unlike the first trip, where I had the very solid destination of England to aim for, this time round the destination was vague. It was San Francisco, it was Alaska, but for no other reason than them being convenient markers on the map. There was no one I loved living there. Home wasn't there either, and I still maintain that an adventure needs a pull, as well as a push, if you're to avoid getting stuck in the middle. I certainly had the push – the desire to get on with life, and to get back on the road – but I hadn't quite worked out the pull yet. 'Give it time,' at least that's what I told myself.

***

Around midday, I passed through a town with a magnificent old wooden house that looked for all the world like one the Addams Family might have lived in. A passing girl explained that it used to be owned, or at least lived in, by a group of hippies who would sit up in the glass tower playing music as this sleepy town slept all around.

This mental image reminded me of Edward Scissorhands, and how he lived alone in that big old house at the top of the hill, until one day the townsfolk came with pitchforks and drove him out. I doubt it happened like that in this case, I just thought it sad that such a beautiful old building was left to rack and ruin.

But Pennsylvania in general was in that sort of state, teetering on the edge of financial survival, what with it being on the cusp of the Rust Belt; an area of north east America that has de-industrialised to such an extent that nothing much is left but the remains of a more confident era. Fortunately, in Pennsylvania's case, huge reserves of natural gas have recently been found beneath the ground, so much of it that a regeneration of the entire state might just take place.

This was explained to me by Richard and Lynne, a couple of retirees I met in the first instance at a lookout point, across a beautiful valley, and then later that day at a McDonald's, where both of us had by chance decided to stop for lunch. Outside in the car park they handed me $20 and told me to put it towards whatever I might need along the way. I thanked them enormously, buying a cheeseburger and coffee with it, before consigning the rest to petrol.

It was in that same McDonald's that I got chatting to a man who was inquisitive about my Indonesian jacket and the bike that was parked outside. Having broken the ice, this seemingly educated and well-dressed man asked, completely serious in his concern, if I thought the Iranian gas stations owners over the border in Canada would one day form a Muslim army and march on America.

I wasn't sure if he was serious at first, explaining that I'd been through several Muslim countries on my travels – Pakistan and Indonesia – and how I found the people there to be incredibly friendly and polite. I told him I thought they were little different to you and I, getting on with life and most of them not thinking about blowing people up at all. They might wish to come to America, but only for a better life. I could see in his eyes that he wasn't quite convinced by what I was saying, and that his mind had already been made up.

I felt sorry for the man if I'm honest. For whatever reason, from whatever source, he'd come across an idea, and a fear, that was just beyond belief, and yet he believed it, and considered it so possible that he thought to ask the stranger he'd just met in McDonald's if he too thought it was likely to happen. The media, politicians, his peers; where does a man get an idea such as that?

The irony of it was that as I'd been passing through this valleyed part of Pennsylvania I couldn't help but think how much like parts of Indonesia it was. Not necessarily the landscape or the foliage, just the way in which the road ran through the valley, houses and businesses built alongside it, communities stretched along its length, and while here they have churches, and there they have mosques, and here you get petrol from a petrol pump, and there you get petrol from a glass jar by the side of the road, the actual nature of life and the way it was structured around the road was completely similar, whether here in America or there in Indonesia. If only the man could have seen that.

I camped wild that night. This was as much a budget consideration as anything else; I simply couldn't afford to stop in hotels or motels. And while on that first trip it had taken me almost two months – right in the heart of Sumatra – to muster the courage to give wild camping a go, I felt it best, here in America, to just get that first night over and done with, because it is scary, the idea being to camp in a place where you're probably not allowed, with nobody seeing you, and you're there just long enough to get some sleep before getting straight back on the road the next morning.

I'd wild camped in Indonesia, Thailand, India, Pakistan, Kyrgyzstan, Kazakhstan, Russia, Ukraine, Poland, Germany and France. Sometimes I enjoyed it, sometimes I didn't. The best part about it is parking the bike right next to the tent, only unloading what you need and leaving the rest just sitting there, waiting until morning when all you need to do is pack away the tent and sleeping bag, strap it back on the bike and get going again. It all becomes quite routine after a while.

The area I was passing through now was mainly rural, with thick forest scattered along the length of the road, some of the trees covered in a strange kind of pink candyfloss that made me wonder what it was.

As I rode along I looked to dart up a fire road, or down a path leading into trees. But always traffic would be behind me or coming the other way, and I never saw the right moment or opportunity to make a dash for it. I carried on riding until I came upon a gas station on the right hand side of the road that looked to be the heart of a small hamlet.

I asked the clerk inside the gas station if he knew of anywhere that I might be allowed to camp that night. He had a think and I hoped he was going to say that I could pitch the tent on the grass out the back of the building. Sadly, he couldn't think of any place, but there was a customer in the store who reminded the clerk of Beaver Creek. 'Oh yes,' said the clerk, 'down by Beaver Creek.'

Having followed the man's directions along an increasingly quiet and remote single track road, I turned off at the sign for the creek. The road was now gravel and more forested than before, feeling like I was driving along a road you might see in a horror movie, the lead character in search of the missing girl, buried alive in the wood, the soundtrack creepy and you not wanting to look because you know something bad is about to happen.

After a few miles the road came to a dead end, circling on itself to form a small parking area right down by the edge of what was a huge man-made reservoir, surrounded by forest, and with an army of mosquitoes out in force. I sat on the bike at the edge of the water, swatting them off. I didn't get a good feeling about this place and just as I was about to drive off and look for somewhere else, a couple pulled up in an SUV, winding down their window and explaining they were looking for deer. We made small talk, before they said goodbye and turned around and drove off.

Once they were out of sight, and with the light almost gone, I kicked the bike into life and raced across the top of the reservoir to the far side of the water, figuring I'd just brave it down here for the night. Sure enough there was a small clearing, well out of sight; the plan being to put the tent up here. It was now dusk, with a mist spreading across the water, no sound but for my heavy breathing and the sigh of the trees as they creaked in the breeze.

Just as I was about to unload my gear I heard another vehicle crunching along the gravel and coming to a stop back on the other side of the water, over where the small car park was. I couldn't see the vehicle, or the two people that got out, but I could hear them as they began walking in my direction, their voices growing louder until they were well within earshot.

I reasoned that I couldn't have them come around the corner and suddenly find me cowering here, so I kicked the bike into neutral and pushed it out on to the path only ten yards in front of them, not quite sure who or what I was about to face.

It was a couple walking their dog, and despite a hairy, foreign-accented man in a bright orange jacket pushing a motorbike suddenly appearing from nowhere by the side of this remote reservoir, the pair didn't even flinch – just smiled and said hello as if this scenario were completely normal.

We talked for quite a while about the area and how the reservoir was once a thriving place, with a campsite just off into the woods where families from around the area would come and camp up for the summer months, the kids able to play in the water. The campsite has since been closed down due to budget cuts and barely anyone comes any more. It seemed like such a shame.

I asked the couple what the pink candyfloss was that I'd seen in the trees on the way here. They explained that it was moths that every seven years would show up in town, build nests in the trees and over the next few weeks strip the trees completely bare, killing many of the trees in the process.

'Nothing you can do about it,' said the man, and we all stood on the spot, staring at our feet, making small talk until they returned to their vehicle and drove off, leaving me finally alone in Beaver Creek.

In the end I put the tent up in that tiny oval car park, sitting it on the gravel beneath a sign that read 'no camping,' hoping to be gone by the time the ranger came the following morning.

Inside the tent I threw my sleeping bag and roll mat, plus my jacket to form a makeshift pillow. The rest I just left on the bike, even the key, which I would always leave in the ignition so that I never would misplace it. I cooked up a supper of instant noodles, making sure to tie up and hang in a distant tree anything with a scent that might attract the bears. I wasn't even sure if there were any bears in these woods or not.

With that I crawled into my tent, it now completely dark, the sound of the sleeping bag being zipped up, then the flap of the tent, feeling slightly safer now, even though it was only a sliver of fabric between me and the outside world. Strange how this makeshift set-up would make you feel so safe, almost a sense of being at 'home,' which in a way you are when on the road. Now I would lie back and try to get comfortable, which was never easy as the stones and the earth beneath you would push into your back, and your neck would get stiff and your hip would gradually become sore.

Then, to top it all off, just as you get comfy you would hear a noise outside and sit up with a jolt, grabbing the Chinese knife that is beside you and slowly pulling down the zip on the tent and peeking out to see if anyone was there. A monster, a bear? More likely an owl in a tree or a beaver doing more work on the creek. And then you would lay back down, fall back to sleep, and half an hour later go through the whole rigmarole again. You never slept well. You always woke tired and stiff. But your night's sleep was free, instead of fifty quid, and that was the whole point.

***

For breakfast that morning I stopped in the small village of Polk. It was just another name on the map the satnav was leading me through. I'm not sure how much I liked this, blindly following arrows blinking at me from the bag on the petrol tank; I had no real sense of knowing where I was going, a sense of being led instead. But perhaps that's what I needed for the time being. It allowed me to concentrate on the riding and everything else that goes with that, while leaving the navigating down to someone, or something else.

On this occasion the satnav brought me to the breakfast table of a man named Jim Miller, a convenience store owner who didn't know what to make of me at first; this stranger wandering through the door of his rural shop in Pennsylvania. But having parked up outside this barely signposted store – it made of wood, and nestled within a row of wooden houses, across from the wooden church – we greeted each other and I asked whether he had coffee. I bought a cup of that, a breakfast muffin from the hot counter from the back of the store and, as I paid – apprehension thawing – we got into a conversation about how our lives came to have crossed paths that day.

Jim had lived in this community all his life. It was his world, but he had a keen interest in what was happening beyond it. He asked me about England and whether it was true what he was hearing from American politicians and TV pundits about how bad the NHS was; this in connection with Obama's intention to introduce something similar to America. I told him that in my opinion it's not perfect, but it's alright. And that to be able to go and see a doctor or go to hospital without having to worry about how you were going to pay for it was a good thing.

Jim explained how he had to pay $400 a month for him and his wife to be covered by private health care. There was also a significant excess to pay – around two to three thousand dollars – with every chance the insurance company won't pay if they can find an excuse not to. I asked what about the people who can't afford the $400 a month and he talked through a scenario where the state might cover it, or that you might have to sell your house to pay the bill or not seek medical treatment at all, simply because you couldn't afford to.

By this time we'd taken a pair of coffees to the seating area – a separate part of the shop, like a knock-through to the house next door – where every Saturday night a band plays to entertain the locals. We talked about Mormons and how a community of them lived down the road, and that I might see them on my journey west.

It was also interesting to discuss the way in which the rural landscape of America was changing and how many people were moving to the city to find work. We talked about what that meant for rural Pennsylvania and how something similar was happening in the UK, where the old industries are dying and what with the cost of fuel and transport – not to mention the lack of jobs – there was an increasing number of people leaving their rural roots behind. And to what end?

We also talked about 9/11 and the impact that had on the psyche of the nation, that sense of living with the fear of another attack. My mind linked this back to the fears of the man I'd recently met in the McDonald's, with his fear of Canadian gas station owners. Jim explained that in the aftermath of 9/11, many Muslim-owned stores went out of business or came under attack, simply because they were Muslim.

There were other things we talked about, but having lost the diary in which I'd made note of it I don't now remember what they were. I just remember Jim to be a wise and open-minded person. I enjoyed talking with him that day. In fact we must have talked for almost two hours. And to think I rode straight past the shop, thinking I'd stop a little later for breakfast, but then experienced a massive urge to turn around and go and get something from that shop.

It made me wonder if there was something in that; and that somehow you can detect another soul you're meant to meet. Maybe there are a thousand shopkeepers in Pennsylvania who I could have conversed with that morning, or perhaps there was only one, and somehow, with the help of satnav, I managed to find him.

Chapter Four
Ohio and Detroit

Having left Polk behind I was now left aiming squarely for Detroit. I was heading there because I knew a man named Vermin, our paths crossing on a popular internet forum a few years before; the same forum I'd used to help me out with the DMV back in New York. Vermin lived just outside of Detroit and owned an old Honda PC800 named Cack, a bike he'd completely bastardised over the years. He'd sprayed it fluorescent orange and yellow, covered it with stickers and mounted a set of antlers above the headlight on the front fairing.

He'd also modified the exhaust pipe so you could insert a tin of beans when you were riding, meaning that they were warm by the time you arrived at your destination. The exhaust then bent upwards, rising vertically above the level of the seat, with a 'flapper' on the top, the sort you might find on a big old American truck. It was an awful machine, but Vermin had ridden this thing all over America and down into Mexico as well. He wrote up the most incredible stories and I admired, and was even jealous, of his carefree attitude to life.

I'd actually met him two years before, back when I'd gone to see Mandy in Toronto with the offer of commitment and found myself too late, and so instead of flying straight home I accepted Vermin's invitation to go and hang out with him for a while down in Detroit. Vermin even offered to lend me Cack, so I could go for a ride down to Florida or across to California if I liked. But another adventure just wasn't what I wanted back then. I certainly didn't want to be on the road. I wanted to be at home, hiding from the world for a while.

Now, two years later, I was back in America and heading in his direction again, this time on Dorothy, following signs for Cleveland but trying not to end up in the middle of the city. I was intending to trace a route to the south of its centre, in the hope of missing the worst of its traffic, something which only seemed to be getting thicker and thicker; the rural pleasantries of Pennsylvania replaced by the industrial sprawl of Rust Belt Ohio, the border between the two states being crossed not long after leaving Jim's convenience store in Polk.

The trouble I was having now was staying off the interstate. Despite programming the satnav to avoid them it kept wanting to send me on to roads of three-lane traffic, travelling way too fast for our speed. I resorted to intuition and road signs, the only physical map I had being one I'd picked up in a book store back in New York. It had a page for each state, which given the size of the average US state meant only the big roads were marked and so it didn't really serve any purpose at all.

But if I was having problems then so too was Gary, a man on a bicycle travelling in the same direction as me – along the shoreline road of Lake Erie – and so having blazed past in a haze of astonishment, I stopped a little way ahead to see if he needed any water.

Gary turned out to be the ripe old age of seventy-seven, and cycling all the way around the shoreline of Lake Erie, a distance of over 600 miles. Having introduced ourselves, Gary explained how his cycling adventures had begun back in his early sixties when he went on a guided tour of Alaska, travelling by 4x4. On the drive up there he met several cyclists, making the gruelling self-propelled slog to the top of the world. This inspired him, and not long after returning from the trip he bought his own bicycle and set about planning his own adventures.

In the years that followed, Gary cycled around Australia, through Central Asia, down along the Pan-American Highway to Argentina and up to Alaska himself. I think he'd even toured Europe and still had plenty of places he wanted to go to. I don't quite remember how long this trip had taken him, but like me he had camped wild in a tent and lived on the cheap. The day I met him was Gary's second to last on the road, him hoping to be back home in Ann Arbor the very next day.

I asked Gary why he did this, because to me he looked in pain and didn't always describe the experience as an enjoyable one, something I could well associate with. For him it was about the challenge and setting yourself the target and trying to get there, regardless of the suffering involved. For him it wasn't about what he saw or even where he went, just that he made it to his destination and could for a moment feel satisfied that he'd done it. Then, as he accepts, his mind turns to thoughts of, 'What next?' And straight away he's planning his next adventure.

Gary asked me about my bike and how much one similar might cost, as he conceded he was thinking of using an engine for the next trip. He was getting too old, or so he told me.

Before going our separate ways, Gary gave me his business card, his profession marked on it as 'Ski instructor, Boulder Colorado.' He was an inspirational man, and I think the sadness I felt when I rode away was of imagining that one day Gary will disappear from this mortal coil, and so too will his amazing tales of adventure. It just doesn't seem fair or right that a man can do so much with his life, and then for it almost to count for nothing. Perhaps it's a convincing argument for sitting on your arse all your life and not doing anything with it, and if you're happy with doing that, I guess why not, as it seems to count for nothing in the long run.

As for me, I'd didn't quite make it to Vermin's that day, camping instead on a site in the pleasant town of Sandusky, built on the banks of Lake Erie, and said to be home to one of the biggest roller-coaster rides in the world, though I never saw it. I just found a Subway sandwich shop and ate my sandwich before heading off to find the campsite, because for whatever reason I couldn't stomach the hassle of looking for somewhere to wild camp for the night.

Despite the price of $15, I much preferred this night to the one before it; the peace of mind of being on a proper site, with a proper tent pitch, with a shower block and toilets, and other people around. You definitely sleep a lot more soundly than when camped out in the wild.

The following morning I traced a wide arc around the city of Toledo in order to avoid getting caught in the traffic, finding myself on the long straight roads of the farming district, fields of corn off to either side, towering white grain silos shadowing isolated farms, then villages and hamlets built alongside the road where I'd stop for gas and end up chatting to people who would always enquire about the motorbike and where I was heading. It was a detour to see Vermin, forcing me north, for eighty miles, a distance I'd have to backtrack when I left, but I just felt the urge to go there, so I went.

***

Vermin didn't actually live in the area any more. He'd moved away a year or so before with his family to Colorado Springs, almost 1,500 miles to the west of here, but just happened to be in the area visiting his parents the same time as I was passing through.

There was no one home when I got there, so I sat on a chair in their garage, waiting an hour or so until they all finally arrived. His parents – Gil and Myrna – were a great couple, Gill himself a keen cyclist just like Gary, once riding from Tampa to Detroit (1,200 miles), and then another time from Seattle to Detroit (2,400 miles). The couple were about to downsize into a smaller place closer to the centre of Brighton.

I talked with Myrna about how strange that must feel, this being the family home in which the previous two generations of the Vermin family had been raised. Myrna was quite pragmatic about it all, seeing it just as a shell and a place not needed any more. There would soon be a new place to call 'home'. I admired the way in which she had rationalised this, her ability to let go of what was really just bricks and mortar.

Vermin himself hadn't changed one bit; a tall sinewy character with short cropped hair and glasses. His real name is Phil but Vermin was the name he often liked to go by. I think it was his alter ego, his riding name, and I could associate with this as I'd done the same with Dorothy and liked to think that I too had an alter ego whilst travelling these big trips. I was certainly more brave and decisive whilst travelling, and perhaps to be called Phil was a reminder that his life wasn't as exciting back in the 'real' world as it was when heading down to Mexico or wherever else he and his bike had been.

You could say Vermin was a complex character. But not really. He just hates the system, and the 'man,' and the 'cubicle,' and wishes the world was a little less keen to strap people to desks or routines and make them work like obedient dogs. He's an old hippy at heart, with his rants about the 'angry white man' – a nod to the white, right-voting old men of America – both amusing and ironic. Vermin has a friend named Gator-Jane, living in the swamps of Florida, who has dead alligators and snakes in his freezer. Vermin said I should go and visit him. I'm not even sure he exists.

The last time I met Phil I was in a bit of a mess and not much company. This time I was glad to be meeting him – his wife Linda was back home in Colorado Springs – under different circumstances, when I was leaning into the wind, with my sails at full mast and far more positive about life and its outcomes. That evening we all sat around the dining table, on the veranda, overlooking a small lake where wildlife would often be seen, not another house in sight. It was easy to see why Gil and Myrna would miss this place so much.

Myself, Vermin and his son Drew later headed into town for a beer in one of the sports bar, the kind of place you might drink Budweiser by the bottle and watch a game of American football on TV. This was a nice part of the world, not just the town itself but the surroundings and how there are so many lakes, houses built alongside them, the land much flatter here than it had been across Pennsylvania. This was now Michigan, the fourth state of my adventure. Next it would be Indiana, Illinois, and after that I really wasn't sure as the options from here would be endless.

I could either maintain this trajectory, spearing west across Iowa and Nebraska, possibly taking Route 30, the Lincoln Highway, all the way from here to San Francisco, the point at which it ends. I could also drop back down to try and rejoin Route 50, the Lonely Highway, which would also take me all the way to the Pacific Coast. Vermin thought it would be a nice idea to head west, riding until I hit the Mississippi River – a few hundred miles west of Chicago – at which point I could trace it south until I hit St. Louis, then head west along Route 50. I said I would just go west, in the direction of Chicago, and make the rest up from there.

Vermin offered to ride with me all the way across to Colorado Springs, him on another bike – not Cack – but still a proper one with a proper top speed. I've had people say this to me before and generally it doesn't last. They spend ten minutes at 37mph, get fed up and ride off, telling me they'll meet me when I get there. I told Vermin this but he was adamant he wanted to ride with me and I too liked the idea of it; a bit of company on the long stretch across the Midwest.

The following morning we loaded up our gear, said a fond farewell to Gil and Myrna, before hitting the road. Five minutes later we pulled over and both agreed we couldn't ride like this, not for 1,500 miles, him hovering in my rear view mirror, struggling to go so slow. And I didn't like it either, feeling as though I was being pushed from behind. I also find the mask starts to slip after a while and beneath it I can be short-tempered, moody and taciturn, which is not something I wish others to see.

It was at this moment – saying goodbye in a parking lot by the side of the main road – that I noticed three broken spokes in my rear wheel. I'd bent down to lube the chain, grabbing the spokes in order to spin the wheel and feeling one loose, then another, and another. It felt like Kazakhstan all over again, only at least this time I carried some spare.

Vermin told me that there was a Honda dealer just along the road and so I insisted he get going and that I'd hopefully see him in Colorado on my way through to the coast. The spokes were just one of the rigours of the road, a hiccup, and there was no point ruining his day as well as mine. I waved him off and turned to face my old bike and its broken spokes, in a town less than thirty miles west of Detroit.

The staff in the Honda dealer were sympathetic, though sadly couldn't replace individual spokes – for liability reasons – their only option being to replace the whole lot, at a cost of almost $200. I couldn't afford that, as it was almost a third of my total budget.

I asked instead if they'd mind me using their car park at the front of the building to try and repair the wheel myself, using the spare spokes I carried with me. They were fine with this and told me to let them know if I needed any tools. You could see they wanted to help, but I think their manager had reminded them that this was a business, needing to make money, and not a charity to help out foreigners riding 105cc Hondas across the world.

The task of replacing spokes was much harder than I'd imagined. It took me three hours to figure out the way of doing it, realising how you had to remove neighbouring spokes to get the broken ones out, and then remember which went in where and which hole they should go back through. Despite the trials of the task in hand, it was a pleasant morning, one of those on an adventure that you could never foresee, and when it happens, you just get on and deal with it, and learn as you go along.

Midway through the repair I struck up conversation with a man who turned up on a gorgeous black Ducati sportsbike. He was friendly, quietly spoken and engaging to talk to. He'd been an accountant and done well in life. He was now retired, and quite shy in the way that he conducted himself. We talked mainly about Detroit and what was happening there, and how it was hard to imagine that less than thirty miles down the road was one of the most violent cities in America. This after all was peaceful middle-class white suburbia.

Again, the issue of public health came up, and of course talk of

Obamacare. For this man it was a simple case of providing for yourself, and the onus on you to work hard enough to afford to pay for medical insurance. It was not, in any uncertain terms, the duty of the state to provide care for you. When presented in such a way it was a very difficult position to argue against. People should take responsibility for themselves, but at the same time I knew myself how easy it is for people to fall and if there's nothing there to catch them then it's a long way to the bottom. And even harder to get back up again.

As far as this man was concerned, a move towards government healthcare – in the form of Obamacare – was a move towards communism, as though only two extremes existed; and so if you weren't all out capitalist, then you were all out communist. There was nothing in between. I tried to explain that in England we have a national health service, but we're far from living in a socialist state. But this man had drawn his line in the sand and that's just what he thought.

It made me realise just how tough it can be in America. If you're succeeding, you're fine and possibly healthy. If you're failing, and having a tough time, then you really are in quite a lot of trouble. It certainly made me grateful to be born in Europe, though of course, they would say the same about where they were born.

With the spokes finally fixed, the day was half gone and I wasn't quite sure what to do with myself. I thought about riding back to Phil's parents' house, which was only fifteen minutes down the road, but I hate saying goodbye, then hello again, then goodbye again. It just gets messy. Instead I decided to head east to Detroit to have a look around, it being only an hour's ride away. Besides, having passed through it those few years before – back when I first met Phil – I was keen to see it again, as there is just something so fascinating about it.

The first time I visited the place I compared it to a circular doughnut (the type with the hole in the middle) and how the ground around the doughnut is relatively peaceful, white and prosperous. Then you enter the dough of the doughnut and suddenly the world changes. It becomes poor, destructive and unavoidably black. These suburbs go on for mile after mile, until you suddenly emerge at the centre of the doughnut – where the hole is – only to find the downtown district is relatively wealthy, white and prosperous again. The change between the two extremes is sudden, from one block to the next. And the contrast between the two is vivid.

Fortunately, there is an interstate connecting the outside of the doughnut with the middle of the doughnut, meaning that most people don't have to drive through the horrible outer circle, but not being allowed to ride on the interstates meant I had no choice but to ride straight through the batter, which I have to say was one of the most depressing and upsetting sights I'd seen from the saddle of this motorbike, and that includes the slums of Kathmandu and Delhi.

I think it's like that because you just don't expect it. This is America after all, the *greatest nation on earth*, and yet here is one of their major cities, and it looks like it's been in a war. There are houses burnt to the ground, others covered in graffiti, whilst the roads and pavements are full of craters and potholes. Everywhere you look is a desolate wasteland; boarded up shops and the general sense of despair, with street lights long since extinguished.

At least in the worst parts of India and Nepal you still got a sense of hope and determination. Even amongst the rubble of Kathmandu there are markets taking place, and the simple fountain of life bubbling away, despite the conditions being so harsh.

What was so upsetting about Detroit by comparison was that there seemed to be no hope, no optimism, no spirit in the air. It was a dead city, and this was a dead road (crossed by Eight Mile Road of Eminem fame), overgrown with large swathes of neighbourhoods abandoned. The only buildings that seemed to be prospering were the churches and the big corporate fast-food chains, which perhaps tells us something about what might have gone wrong here in the first place.

There is a huge debate as to what went wrong in Detroit. Those on the right (the Republicans) blame the blacks for burning down their own neighbourhoods back in the riots of 1967 and more specifically the black mayor Coleman Young – serving from 1974 to 1993 – who Republicans claim used Detroit as a socialist experiment that went catastrophically wrong, the city slipping from two million residents in its heyday, to little over half a million today.

Conversely, those on the left (the Democrats) blame the failure of the capitalist system to make the American car market a success. That people began buying superior Japanese cars, and that those in charge shipped jobs out to China is what some people see as the reason why Detroit's main industry – car manufacturing – went so badly wrong. They also cite the effect of 'white flight,' and how the relocation of the white Americans to the suburbs, just as industry was collapsing – while at the same time black immigrants from the south were flooding in – meant that there was a vacuum of jobs and opportunities which eventually broke out into the riots that destroyed half the city.

What I did learn was that the way in which the tax system works here – taxes paid by the local community stay in the local community – means that this situation is a long way from ever changing. Basically, the tax generated by the wealthy areas stays in the wealthy areas. So public amenities there get better and better. Whereas in the inner city slums there just isn't enough tax revenue generated to keep things fully functioning, hence why the roads in the suburbs go from being smooth and well maintained to being almost beyond repair the moment you enter the poorest areas of town. And then you reach the city centre – which is overly policed to keep it safe – and all feels and looks well maintained and civil again.

There are positive signs however. Detroit, apparently, is the number one city in the world for urban farming, while in recent years some of the worst neighbourhoods have been improved by the Arab and Middle-Eastern immigrants moving in and beginning to rebuild the place. Artists and musicians are also making the most of the abandoned buildings and factories, while the road I would take out of the city – Old Ford Road –

seemed to be more prosperous than the road I took in earlier that day. I certainly had a soft spot for this place. I felt for it. I felt it deserved better and I hope one day it gets back on its feet and proves that regular people can perhaps succeed in a city where corporate America (or human nature, perhaps) seems to have failed.

Chapter Five
To Chicago

I slept that night behind a mound of dirt in a lay-by just outside Ann Arbor (where Gary lived), before riding into town first thing in the morning for a coffee. I sat in a seat beside the window, keeping an eye on the bike outside. I wore my cap to hide my scraggly hair. I guess in a way I was homeless. That's what it feels like on these adventures. Your bike outside with literally everything on it. It's your lifeline. Without that bike I would be in a foreign town with no reason for being there, the trip would be over. I would have nothing else to do but come home and do something else with my life. This means that you do worry and fret about the bike, as if it were a child, and the thought of losing it catastrophic.

Later that morning I found another broken spoke, noticing it when I stopped to check if the ones I'd fitted the day before were holding up okay. Thankfully I still had plenty of spares, and now with practice I was able to repair it much quicker than the three from yesterday. A police car circled through the lay-by I was parked up in, making clear sight of my foreign numberplate. It was reassuring that he didn't stop or ask for any explanation. I think the policeman back in New York had just been over-zealous.

As for the spokes, it had been suggested on Facebook that if they kept on breaking then I was to try strapping tie-wraps around each of the points at which two spokes crossed. This would reinforce them, and prevent them from vibrating loose and snapping again. I was five tie-wraps short of doing them all, but a couple in a motor home, who had been watching me struggle with the repair, kindly offered me the rest.

I continued on that day through Michigan, travelling from Detroit to Chicago along Route 12. The world here was flat and featureless, pockmarked by small towns with little life. This wasn't a place I'd like to have lived. As mentioned, this entire region, from the Midwest to north-east, is known as the Rust Belt, with much of it suffering from the onset of de-industrialisation, much like some of the towns of Yorkshire and Derbyshire that myself, Greg and Rob passed through on our route down to Heathrow. Places such as Detroit are the focal point, but all outlying areas are affected (apart from places such as Ann Arbor, but that had the universities), with some people choosing to migrate to where the new jobs are (Texas and California), others staying put, riding out the storm, waiting for...

Waiting for the world to change I guess.

***

Despite aiming for Chicago, I camped that night at the Indiana Dunes State Park, ninety miles shy of the city and on the shores of Lake Michigan, about to pay $15 for my own pitch before meeting Bojana and her boyfriend Adrian, a couple originally from Eastern Europe, now living in Chicago, who asked if I'd like to share their pitch, together with their friend Faisal, an Indian student here. The three of them were taking a weekend break from Chicago.

Having dropped off our things at the campsite we headed back to the beach for a swim, before driving in their car to get some food from a local gas station. I remember vividly the Foo Fighters playing on the radio; the acoustic version of *Times Like These*. As I relaxed in the back seat in a car full of new found friends, never had a song been more apt to sum up a moment such as this one.

During those times of despair back in England, I'd really begun to wonder who I was, and if I'd ever be myself again. At times I doubted I ever would, and it was a horrible feeling when the person you hate most in the world is staring back at you in the mirror every day, and all you really want to do is smash the mirror until your knuckles bleed.

I was just grateful that I had *this* to keep me going. As dark as the tunnel sometimes got I could always sense the desire to one day get back on the bike and start riding again. Without this, the tunnel would have been completely dark, and I imagine that for those in that situation, with no light to head towards, the decision to end it all must become a natural one.

I think generally you can see this in people's eyes, which is worth looking out for, because self-destruction, self-sabotage and the enemy within are not usually conducive to people asking for help themselves. Destruction is what you seek. Not help, and certainly not judgement. Sometimes just a cuddle will do, as sad as that sounds.

***

On my way into Chicago the next morning I passed through Gary, Indiana. An ominous black car with blacked out windows pulled over to observe me as I took photographs of the city limit sign.

Gary is where Michael Jackson was born and all in all reminded me of the worst parts of Detroit, with its wasteland of abandoned buildings and general air of decay. A redneck in a pick-up truck pulled up beside me at a set of traffic lights, calling out from his cabin: 'Hey, you'd best be careful around here.' And so I might; nineteen people had been gunned down in drive-bys the night before in the Chicago area, with the city famous for its violence and crime.

I have to say, both here and in Detroit, I never felt any threat or danger. In a way I was a sitting duck and an obvious target; a foreigner on a slow bike travelling through the worst parts of the city, with a target on the side of his helmet. But at such times I just kept on riding, minding my own business, and I think that's all you have to do, like going out to a nightclub and keeping your head down to avoid any trouble, though it's always there if you want it.

As for Chicago, I have to be honest in saying that once you've ridden through the hideous suburbs to get to the glorious centre it does kind of take the shine off things. You go from the run-down black part of town, to the run-down Hispanic part of town, then to the black again, then you turn a corner only to be greeted with a manicured golf course and white joggers pounding pavements beside a pristine waterfront park. I mean, are you really to believe that all those Starbucks coffee shops, museums and art installations are a true reflection of what's going on here? I didn't think so at the time.

It didn't help that Chicago was full of so many homeless people. On every corner, outside most shops, people were begging. You could walk past them and pretend they weren't there, but they were there, and I saw each and every one of them, feeling as though I had more in common with them than I did with anyone else this day, much as I'd felt with the homeless of Darwin. I think that still remained my biggest fear in life; that I would end up like them one day, such was my ability to self-sabotage everything that was good, plus my inability to make things stick, and keep them stuck.

By now it was raining heavily so I parked the bike beneath the underpass and took a stroll around the main tourist area, centred around the Art Institute of Chicago.

I had another internet friend who lived in the city, Hollie, who had found me on Facebook having read about my adventures from Sydney to London, as she too had a CT110. Having spotted that I was now in America she contacted me to say that I was welcome to stay at her place any time. I let her know the night before that I would soon be in Chicago if her offer still stood. She said it certainly would, but that she wouldn't be in all day Saturday. And today was Saturday, which meant I was left with nothing much to do but take a walk around Chicago in the rain.

I took a stroll up the 'Bean,' an epic art installation that is simply a giant mirrored jellybean-shaped object, as big as a barn, the contours of which do weird and wonderful things with your face. You could walk beneath it and generally kid around. Families from all over the world were there. These are the times you feel alone, when you're in a city looking at a tourist attraction and everyone else is with their family or friend and you're there on your own, nothing to hold but your helmet.

There was also a water feature with a tall monolith in the middle of the water with a computer generated image of a smiling black child's face, that slowly changed expression, and then to another face completely. Behind it was an open-air arena on which concerts were regularly performed. Today, in the rain, came the sounds of Alaska, with dozens of artists scattered around the grassy arena making sounds with strange instruments, with no note sheets, just making whichever sound they thought would fit best. They were doing it to 'help' the native people of Alaska. I thought to myself they would be better off helping the people on their own doorstep, but that was just the cynic in me creeping out.

To escape the rain I finally headed to my second home, McDonald's; my sanctuary in the midst of all of this. I went there because the food was cheap, it was consistent, you didn't have to add tax on to the price and you didn't have to tip. More important was that in a McDonald's – as they all look and feel the same – I felt I could relax, because for a while I was in a place I recognised and was familiar with. On the road you're certain of nothing. In McDonald's you know you can get a burger and a coffee for $2.17. And that was important.

In this McDonald's I met a lady by the name of Lisette. Lisette had been homeless for two weeks and explained to me that she couldn't get a job because on her police record it showed she had a felony for marijuana possession. She looked a complete state; a middle-aged black woman, slightly glazed eyes and slurring. She had no teeth. I felt sorry for her and asked what she wanted to eat. She'd have two cheese burgers and a coffee. Done.

While we waited we just chatted about life; mine on the open road, hers in the gutter. What do you say to that? What can you do? At times like these I wished I had a magic wand that I could wave and suddenly Lisette would have a new set of teeth, and a decent home, and a stable life and whatever else it is people need to feel free. When her coffee came she added to it a total of eight sugars, so I don't think there's much that can be done about the teeth.

Later on, as I was trying to pass the time away, I got talking to the busker who was playing saxophone beside the spot I'd parked the bike beneath the flyover. On arrival I'd thrown a few dollars into his collection in the hope that he might act if someone tried to steal anything from it. But as I returned to the bike this time we got chatting.

Jacques was almost sixty years of age, a slight man, hardly any meat on him, sinewy in the extreme, wearing a yellow rain mac and hood. We made small talk about the downpour then, curious, I asked him about his life and how he busked out here for the money he needed to live on. He said it was the saxophone that had kept him out of trouble during his youth.

After that I asked him about Chicago. He said it was getting worse; the violence, the drugs, the guns, the shootings. He said for a black kid growing up in the rough neighbourhoods there's no real way out. For him it was his saxophone, that's what kept him on the straight and narrow. Now he says schools don't run music classes, or even gym classes. So you've got these kids with no purpose, no role models (except for rappers) and it almost becomes inevitable that they're going to get into drugs/gangs. And the gangs don't know how to deal with confrontation, except with a gun, hence nineteen shot dead last night.

Jacques said the police largely leave the worst areas unpatrolled. He believed that if they tried to intervene the violence would just spill into the richer neighbourhoods. Basically leave them to it, and let them kill themselves. I later learned how it was referred to by some as the principle of the 'self-cleaning oven;' effectively it being left alone to bake off its own mess. To me it was an epidemic of violence just waiting to spill over into the rest of the city streets, and surely the problem can't be ignored forever?

What bothered me most was that when I made mention of these people I was meeting on Facebook, some of the more affluent Americans who had 'friended' me over the years told me to ignore what I was seeing, and come to where they were, as it was a whole lot better in their version of America. They said that Lisette was undoubtedly on meths and how really it's just a simple case of trying harder in life.

This really pissed me off, because I thought how easy it is for them to say that; to tell someone in that position to try harder. I mean, if you're born in the positions most of us reading this are born in then we don't really need to try very much in life in order to maintain the status quo. Our parents give us a good education, they teach us to work hard and respect others. They send us to university. They plant seeds of expectation which most of us meet. To do relatively well in life is therefore almost a given.

But what if you're born at the bottom, surrounded by the very shittiest side of life. No one cares what you do or what you become. A good education is a distant dream and the most you can hope for is a job that most of those criticising would never wish to do, and if you do get that job, then those same people will still look down on you.

So no, I don't think it's as easy as telling someone to try harder; if it were, then those criticising would all be multi-millionaires, because they'd have climbed out of their middle-class suburbia instead of maintaining their own status quo.

I think it was at this point – and I was told as much – that I came to the conclusion that there really are two Americas within America. There's the one that we see on *Man vs Food*, the TV show where the presenter travels the nation's diners trying to eat their mammoth portions in a display of greed and gluttony – the vision of America it wants us to see. And then there's Detroit, and Gary Indiana, and downtown Chicago, where you meet people like Lisette and Jacques and the two are completely separate worlds; one where people can afford health care, and to live in the nice parts of the city, and have access to a decent job, and the other, in which nineteen people get shot in an evening, and nobody really gives a shit.

I had to concede however that maybe this adventure, born as it was from the darker recesses of my mind, was perhaps having an impact on the way I was seeing things. Maybe my mind only looked out for the bad things, and the people struggling in life. I think that's the thing with depression (I hate that word); not only do you see your own gloom, you see everyone else's as well, and just as you'd like to do something about your problems, you'd like to do something about theirs as well. And knowing that you can't do a damn thing about it only serves to make matters worse, until the point at which you really do feel lousy.

Equally, perhaps in being born and raised in a northern mining town with only one black family for miles around, I was conditioned to make the distinction between race and colour more than someone who grew up in a city for example. Future generations might not have the same attachments that people of even my generation have. It would be nice to think that would be the case. As it is, the elephant in the room for America, as far as I could see, was that there is a huge racial divide. Who causes that and why it continues I don't know. But to pretend that I couldn't see it from the seat of my Australian motorbike would be disingenuous.

***

Finally came word that Hollie was home and having said farewell to Jacques and handing him $20 for his accommodation that night, perhaps for no other reason than to assuage my own guilt, I hit the road in what can only be described as a torrential downpour. The gutters were overflowing, puddles were already as high as the foot pegs and to ride along it in was like continuously having buckets of water thrown across your face. But I danced along the road that night, glad to have a destination to head towards.

Hollie lived in a Mexican part of town, the buildings two storeys high, with colourful murals painted on many of them. I saw Mexican bars and Mexican cars. Hollie lived up a quiet alley, with so many telephone and power cables strung along it I think you could probably have swung from one end to the other without touching the ground.

I parked the bike in the alley, went up the steps and banged on this stranger's door. Hollie answered and thus was spoken the weirdness of virtual friends meeting in the real world for the very first time. But it was very good to see her; like the meeting of long lost friends.

Hollie shared her flat with a massive dog named Louie. He was so dopey looking and drooling from his chin, much like the one in *Turner and Hooch*. I'm not normally a big fan of dogs, but I liked this one, and sleeping as he did beside the sofa, he kept me good company that night.

Hollie told me how one day she wants to ride her CT all the way down to South America. She was a cool chick, previously working in a custom bike shop and telling me I could stay as long as I liked. I told her that if I ever make it to Alaska then on the way back down we can perhaps meet up and head to Central America together on our bikes. I didn't stay that long, only a couple of nights, but it was long enough to get a taste for the place and make preparation for the journey ahead.

One of the evenings, after she had finished work, Hollie arranged for us to go for a ride through the city with a few friends of hers; the plan being to head towards the beaches on the north side. I also knew some other people in Chicago – other friends from the internet – so met up with them as well; Dave and his girlfriend Kara, both riding a gorgeous café racer that Dave had restored which was clearly his pride and joy. Our convoy of four bikes lit up the city streets; me and Hollie on our CTs, Dave and Kara on their café racer, and Hollie's friend Jonathan on his modern Ducati.

It was a warm night; no need for a jumper, the streets of Chicago so straight and grid-like. It felt different from New York, definitely different from Detroit. This northern side of the city is quite safe; it's to the south, the part that I'd passed through on my way in, that has all the problems. Having pulled up at traffic lights, Hollie pointed out that I had no back light and how it only illuminated when I hit the rear brake. The only solution to this, to avoid drawing the attention of the police, was to ride with my foot partially on the rear brake lever, just enough to keep the light activated, with intention of picking up a new bulb the following morning.

We rode on, through the thinning city streets, coming to a rest in a car park beside the beach, where we walked across the sand to the water's edge. The moon reflected across it. The water was relatively calm as this wasn't the ocean but a lake, Lake Michigan. I'd read that it was once heavily polluted, but in recent years efforts had been made to clean it up, with a tall lifeguard chair suggesting people now swam in it.

We rode a little bit further to another spot, one where we could look back along the shore to where the skyscrapers of Chicago rose from the ground and pierced the dark blue night. A police car circled past making a loudspeaker announcement about everyone needing to be out of there because soon they were going to close the park, the time getting on for midnight.

We hadn't left by the time the patrol car circled back around, it pulling to a stop right behind us. 'Who's bike is that?' shouted the policeman from his open driver's side window, pointing to the red CT with UK numberplate.

I walked towards the police car, fearful of what was to come.

'That's an old Trail 90, what year is it?'

'It's a 2004,' I replied.

'They didn't make them in 2004,' he continued.

'They did in Australia.'

'Is this from Australia then?'

'Yes,' I said.

'How did you get it here?'

'I rode it.'

The policeman was so amused by this that he told us not to worry and that we could take as long as we liked. He explained that they cleared everyone out of the park to prevent homeless bums and other such people (it could have been me wild camping) from sleeping there over night. I wished him goodnight and watched as he drove off, police lights still twirling a bright red and blue. I returned to the group and carried on taking snaps of the Chicago skyline, twinkling in the late night sky.

We arrived back at Hollie's house way past midnight. We parked the two CTs up in the street and hit the sack, but not like that. What a good few days it had been. I'd made some good friends, learnt a lot about Chicago and the people that lived here. More than that I'd had a good opportunity to take a breather before pushing west, as from here on in I would be crossing the prairies of the Midwest, through the Bible Belt and on towards the looming shadows of the Rocky Mountains.

Regardless of what happened from here, it was nice finally to be back doing something that I could just get on with and chop away at. I didn't have to think too much or question what I was doing. I just had to ride. And it did feel like I was leaving some of my troubles behind. I was just grateful this time – unlike the first time – that I understood the dynamic of it a little better. I didn't see this as my solution, or my answer to life. I held no hope in it fixing me, or curing me. I was doing it because it's just what I felt I needed to do.

This trip was certainly an important part of moving on. I still found that hard. I still had an inclination to just turn right and head back up to Canada and knock on Mandy's door, whether she wanted me there or not. But I couldn't be so selfish. Passing that vertical alignment with her house up in Canada had been a difficult but necessary step. It represented me leaving that period of my life behind and moving on. Who am I kidding? We never move on. We just try and paper over the past. And in the meantime, all that's left is the road.

Chapter Six
Route 66

I decided to take old Route 66 out of Chicago. This is the famous highway heading all the way to Los Angeles. I had thought (like Vermin suggested) about heading due west until the road hit the banks of the Mississippi, and then I could trace it south until St. Louis, and then west towards the Rockies. But for so many people Route 66 is such an iconic road that the opportunity to ride it for myself was too powerful to resist.

I'd heard much about the road; about how it no longer exists in its entirety and how you have to hop on and hop off it as you trace its path all the way from Chicago to Los Angeles, a total distance of almost 2,700 miles. Of course, the road hasn't always been broken up like that. Back when it first opened in 1926 it was a solid ribbon of road – later becoming known as the 'Mother Road' – transporting entire families and communities from the hardship of the industrial north-east of America, to the more optimistic climates of the Pacific Coast.

Sadly, just like most things, progress came along and made the road redundant almost overnight. It was decommissioned as a federal highway on June 27th 1985, the day the interstate was completed. From receiving a steady flow of traffic, the towns along the route one day fell almost silent, bypassed completely, with many of them struggling to remain in existence ever since.

Scottish comedian Billy Connolly filmed a TV series about the road not so long ago. It painted quite a sad picture of people hanging on by the skin of their teeth, doing their best to preserve a way of life that to many is now considered outdated. It's just fortunate that in recent years efforts have been made to promote the old road and increase the numbers of tourists and travellers along the route.

More important than the road was that ahead of me now sprawled the vast expanse of the American Midwest. If you look at it on the map you can see that from Chicago all the way across to the Rockies there is nothing much but prairie. Of course, I'd tackled such vast places before; the Australian Outback one example, the main roads of Kazakhstan being another, but somehow the vastness of the American continent just felt a lot more intimidating.

Maybe it was the thought of twisters, or memories of *The Texas Chainsaw Massacre*; that sense that you're about to let go of the handrail and take a step into the unknown. It doesn't help that there are so many routes across it. As well as Route 66 you could take the Lincoln Highway, running through Iowa and Nebraska. Or Route 50 – the Lonely Highway – passing through Missouri and Kansas. Or you could take any number of other main and back roads and get lost out there forever.

Thankfully, despite the broken spokes and the signs of old age from the engine, the bike was still doing just fine. I'd changed the oil twice already, and fitted a new rear tyre back near Detroit, during one of those spoke fixing occasions. It was the highways that were proving to be hard work, just trying to keep up with the flow of traffic and get out of the way of the big trucks that squeezed us into the gutter.

The question still remained as to where this adventure might end; in San Francisco or in Alaska? I thought about this a lot while riding. The concern was that I'd left it too late in the season to go up to Alaska. I'd read that the end of September is the absolute latest to be heading up that way and it was the end of August already. I still had to get to San Francisco, and Alaska was another 3,500 miles north from there.

I could if I'd have wanted gone straight up from Chicago to Alaska – shortened the distance by a great deal – and perhaps made it with plenty of time to spare, but I'd always had my heart set on getting to San Francisco, and to miss it out would have felt like cheating. Besides, this route across the Midwest was going to take me through the state of Kansas, and as I was riding a bike called Dorothy, named after the previous owner's favourite character from *The Wizard of Oz*, my childish side couldn't help but get excited by the prospect of that.

And so it was, Route 66, heading out of Chicago, the road beginning almost exactly outside the McDonald's where a few days prior I'd met Lisette and heard her story. From there it heads west along Roosevelt Road, before turning on to Ogden Avenue and following that in a south westerly direction, all the way out of the city, following the brown historic route signs as you do so.

On the way out I stopped at the bike shop where Hollie used to work – where Jonathan still does work – picking up a couple of bulbs for the rear light to get that working again. By choice, I think Jonathan would have grabbed a bike from the shop and come along with me.

I suppose that is the impression people get; of being on a fabulous adventure full of excitement and joy. I think they would be less keen to sleep in hedge bottoms or be caught out in the rain or have spokes break on them in the middle of Detroit. For what it's worth, I look at other people's lives and wish mine was like that: when they seem to have everything sorted out; a place to call home; someone to love, and someone who loves them; a good routine; friends and family close; interesting hobbies and a job they like. Though I don't think it pays to wish for a different life, not unless you know all of the facts.

Once clear of Chicago the world really opens up and flattens out. There's a lot of space out here. Everywhere you look you either see fields or roads, or roads through fields. At times the old road would run parallel with the new interstate, just a wire fence between them, leaving me to look across at the massive trucks travelling at more than twice my speed. Had I been on a faster bike I would probably have joined them on the interstate, but that was beauty of this bike, it forced me to take the road less travelled, directing me through the places that most visitors – and locals – would consciously avoid.

The road would then hit a town, such as Wilmington, where at the side of the road a giant green man stands, almost as a guardian of the past. His name was Gemini Man and he symbolised everything about Route 66; the nostalgia, the kitsch, the remnants of what was perhaps back then a more optimistic future, where giant green men were cool and good for business and people would pull over to have their picture taken with it, as I was doing now.

I met an Irish couple here, travelling Route 66 in a rental car, hoping to reach LA in just two weeks' time. They had a route mapped out, a plan, an itinerary, and were the first foreign tourists I'd met since leaving New York. They weren't ever so friendly at first (or just nervous). I got the impression that they were a bit upset to have met someone else travelling the route, as they gave off the sense of wanting to be pioneers of the road that day, and they couldn't do that if they found themselves part of a procession. We took each other's photos and carried on.

I wrestled with the road to stay on it. There are just so many twists and turns, endlessly having to keep your wits about you so you don't end up on the wrong road. At one point I followed what I thought was a signpost for Route 66, only to find myself heading up a farmer's field, having to ask the farmer which way the old road went from here. I found it all quite frustrating. I don't know why. I think it's because I had a mission to try and reach St. Louis that evening and just wanted to get it done, not faff around chasing nostalgia.

Ninety-eight miles out of Chicago I found myself in the town of Pontiac. By Route 66 standards it's quite a big town, with a museum in honour of the iconic road. I parked outside it, but didn't go in, as I'm not that big a fan of museums. I'm probably not a good tourist full stop. I mean, the Taj Mahal as I passed through India was alright, but it wasn't the highlight of my Indian adventure. I preferred instead the dark alleyways, where you sit on a step drinking a five-rupee shot of chai tea, served in a porcelain cup that you smash on the ground when you've finished. It's things like this that are worth going to India for, not an old building, as nice as it was.

Here in Pontiac it was now lunch time and while I never did have a big appetite whilst travelling it was simply time, after all morning on the road, to have a break from it and recoup. I found a small bakery, serving fresh pots of coffee in polystyrene cups with a cabinet of doughnuts, all covered in a brightly coloured glaze.

'Been a lot of drought,' said one of the old timers I got chatting to in the queue. 'You'll see a lot of that on your journey west,' he continued. Indeed I would, reading later how back in 1930s this entire area was known as the Dust Bowl; the combination of drought and new farming methods sending huge clouds of dust into the air, transforming into storms that blew as far east as New York.

Visibility was cut down to a few feet, forcing many people to flee their homes and head for the Californian coast. With the Great Depression still raging it was a difficult time for everyone, with it not until post World War II that the industrial machine of America got into full swing and made it the superpower that it is today.

I'd never had much interest in American history before; in the past it had no relevance to me. But out here you can't help but think about how this was all formed: the voyage of Christopher Columbus in 1492; then over the coming years the European colonisation of a land already inhabited by indigenous people, with the first British colony formed way back in 1607.

This exodus from Great Britain, I learned, came largely as a response to the religious persecution of groups such as the Quakers and the Puritans, sailing to America in search of a place to worship free of persecution, not to mention the opportunity to own their own land for the very first time. And from that a new nation was born.

By 1770, twelve more colonies were established, with a total population of around two and a half million. Tensions between the new colonies and the British Empire from which they came continued to grow. In 1775 the War of Independence began, the new colony refusing to pay tax on imported tea and throwing it all over board in a mark of defiance known as The Boston Tea Party, which set in motion the war that was eventually won in 1783; America allegedly the first colony to successfully revolt against colonial rule.

From that point on, western expansion of this new nation began, with Thomas Jefferson purchasing land from the French west of the Mississippi, effectively doubling the size of the American territory overnight. The year 1861 brought the American Civil War; which in a way could be construed as the agricultural south trying to do to the industrial north what the north had previously done to the British; beat them, and go it alone. An estimated 750,000 people died, the war lasting four long bloody years.

In the twentieth century, America was initially reluctant to enter World War I. There was Prohibition, the building of the first mass-produced motorised car by Henry Ford, and Mickey Mouse was born. Then came the Great Depression, the roaring forties, the involvement in World War II, Pearl Harbour, the Cold War, the first man on the moon, Vietnam, the assassination of JFK. Then later, the First Gulf War and, in this century, Iraq, Afghanistan, and the sabre-rattling over Syria and Iran.

It felt then that I was passing through a nation built on the actions of defiance and western expansion, and I have to concede that not at all times did I like this place. I felt that it had a high opinion of itself, 'the Greatest Nation in the World,' which is an easy thing to claim if you've never left your own shore. A man in New York argued with me that it was also the freest nation on earth, though he'd never set foot outside of America, so how could he say whether it was or not, only regurgitate what he had been conditioned to believe.

I felt there was a lot of fear here as well, more than I'd encountered in any of the other countries I'd passed through so far. I wondered if it was because, having fought to claim their own freedom and land, the American psyche is one that believes that someday, someone else will come along and try and do the same thing to them.

To my eyes, this had resulted in a fear of communists, of black people, of Muslims, of the State, of God, of paying for someone else's health bill. To extend this line of enquiry makes you question if it is this latent fear that gives rise and sustenance to the American propensity for gun ownership. Guns as a means of defending themselves and their country; a weapon against their own fears perhaps.

I certainly struggled with it at times during these early few weeks. I don't know if it was my own mood, still low at times, or the route that I'd taken, with my passage through such places as Detroit and Chicago revealing a side of America that rarely gets talked about, standing at odds with the image the nation generally projects of itself.

What I'd seen was confronting, and at times upsetting, but it was what it was, and all you can do is sit and look at it all, and try to take as much of it in as possible as you slowly drift on through. The people though, even if I didn't agree with them, had all been warm and kind, just as they had been across the rest of the world. I wonder if that's because they're human beings first and foremost, and Americans second.

***

Despite best intentions, I never did make it as far as St. Louis that evening. Somehow, despite the satnav, and the route signs, I managed to get lost, riding the back lanes of rural Missouri, tracing the edge of corn fields, having to go back on myself and generally becoming a little flustered until I finally landed in Carlinville, a small country town some seventy miles to the north of St. Louis.

I found myself in the town's main square, around which all the shops were built. There were four main exits from it. I wasn't sure which one to take. I turned left, only to find myself at a dead end, overlooking the old Country Hall, a grand old building that looked a bit like the one struck by lightning in *Back to the Future*. I photographed it, before spinning around and heading back up to the main square in the centre of town, determined to try again.

I stopped to ask directions from two men sat on a doorstep smoking cigarettes. They turned out to be recent arrivals from Vietnam and whilst friendly, didn't know their way around either. As I chatted with them I tried to imagine what their journey must have entailed: growing up, a sense of discontent, hopes of one day living in the western world, saving money, booking tickets, landing, arriving here and getting work in a local restaurant, in a town in the middle of nowhere. It reminded me of something;

Sonder; 'the realisation that each random passer-by is living a life as vivid and complex as your own – populated with their own ambitions, friends, routines, worries and inherited craziness – an epic story that continues invisibly around you like an anthill sprawling deep underground, with elaborate passageways to thousands of other lives that you'll never know existed, in which you might appear only once, as an extra sipping coffee in the background, as a blur of traffic passing on the highway, as a lighted window at dusk...'

Taken from the online Urban Dictionary.

One of the men thought he knew of a campsite on the edge of town and sent me off in a direction where all I found was another McDonald's, resigning myself to another coffee and cheeseburger, just to stay on budget, which by this stage was just about hanging on in there. By chance, I parked beside a car with an open window. A girl was sat inside the car reading a book. We exchanged pleasantries, before I headed inside and took a break from the road for a while.

On the way out – it now dark – the girl was still there, still reading her book with the interior light illuminating the words. I was curious to know why she was still there, so asked her. It transpired that her friend worked in McDonald's but couldn't drive. And so this girl – Nikki – would drive her the forty miles from home, and instead of going backwards and forwards to pick her up at the end of her shift, would bring a few books and, for the eight-hour shift her friend was on, sit in the car and read them.

Nikki was a great girl: a big smile, easy to talk to and it was just one of those moments where you're stood in a fast food carpark, talking to a stranger in the car next door, and it's dark, and you don't know each other, but it feels like you know each other, and it's completely surreal because at the end of it all you ask if she knows of any campsites around and she says, 'yeah, down by Beaver Dam.'

And that's where I camped that evening, in a clearing in the forest, the entire place to myself.

***

In St. Louis the next morning I decided that I should go and visit the Gateway Arch. This is an easy building to find as it stands 192 metres tall (630 feet) and rises like a steel rainbow from an area of parkland right beside the Mississippi River. It was built in 1965 as a monument to Westward Expansion of the United States and 'typifies pioneer spirit of the men and women who won the West and those of a latter day to strive on other frontiers.' A monument to imperialism I guess.

It was actually in 1804 that two explorers – William Clark and Captain Meriwether Lewis – set out from St. Louis on what was called the Corps of Discovery, an expedition commissioned by then President Thomas Jefferson in order to map and explore that land he'd just purchased from the French. A total of 33 men left on the expedition, it taking them over a year to reach the Pacific Coast (the place I was heading to). At which point they turned around and came back again.

For the expedition, the US Mint prepared special coins inscribed with a message of friendship and peace, called Indian Peace Medals, which soldiers distributed to native people they came across on their expedition, the coins symbolising US sovereignty over indigenous inhabitants. I think it's fair to say that the indigenous people of the land suffered in all this: the western expanse of the Europeans; the taking of the land; being forced on to reserves, well away from the places they would have chosen to inhabit.

You'd like to think that if the same scenario played out today, and we discovered new territory, maybe even on the moon, but the moon already had tribes of moon-men, then we would work together and strive to get along. Or would we once again take what we wanted and not really care about the men who already live on the moon? Maybe it's a simple case of survival of the fittest, a reminder that men are tribal, and conflict is inherent. Conflict seems inherent in relationships and families, let alone nations. So perhaps it'd be unrealistic to expect anything other than bloodshed.

To get a better picture of the arch I decided to push the bike between the security barriers and up on to the mound of grass in front of it. Having done this I took quite a few photographs, from various angles, moving the bike around and repositioning it for ten minutes or more. It was then that a security patrol car approached, the two officers (wearing shorts, with fat calves, dark glasses and pistols in holsters) getting out and walking in my direction. I knew I was in trouble; I knew I shouldn't have been on here with the bike and certainly didn't imagine this was going to end so well.

One of the officers demanded my passport, which I handed to him. He then proceeded to ask a series of questions about what I was doing in St. Louis, how long I'd been in America and what the purpose of my visit was. I explained what I was doing – riding the old bike across – apologising for bringing the bike up here and explaining that it was just for a souvenir snapshot. The officer radioed my details to what I assumed was a central command centre, waiting for them to be processed and come back with a verdict as to whether I was who I said I was or not.

It all reminded me of something John had told me back in Equinunk, about the security in Times Square, Manhattan. John's belief was that the reason I was able to push the bike up on to the pavement and position it right in the middle of the pedestrian part of Times Square for a photograph was because facial recognition cameras would have detected me – along with everyone else – the moment I entered the area, cross-referenced the image of my face with that taken by border control when I entered the country and verified whether I was a known threat or not.

I questioned the plausibility of this, before remembering how Facebook is already doing this whenever you upload a photo, detecting who is who. And that's only the technology we know of.

As it was, the two security guards here in St. Louis were happy that I posed no threat, insisting I go back out through the security gate and park the bike in a proper location next time. I rode down and parked it alongside the Mississippi River, a wide brown vein of water passing right through the heart of St. Louis. There was a steamboat moored nearby, old rusting factories on the other side of the bank, and high above it all towered that huge silver rainbow.

It was only $10 to take the tiny four-man lift to the top of it, which I did, hearing how the lift was very clever in the way it was able to move up and across, crab-like, as it climbed the leg of the arc. At the top you emerge in a slender viewing capsule, windows on either side and room for some forty people.

For a while I was too nervous to look out the window. It was that sense of being so high up, with nothing really beneath your feet, except for a long drop to the ground. After a while I pushed my nose right up to the glass and looked out, first to the east, back in the direction of New York, perhaps now a thousand miles away, and then to the west, across that land that Lewis and Clark, only two hundred years before, had first explored, planning to follow in their tracks on my old Australian Post bike, the one I'd ridden some 25,000 miles to get here.

It was a shame that Dorothy had lost some of her allure and mystique of that first trip, where she really had become her own character. Though in truth, I'd probably been guilty of giving too much life to an inanimate object, possibly in the belief that if I gave life to Dorothy then I wouldn't feel quite so alone on that nine-month journey from Sydney to London.

The obvious truth is that I was alone, and I think that's what had scared me about doing this second trip; being on my own again. I wondered if this is something that bothers all of us at times; that sense of living and dying alone. Hoping we won't, but knowing that we probably will, as grim as that might sound.

Having returned to the bike I decided from here that I wasn't going to continue along old Route 66 as it just wasn't for me; I neither had the time, the money or the pace to explore it properly, and to be totally honest, it was quite disappointing in comparison to what I'd been expecting. The other route – along Route 50, the Lonely Highway – which passed through St. Louis, was not only more direct, but also a lot less complicated and hard to follow. It would also take me straight through the heart of Kansas, and Dorothy was excited by the prospect of this.

***

Heading out of St. Louis I passed through some more run-down neighbourhoods, not realising at the time that this was the third most violent city in America. Flint, in Michigan, was first; Detroit was second; meaning I'd passed through two of the top three. Once again, it's hard to avoid the visual evidence that the worst bits are always the black bits, and as I rode out through another ghetto I couldn't help but wonder why it is like this. I mean, is the trouble in these neighbourhoods because the residents are black, or is the trouble in these neighbourhoods because the residents are poor, and just so happen to be black? Later I read a little about it, to try and make sense of it for myself.

I read that the first African slaves arrived in Virginia in 1619. Slavery was made illegal in Northwest Territories one hundred and sixty years later in 1787, but with demand for cotton increasing, so too did demand for slave labour, giving rise to the Underground Railroad; a chain of sympathisers helping to traffic Africans out of the south, to the sanctuary of the north.

Laws were in place to stop the slaves from escaping, with people punished, and hanged, for trying to do so. Finally, in 1808, there was a ban on the importation of slaves from Africa. In 1820 it was banned completely in the north, but not in the south. However, the famous Dred Scott case of 1857 cited that congress did not have the right to ban slavery in states, and furthermore, that slaves are not to be classed as citizens.

Even Abraham Lincoln – often credited for abolishing slavery – was once quoted as saying: "I will say then that I am not, nor ever have been, in favour of bringing about in any way the social and political equality of the white and black races; I am not nor ever have been in favour of making voters or jurors of negroes, nor of qualifying them to hold office, nor to intermarry with white people...

"I will say in addition to this that there is a physical difference between the white and black races which I believe will forever forbid the two races living together on terms of social and political equality. And in as much as they cannot so live, while they do remain together there must be the position of superior and inferior, and I, as much as any other man, am in favour of having the superior position assigned to the white race."

(Debate at Charleston, Illinois, September 18, 1858)

Then came the American Civil War, slavery used as a justification for that, though it was a war that had been brewing between the industrial North and agricultural South for quite some time. The true aim of the war was to preserve the Union; to preserve the United States, rather than have it split into two opposing parts. Of course, the North won, the Union survived, with the Emancipation Proclamation of 1863 deeming that a person held as slave shall be free, except those in border states where slavery was still allowed.

It was only in 1869 that blacks were classed as American citizens for the first time. A year later they were given the right to vote, but with legalised segregation continuing under Jim Crow laws for another 100 years, this gave rise to separate schools, hospitals, streetcars, public waiting rooms, restaurants, boarding houses, theatres and parks. It was in 1964 that President Johnson finally signed the Civil Rights Act, prohibiting discrimination with regard to race, colour, religion or national origin, this all taking place just a lifetime ago.

The succeeding years brought the race riots of Detroit and Newark in the eighties, and later Los Angeles in the nineties. Malcolm X was assassinated, so too Martin Luther King. Now you have Barack Obama in the White House, but is it really plausible to think that after the events of the last four hundred years or more, that black America can pretend everything's forgotten and move forward, united?

It would be nice to think so, but I just know with myself that once too much water has passed beneath the bridge, no amount of back-pedalling can change things. It takes time, patience and forgiveness, on both sides. Trust is important too, and I would say, from my brief experience so far, that it is trust that seems to be so lacking between these two colours of America. And it does no one any favours for one party to tell the other that it's a simple case of trying harder, not after the events of the past.

As a counterpoint to all this, as I made my way out of the city in the direction of the Lonely Highway, a man pulled up alongside me at a set of traffic lights. He was a black man, wearing a suit and tie and driving a top-of-the-range Cadillac Escalade, an expensive SUV.

'Where are you off to?' enquired the man from his driver's seat. 'San Francisco,' I replied with mild embarrassment. The man laughed in a kind hearted manner, wishing me the best of luck on my journey ahead. In return I complimented him on his car. 'Thank you,' said the man. 'I've had to work long and hard for this.'

A simple act of *trying*? Perhaps it is. Though surely the same must apply to all of us.

Chapter Seven
Across the Midwest

This night on the road was possibly the worst of any I'd encountered in the last 25,000 miles. From St. Louis I'd ridden all afternoon, along this Lonely Highway, which wasn't lonely at all. It was full of trucks and traffic and endless little towns, down on their luck; dead fields of corn after the drought had struck; and one gas station, where I sat drinking my coffee and eating my sandwich in the canteen section while having to listen to some guy talking about Obama and how he's a 'moslem' and not even American and how no way should he be President.

I just kept my head down. Clearly they weren't keen on outsiders around here and if any of them spotted my Indonesian biker jacket, and knew it to be the most populated Muslim country in the world, I might well have been chased out of town. You'd like to say something, try and reason with the man, perhaps try and convince him that not all people of that religion are evil, but that would have done me no good, and so I kept quiet and ate my sandwich.

As for this night on the road, I'd passed through a few towns along the Lonely Highway, asking at several gas stations if there were any campsites or creeks where I could camp. I think when doing this you secretly hope they'll say, 'Sure, come and camp on my land.' But not this night, and by now it was getting dark and even outside of the towns there just didn't seem to be anywhere to pull off the road and pitch a tent out of sight. Everywhere was either farms or fields, with private land ownership meaning every inch of it was fenced off or too exposed for wild camping.

In a way this was no different to riding across Indonesia, or other places where there just seems to be no space beside the road left vacant or accessible to rough campers such as me. Indonesia thankfully had a network of locally owned guesthouses, some of them brothels, which were cheap, quite grim, but they did the job of providing you somewhere to sleep. Here in America, where land ownership is absolute, and hotels too expensive, the biggest problem I was having was finding a place to sleep at night.

In the town of Tipton – it now almost dark – I stopped at an ice-cream kiosk having spotted a biker sitting on one of the benches. He rode a Harley Davidson and was with a woman who had a set of comically enhanced breasts. I asked them (the couple, not the breasts) if they knew of anywhere nearby I could camp for the night. They were quite dismissive and unhelpful, mentioning something about a park just down one of the side streets. I thanked them and headed in that direction, finding the park to be surrounded by houses, and people walking their dogs. This wasn't a good place to sleep, it was too exposed. I imagined I'd soon be woken by the police and moved on.

I rode back towards the main road. As I stopped at the junction I looked to the left along the rural road that meandered off into countryside. Just beyond the last house was a trail leading off into forest land. The last house overlooked this path and I thought that if they saw me go down there they'd no doubt call the police, but it was dark now, and that was the best chance I had of finding a place to sleep.

I turned left out of the entrance to the park, rode the few hundred yards until I was almost at the turn for the dirt trail to my right. I scanned around, making sure there was no traffic, then darted down the lane.

As the headlight on the bike is permanently illuminated whenever the engine is running, I cut the engine, knocked her down into neutral, leapt off and pushed like crazy down the trail – hoping that the people in the last house hadn't seen me – until I hit the cusp of the bushes and the forest. I kept pushing, right through the branches and along the remnants of an old trail, long since overgrown, just pushing and pushing, as hard as I might, the bike and me galloping over the ruts and dead branches, wading through the trees until all of a sudden the trail came to a halt at a dried-up riverbed.

I put Dot on her stand and looked around. I looked behind to see or hear if anyone had followed me. I looked over the other side of the dried-up riverbed to where there was a tall fence with a farm installation on the other side, perhaps a good stone's throw away. I could see the light on top of the barn above the fence, but no one could have seen me over the fence, though I did hear voices in the yard.

By now my heart was beating like a drum. It was made worse by the fact that every time a car drove along the road I'd just turned from, it would shine a faint beam of light through the trees and on to the small clearing on which I was stood, which made me think it was the torchlight of the person looking for me. I stood like this for ten minutes or more, perhaps even twenty. I was in an eerie dark forest; all the light had gone. I shouldn't be here, but I had nowhere else to be. I would have to sleep here, and hope that no one would come.

To make matters worse, in my panic, I thought it was time I did an oil change, because with a knocking noise beginning to be heard from the engine I thought for some strange reason it might help. So right there, in the middle of the forest, I dug a small ditch beneath the engine and, not proud of this, undid the engine bolt until the oil started flowing out and into the hole I'd dug in the ground. Returning it to nature, I justified to myself, knowing I shouldn't have done it. I was just desperate to do anything to keep this bike running as it was my lifeline.

While doing this I dropped the engine oil bolt in the dirt and couldn't find it anywhere because it was pitch black now. I didn't have a torch, and I couldn't have shone one anyway because it might have given my position away. My mind was telling me that any minute someone was going to wade through the bushes and scream at me for being there, or point a gun at my head, and I would have a bike without an engine bolt, draining oil into the earth.

I could have hit myself. And did. It was a horrible evening, one where you could tear yourself limb from limb. I don't think I was thinking rationally. I don't think I was sane. I was alone in America, deep in the Midwest, at night time, camping in the dirt.

Finally I found the bolt, wiping off the soil and debris, before screwing it back into the sump, replenishing the oil and putting up my tent. I threw in my sleeping bag, got in that, gripped the knife, lay on the hard dry ground, and slept until 4.30am, when the alarm clock on my sim-less mobile phone woke me from my slumber. I quickly packed up my things, and under the cloak of darkness, pushed the bike back out along the path, fighting with the trees and branches, hiding amongst them until I could check the lights of the last house were still out and there was no one out on the road.

Coast clear, I pushed like crazy, back along the dirt trail to the road. At the end I fired Dot into life and, having already put my helmet and gloves on, raced straight off, back up to where the ice-cream kiosk was, as a gas station was located on the opposite side of the road and was already open for the day. I bought a coffee and sat on the step outside, looked upon suspiciously by the people around me. I checked the bike's valve clearance with the feeler gauge, before thinking I'd got nothing better to do than hit the road and hope this day was a better one.

**

Instead of staying on Route 50, which by this time would have been dual carriageway all the way into Kansas City, I took Route 5 running due south for around 70 miles until it hit Route 54, running almost parallel east to west to Route 50, but hopefully a little bit quieter, with less heavy traffic. By taking this route I would bypass Kansas City completely, which in a way was a shame, as I'd heard the town was famous for its BBQ food and I think to be doing this trip on a 'proper' bike, on a 'proper' budget, being able to find a decent hotel and spend my nights meandering around the city, would have been quite pleasant.

Sometimes I did resent the way I travelled; with haste, on a low budget, often desperate to be at the next destination. Though equally, I chose to avoid the cities as they just made me sad. I rarely saw anything that I liked in them. They were difficult to navigate, dense in traffic and largely all looked the same. Too many people in too small a place. And on a bike like this it just felt like an unnecessary chore, hence the reason for avoiding Kansas City this day.

Fortunately, Route 5 was the quietest road I'd been on for a while and with it being so early in the morning there wasn't so much traffic around. As per usual I stopped at my favourite fast-food diner for breakfast – talking to the counter staff about local sights that might be worth seeing (a lake, I skipped) – before taking something of a shortcut, finding myself riding amidst a world of water, where perfectly still lakes cut across the land and long flat bridges carried you from one bank to the other. Combined with the thick forest surrounding it, it seemed a nice change from Missouri's flat agricultural land, which is mainly all I'd seen of it so far.

Route 5 finally dropped me down to Route 54, which, for whatever reason – it's hard to pinpoint exactly why – just seemed a more pleasant place to be than Route 50. It was quieter for a start, and felt like a road that served communities, rather than one designed simply to get you somewhere. Odd to think of a road as having a soul, but that's what Route 54 seemed to have; a simple liveliness about it as it rolled gently across the landscape, meandering left and right, through small dilapidated villages, past fields of burnt-out crops, the air so hot and still.

I didn't stop much out here (only to take a photo of Dorothy beside the Kansas state sign). I didn't have reason to, and there didn't seem much worth stopping for either. This was short-sighted really, as I bet all of these down-on-their-luck towns would have a story to tell, about their rise and their fall, the shops that have closed down and the people that have moved away, or still live here, scratching out an existence for the simple reason that this is their home and that's where they belong.

I passed through these places, wondering what it must be like to live out here, so far from the coast, landlocked for thousands of miles. No wonder some of them were a little bit insular. The world to them was small out here.

It was out here in the middle of Kansas that I ran into Klara and Flo, two young German cyclists riding across America on a pair of push bikes. I saw them at first as two dots on the horizon, travelling in the same direction as I was, gradually catching up with them until I pulled alongside and slowed to ask if they were okay for water. They were fine and so I carried on, stopping in the next town, a few miles away, to wait for them. I reasoned it would be good to share the joys of the road for a moment.

The two cyclists finally came to a halt in the Dollar Store carpark where I waited for them in the shade. It was midday and stinking hot. They wore dark lycra, helmets and were covered in sweat. Their skin was red from where it was exposed to the sun. I was always fascinated by cyclists doing this kind of long distance touring. It seemed like a sufferance, averaging around 100 miles a day, having to pack and plan for the limitations of what could be carried by bicycle, not being able to rush through the bad areas like even I was able to do, having to pedal through them, so vulnerable in so many ways.

The pair told me how they had started in or around Washington, riding the Appalachian Trail, passing through West Virginia and Kentucky, their intention to make it all the way to the coast and possibly drop down into Mexico after that. I asked them how they had found it so far and they said many of the areas they had passed through had been incredibly poor. They said that a lot of time they found it hard to explain to people where Germany was. Some of the locals thought you could ride there, not realising that it was on the other side of the Atlantic. But like me they'd only met good people, who had helped them, or people of the other persuasion, who had baffled them. But they were enjoying it, and it was a pleasure to have met them this day.

The rest of the day was simply spent riding along Route 54, before later drifting into the centre of Wichita just as evening approached. To me Wichita was one of those towns that you've probably heard of, either from a movie or a song or some other piece of pop culture, but you have no clue what is there or even where it is in relation to the rest of America. All I knew was that when I saw it on the map I was excited that my route would take me there.

It's definitely not a big place. Instead of the vast expanse of Detroit and Chicago, there was instead a moderately long entry road, lined with cheap motels and liquor stores. It was downbeat and downtrodden, Chinese and Mexican restaurants inhabiting the tired single-storey brick buildings, serviced by parking lots cracked by weeds and guarded by broken wire fences. I considered the prospect of stopping in one of the motels (budget notwithstanding), but would have preferred another dried-up riverbed any day of the week.

The centre of town was an improvement, though strangely charmless. Everything was built on a grid, office buildings no more than three or four storeys high. It felt like a place of bureaucracy, and I learnt later that it was in Wichita that the aviation industry grew. Boeing, Airbus and Learjet all still had operations there, with Wichita also home to the very first Pizza Hut. The city now has a population of around 400,000, making it the biggest city in Kansas, bigger than Kansas City in fact. In a way it reminded me of the Australian capital of Canberra, and how you had to know where the pockets of life were or else you'd never find them.

I stopped at a McDonald's just off the town centre. I thought that if I'm going to camp that night then I'm best eating now and so got in line to order a 99 cent cheeseburger and a $1.17 cup of coffee, which was my usual order on this journey across America. As I stood there, lost in my own world as I so often was, I was interrupted by the Asian man ahead of me who enquired as to whether that was my motorcycle parked outside. I told him that it was and he asked where I'd been and where I was going. I wasn't particularly interested in talking about it. It was just life, my life, I didn't think it was at all worth talking about, certainly not at that moment.

The man asked where I would sleep this night, and I said wherever I could find to put up my tent. He couldn't believe it. He couldn't believe that I would just ride along until I found somewhere out of sight, park up, put up the tent and go to sleep. He was quite stunned by this, but obviously, to me, it was just a part of my life out here.

The man was with his son, the pair of them driving to Colorado for the start of the son's new university term. He said they were doing the drive over two days and that the father would drive straight back having dropped his son off. They invited me to sit with them. I waited for my coffee and cheeseburger, and then did so.

The pair were from Taiwan; the father (Kol) I gathered was a relatively successful businessman. He spoke good English, asked direct questions and genuinely seemed interested in what I was doing. I asked what his impressions of America were and he said the country had been good to him, commenting that it was a relatively new country, only a teenager compared to the countries we'd come from, and so still had room to grow and to learn.

He also reasoned that if a man was walking outside and got attacked by another man or a group of men then people – strangers – would rush over to intervene. He said that in our own countries (Taiwan and England) that just wouldn't happen; we'd turn a blind eye and keep on walking. I think he was right, we would. We'd convince ourselves it was none of our business and look the other way. This is what I did like about America, how people are strong as individuals and not afraid to be heard and act when they feel a need to. We in England are often too concerned about what others think to be like this. Perhaps we are cowardly. Perhaps we have less to protect.

The man told me he wanted to help me out. I asked what he meant by this and he said that he was going to pay for me to have a room in the hotel that he and his son were staying in over the road. I told him I couldn't possibly let him do that. But I think as a father, speaking to someone's son, he wouldn't take no for an answer, and was adamant that he was going to book me a room, whether I liked it or not.

I followed the man outside, being told to wait whilst he got the car and then I would follow him to the hotel that was just around the corner. Shortly after a top of the range Mercedes E55 AMG pulled up, the son driving, who was only around 17 years of age. I followed the car to the Best Western that was in sight of the McDonald's we'd just left. Kol told me to wait outside while he went in and took care of the room.

He came outside five minutes later and handed me the key. He told me that I'd never see him again, that he didn't want anything in return, reassuring me that the room was paid for and that I was to have a safe trip. I shook his hand and thanked him dearly, almost to the point of stunned silence, before beginning the task of carrying all my gear up through the lobby of this grand hotel – explaining to the confused receptionist what events had just transpired (a stranger, buying a room for another stranger, who he had met just moments before in McDonald's) – before using the key card to access a beautiful room with twin king-sized beds, a bathroom, a kettle, a TV, clean towels and not a single dried-up riverbed in sight. There was also safe parking for Dot, in the multi-storey next door, chained to the railings with a lock I'd been carrying, with no use for it until now.

I unpacked all of my things, re-organised them, took a shower, then had a long hot bath, followed by some time on the internet uploading photos and sharing my excitement with friends back home. After that I lay back to watch a few hours of TV, before falling asleep.

The next morning, before heading down for complimentary breakfast, the invoice was slid beneath the door. I thought for a moment I would have to pay it, before realising it was just a receipt for the almost $160 room the stranger from Taiwan had paid for last night. One night in a dried-up riverbed, the next in a king-sized bed in a fancy hotel; the surreal encounters of the road.

Chapter Eight
Kansas

I didn't ride far that day. I just didn't feel like it. Instead, I spent most of the morning trying to figure out which way to go, because not far from Wichita, up near Dodge City, there would be a fork in the road and I had to decide which way to turn. I could either carry on along Route 54 until it rejoined Route 50, and from there follow it all the way to Colorado Springs, the town in which Vermin and his family lived. Or I could take the fork to the left, and follow the old Santa Fe Trail, a nineteenth century trading route (now part of the highway system), that was once used to transport arms down to the front line during Mexican-American war of 1846 to 1848.

It was one of those decisions where there isn't really a right or wrong answer; all roads lead to the same place, so it was a question of what I would prefer to see along the way. I really wanted to go to Santa Fe as I knew it to be a quaint rustic town, with a strong Mexican influence and a town centre of buildings that could have come straight out of a *Flintstones* cartoon. I knew this because I'd been there before, ten years prior, when after that summer teaching tennis back in Equinunk I'd taken a three-week organised trip all the way from the east coast of America to the west.

A total of fourteen of us were crammed into the back of a mini-van, with a guide named Abi, a prescribed route to follow, and nothing much to think about because everything was done for you. The route was also different to the one I was taking now. From New York it went down through Washington, then into Alabama and Louisiana, reaching New Orleans where we stopped for a few nights. From there it meandered west, to Carlsbad Caverns, Roswell, then up to Santa Fe and west from there, all the way to the coast.

By chance, we landed in LA on the 10th September 2001, the night before the planes crashed into the twin towers. I'll always remember that morning, waking up on a campsite and being told to go and look at the television in the communal lounge as something bad had just happened.

The rest of the day we all sat pretty much in silence, unable to believe what we were seeing; no doubt the same emotions as everyone else who watched their televisions that day. I remember being in a lift a few days later with an American man, raging and insistent that we just go and bomb the lot of them in retaliation. Sadly, that's pretty much what we did, and I don't think the world's been quite the same ever since.

To think that now, because of those attacks on New York (or those attacks on New York being used to justify what followed), American drones are being flown over areas in Pakistan not far from those I rode through on that first trip (I passed through Abbottabad, the town where Osama Bin Laden was found) killing people – some innocent – in a bid to win this War on Terror.

I can't help but question the irony of that. I think that's why at times I struggled to like this place, because I didn't always like its politics, and as you travel through the guts of America you can begin to sense how as a nation it chose to respond in the way that it did; lashing out, as a victim might, thinking it had the right not to be attacked, a sense of righteousness perhaps, a Manifest Destiny, aligned with that presence of fear of people and cultures they don't always understand. To fight force with force, to wield the biggest gun, in the way that the West was won.

It was perhaps ironic then that the town I passed through next was Dodge City, home of Wyatt Earp, one time sheriff of the town. The town isn't so dangerous now. In fact it seemed to have more churches than any other town I'd passed through. In the centre of town was a museum, featuring a full size recreation of an old 19th century street, complete with wooden shops. Historical re-enactments took place here, whilst out in the parking lot an old black steam train overlooked a gift shop, where you could buy all sorts of trinkets from the past. Across the road was a McDonald's, meaning the trappings of the 21st century were never that far away.

I didn't plan on staying long, I was simply passing through, only my feet seemed to get stuck in the mud, and as much as I tried to plod on I just couldn't seem to muster the conviction to push myself over the inertia. Some days you get like that, when the call of the road just isn't strong enough, and I think by now I'd begun to relax a little more and accept that you get there when you get there, and not a second before.

I hung around Dodge City instead, chatting to some other bikers riding huge and beautifully painted Honda Goldwings, towing matching trailers on the back. It was the antithesis of my approach to travel, with no right or wrong. Just different spokes for different folks.

By evening, I'd conceded my riding day was done and having enjoyed my time in Dodge City – more pleasant than I'd ever expected – I headed out to a campsite where I pitched the tent beside a dried-up lake and watched as the full moon shone into view.

To say the tent only cost $18, it was doing okay, as were the rest of my things. I'd even become quite attached to my J-Lo sunglasses and had refined the packing of my equipment to such a point that I knew where most things were. The saddle bags had kept on ripping. I now fixed them with tie-wraps holding opposing panels together. I was making do, as by this stage I was halfway through my £500 budget, and still with so many miles left to go.

Times like these didn't help – paying $20 for a tent pitch – but sometimes the last thing you need on an evening is not to feel safe at night. And to be truthful, I wasn't quite as destitute as I could have been, mainly thanks to a man named Malcolm, who I probably should have mentioned before.

I'd met Malcolm at a bike event one weekend in England, a few months before embarking on this adventure. Malcolm had asked me for a copy of my first book and told me that if I were ever to do America then he'd sponsor me £200. I didn't think anything of it until he emailed me out of the blue just two days before I shipped myself and the bike over to the States.

'Good news Malcom,' I responded, 'we're on our way.' 'Great,' he said. 'Now give me your bank details and I'll wire you that money.' I told him not to be so daft, but he was adamant.

Reluctantly I'd sent him the details and a little later checked my account only to find he'd deposited £500! Then, when I told him my budget for the entire trip was not much more than that and how grateful I was, and how silly he was, he sent me another £150, to make it up to £650, which was incredibly kind, and meant that I was doing the trip almost in the black, rather than even further into the red, as I otherwise would have been. It was this money that had paid for the satnav.

Apparently, it was upon reading in that first book of my trials and tribulations and recognising those feeling of frustration in not being able to make it work with the person that you love that compelled him to lend a hand. He'd been there, as most of us have – Malcolm was of an age where he had a pair of grown-up sons, and his hope for them was that they never fall properly in love, because to him it only proved to be ruinous.

I found it difficult to disagree with this; the eternal hole in your soul caused by the feeling – real or otherwise – of letting someone go, or letting someone slip through your fingers, really can have a detrimental impact on your mood, and your mind, from that point on. But then again, the pain of that, as crap as it is of times, makes us who we are. It makes us do the things we do. And so I see it perhaps as a double-edged sword. Were it not for the way I had been feeling, I would never have done this, or found need to do this. I would not be here on an Australian motorbike, in the middle of America. Heading west in search of an unknown future. And by now, I was glad that I was.

I had however decided not to rely on satellite navigation quite so much from here on in, packing it away and relying once again on my own intuition. I often think in modern life how there's too much reliance on the things that have the capacity to guide us (removing our own input from the equation), and at times I wondered if there was a correlation between those anti-depressants the doctor prescribed me, this satnav unit that guided me, and even the organised religion the lady in our local post office wished for me to join during my darkest of days.

After all, such things give us a hand rail to hold on to, which seems necessary when we need them most. But later, for me at least, I felt it necessary to let go of that rail, and stand on my own two feet again, as terrifying as that can sometimes be. Which is why I said no to the anti-depressants, the organised religion, and finally packed the satnav away in the panniers, and went in whichever direction felt right. Which of course was west, in the direction of Colorado Springs.

***

The following morning I got the hell out of Dodge, ploughing out across the prairie, my tail feathers on fire and racing hard and fast away from the rising sun. It really is a strange place out here, highlighted by the road signs campaigning against abortion. 'I regret my abortion,' read one roadside placard, accompanied by a picture of an empty armed woman looking forlorn. 'One in four murders are caused by abortion,' read another.

The villages through which I passed felt guarded and mindful of outsiders. They felt like closed communities, and even the traffic from behind felt cold and unfriendly, overtaking too fast and too close, often forcing me into the gutter. Fields of rotating wind turbines sat on the horizon line, almost a surreal sight given the volume of them. The road through all this ran arrow straight across a dusty prairie, passing through small gas station towns as it did so. At one gas station I was made nervous by a group of men in a pick-up truck, eyeing me and the bike up in such a way that made me look over my shoulder for the next twenty miles or so.

The American frontier must have been a wild place back in the day – no certainty about it, gradually encroaching on the land as the new world of the United States advanced west, bridging the gap between St. Louis and California.

The term Manifest Destiny is, to a large extent, the ethos and tone behind that western expansion of the nineteenth century; the presumption that this New World, this United States, had divine right to the land. Basically, with God's blessing, they took it, which is an awkward theory to get your head around and accept, especially when you apply it to what is happening in the Middle East right now and the wars that are being fought there. A new Manifest Destiny; or again just human nature?

It is though perhaps unfair to single America out for acting in such a way. The British Empire has no doubt been guilty of it in the past. So too China, which I saw for myself as I passed through it on the way back from Australia. In the city of Kashgar in the western province of Xinjiang, the rapid migration west of the Han people has eroded and displaced the people and the culture of the Uighurs; a Central Asian tribe, once with its own country, East Turkestan, which in the fifties was annexed by China, their way of life now threatened by the 'pioneers' that surge from the east.

I met Emmett out here, a man in his sixties, also on a bicycle, cycling almost all the way across America, though not all in one go. In fact, he began his journey way back in the seventies, getting as far as Colorado Springs before his life in the army took over and he had to abort his cross-country trip and go through the rigmarole of living and earning and raising kids. Now retired, he explained how once more the world was his, and he had resumed his cross-country journey almost thirty years later, now heading for Cincinnati, and then on to the East Coast, perhaps as part of a third instalment of the trip.

Not far behind him I came across another cyclist, this one Japanese, studying in San Francisco and spending the summer vacation riding as far east as he could before term resumed. I told him he would catch a man named Emmett soon, though I felt sorry for the pair of them, as in the town I'd just ridden through, the temperature was stated as being some 103 degrees Fahrenheit. It certainly was baking hot out here.

To keep the sun off I had all my skin covered: the long-sleeved flannel shirt, BigZoner waistcoat, sunglasses across my eyes and the red and white neckerchief tied across face so that my nose, cheeks and neck were completely sheltered from the throbbing midday sun. This still wasn't enough to prevent a hornet, or a wasp, or whatever it was, from stinging me clean in the throat.

I saw the black dot looming as I rode forward, flying object meeting throat with incredible force. The sting was sharp and painful, providing one of those moments of irrational thought, when you imagine a sting can turn into an allergic reaction which can turn into your throat swelling up, which can mean a loss of breathing, and the onset of sudden death.

I pulled over beside one of those tubular mail boxes with the little wooden flag that pops up to let the owner know they have mail. It was just there by the roadside, the house it belonged to way off in to the prairies, not even visible from the road. There was no one around. Not even any passing cars or windmills. Just nothing. Only me, sat on Dot, with my helmet off, trying to get a look at the fast-swelling lump emerging on the front of my throat. I think nature was trying to tell me something: go easy on Kansas (and America), or else...

It wasn't long after this that I crossed the border from Kansas into Colorado. I'm not sure why but this caused a huge sigh of relief, the sign a good indicator that the Midwest had been crossed and from here the next challenge would be riding up and over the Rockies, a challenge that didn't seem too daunting given that me and the old bike had already ridden the second highest road in the world during our crossing of the Himalayas back in India and then Pakistan.

Meanwhile, in the first town of Lamar I stopped for a respite from the road and to stock up on maps and advice at the tourist information centre in the centre of town.

One of the volunteers, Elizabeth, was a lady well into her seventies, perhaps even her eighties, who had lost her husband four years prior, yet still maintained a cattle ranch, with over one hundred cows. She was an incredible woman, full of life and curiosity, reminding me of Gary (the seventy-seven year old cycling ski instructor I met at Lake Erie) and how at similar ages they're both out there, still doing their thing.

Elizabeth was working with a lady called Judy, the three of us chatting extensively about life and the journeys ahead, all the while a straggle of other travellers dropping by for bits of information on where best to go. These tourist information centres really do offer a great service to anyone heading across the country in the way that I was.

Strangely, as I sat there that day, I thought about the concept of legacy, and how life is often centred around the desire to leave one behind, as no one would like to think they were here, and they were gone, and no one really remembers them. I wondered if that's what I was trying to do with these trips, and maybe even these books; trying to leave my own indelible mark on the world, as small a mark as that may be.

Maybe it's because I didn't have any desire to have children or start a family – not yet in any case – and I couldn't help but wonder if that's a large incentive for having children; so that in that one single moment of procreation you have left a mark that will outlive you and ensure that your name lives on. I don't know which is easiest; to have children, or to ride a motorbike across the world? Perhaps both have their complications, though I imagine having children leaves you with fewer questions, whereas riding across the world only seems to provide you with ever more. Or perhaps I am completely wrong on that, as I might one day find out for myself.

***

That afternoon I rode towards the thin line of the Rockies, across the wilderness of Colorado, being able to just make out the mountains in the distance. It was like riding towards the gates of Mordor, that formation of rocks resembling an impassable fort, in place to impede my progress to the Pacific Coast and San Francisco beyond.

Sadly, the road didn't lead directly to Colorado Springs, but instead to the town of Pueblo, seventy miles or so to the south. That wouldn't have been a problem had the road connecting the two not been an interstate, meaning that I would have to detour west, then back east, adding around sixty miles to the distance. I didn't like the idea of that. Sixty miles is almost two hours of riding at my pace, and already the sun was beginning to sag low in the sky. I checked Google Earth at another McDonald's, realising that a dirt trail known as Overton Road ran parallel the entire length of the interstate.

I took that option, riding it now, the thick and towering line of the Rockies to my left, and the never-ending expanse of the prairies to my right. It was a beautiful evening; the perfect road, the perfect bike, the simple act of riding through a lonely landscape, kicking up dust trails and staring out at the sky; a mellowing redness about the clouds, mirrored in the red tinge of the ground below. It was a dream world, feeling the warm breeze on my face, the loose ends of the neckerchief flapping rhythmically against my sun-tinged neck. An hour's ride to Phil's house. Then a beer. Perfect.

It wasn't to last. As darkness fell I realised the front headlight wasn't working properly and I was still a good thirty miles from Colorado Springs, leaving no choice but to ride without a headlight in the dark. Not only that, but the engine didn't seem to be pulling very well either, struggling to maintain speed and gradually feeling more and more sluggish. From euphoria to panic in the space of five miles or less.

Finally, the dirt trail joined the road network, and through the outskirts of Colorado Springs I did my best to tuck in behind the cars, following their tail lights, hoping that the fluorescent postal jacket would have me seen by other road users that night. The last twelve miles to Phil's house felt like a thousand.

Phil wasn't home when I finally made it there. It was perhaps just before nine in the evening, after almost seventeen hours on the road. I wasn't even sure I'd got the right house as I'd picked up an email back in Pueblo from him saying that he was going to be home. I asked the lady next door if my friend lived here and she didn't know, she'd only just moved in.

I took my passport from the bike, my laptop and camera, most of my paperwork, and left Dorothy parked at the end of the drive. I walked away, feeling for the first time in all these years a strong desire just to abandon it, to do something else with my life and never have to see or ride the bike ever again. After all, I was in a foreign town, in a foreign country, with barely any money, and a friend who I couldn't contact by telephone because I didn't have a sim card, and who wasn't in, and I didn't even know if this was his house.

I walked away from that. I had everything I needed to start afresh. My credit card, driving licence, camera, passport, laptop. I walked through the suburbs and back to a country fair that I'd seen taking place on the way through. It was perhaps a twenty minute walk away, with people who'd been to the fair coming in the opposite direction. They looked so happy with life, and I felt so lousy. Like I had this massive obligation to do this trip, and I just didn't want to do it any more. How quickly your mood can change out here.

Now I walked to pass the time. I walked to avoid answering questions of what I was doing here and why. Dark thoughts that night. Back in the hole. Falling down a well, trying to stop yourself from falling, finger nails grating against the walls, still falling. 'Pull yourself together man. Come on, come on. Come on.' It felt like that time I was trying to find a boat out of Sumatra, riding back to the port, bracing my arms and letting out a primal scream, forcing out the fear and the anger. Roaring until your brain explodes.

I marched back to what I thought was Phil's place. When I got there he still wasn't home. 'Sod it,' I thought, flinging open the side gate that led to the backyard and going for a look around to see if I could make any sense of all this, to see if I'd got the right house.

I saw the garage and the back of the house, and that the lights were on, but no one was at home. There was another gate to another part of the backyard. I pushed through it, not expecting to find much, and yet there it was: the piece of shit that Vermin rode; Cack, the bastardised Honda PC800 with the antlers on the front and the chimney on the back to warm your can of baked beans. I was so relieved at the sight of that bike. My body oozed its tension all over the floor.

I wheeled Dot around and through the gate. I was hungry, so took out my gas burner and heated up a tin of ravioli. Dinner by moonlight, eating it with the folding cutlery set I'd bought from Kmart, back in Equinunk, the day I'd gone riding with John. I sat on the step and filled my stomach with this shit tin of food. Until all of a sudden the family came home, Phil and his wife Linda and his two kids, Dana and Drew, who'd all been out for ice cream. Was I glad to see them!

'How was your ride across the Midwest?' asked Vermin, over a bottle of cold beer as we bummed out on his sofa that night.

And there, from the beginning, I told him.

Chapter Nine
Colorado Springs

The journey from here changes. The start and the middle are done. As I entered this stage of the journey across America, I felt calmer about things and in a better place to slow down and enjoy the world through which I was passing. I was excited about this stage, as it contained all the places I most looked forward to visiting, such as Monument Valley, the Grand Canyon, Las Vegas, Death Valley, then on to San Francisco. I was definitely making good time, with it taking me just under three weeks to get from New York to here. It might seem quick (or slow) to some people, but it was the perfect pace for me, as it was all about maintaining momentum.

I didn't realise at the time but Colorado Springs was founded in 1871 as a place through which the railroad could pass. It later became known as 'Little London,' thanks to its relative luxuriousness that proved popular with visitors from England. And in fact the town's founder, William Jackson Palmer, had close connections with England as it was from that country that much of the railroad's funding had come.

The town also has a long established military history, with Peterson Air Force Base on the outskirts, Camp Carson serving the army and the North American Aerospace Defence Command – or NORAD – built into the mountains overlooking the town. This is where all of America's air defence command is based, and if you've watched the film *Independence Day*, with Will Smith, you'll know it as one of the first places the aliens destroyed in order to give themselves free passage through the American airspace. It's this weird blurring of fiction, sat upon the framework of reality, that makes travel though America so involving, especially given the interaction most of us have had with Hollywood over the years.

I spent two days in Colorado Springs with Phil and his family, the break from the road I needed before pushing west. Crossing America had been a lot tougher than I'd ever imagined. I'd perhaps been guilty of underestimating it, and not entered it with the right frame of mind in the first place. Those first thousand miles or so had really been a battle, those across the Midwest weren't always easy either. But we'd made it to Colorado Springs, still in one piece, everything just ticking along like the internals of a relentless clock.

I did still think about Alaska and whether I would make it there or not. I was optimistic that I might, but realistic enough to know that it was starting to reach the end of the season and that if I wasn't heading up that way soon then it would be too late, and that I would have missed the window for this year. I don't think it mattered really. There would be achievement enough in reaching San Francisco, which was still around 2,000 miles away. The shame in not reaching Alaska on this occasion would be that in September – the month I would arrive there – the Northern Lights shine at their brightest. Thus the title, *Running Towards the Light*, had never seemed so apt.

Such concerns for now could wait, because for those two days I rolled the bike into the garage and closed the door, happy not to have to look at it or ride it for a while. Instead, I was taken sightseeing by the Vermin family – Phil, Linda and their son Dewy who was soon to be joining the military.

Having grabbed an early morning coffee we went for a drive up into the Garden of the Gods. This is an area just beyond the city limits – one of the reasons they chose to build the city here in the first place – like a giant

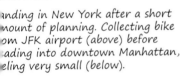

...anding in New York after a short ...mount of planning. Collecting bike ...om JFK airport (above) before ...ading into downtown Manhattan, ...eling very small (below).

From New York into Pennsylvania, staying with Johnny Equinunk (right), shooting with Thomas and Frank (below right), meeting cyclist Gary (bottom) and fixing broken spokes outside Detroit (bottom right). School bus from Camp Equinunk (below).

Spooky old house, Pennsylvania

Derelict Grand Union Station, Detroit

From Chicago along Route 66 in the direction of St. Louis, stopping to admire Gemini Man in Wilmington (below), before pushing on for a photo beneath the Monument Arch in St. Louis (bottom). Parked outside Route 66 museum in Pontiac (right).

Meeting people across the Midwest; cyclists Klara and Flo (left), tourist information centre Elizabeth (centre), cyclist Emmett (right), and Vermin and son Drew in Colorado Springs (below).

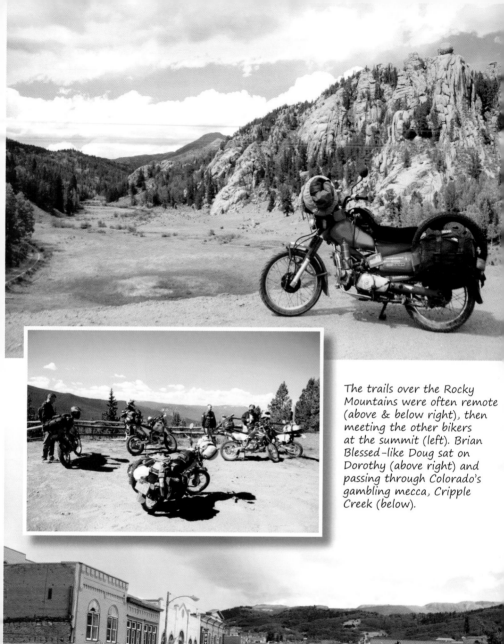

The trails over the Rocky Mountains were often remote (above & below right), then meeting the other bikers at the summit (left). Brian Blessed-like Doug sat on Dorothy (above right) and passing through Colorado's gambling mecca, Cripple Creek (below).

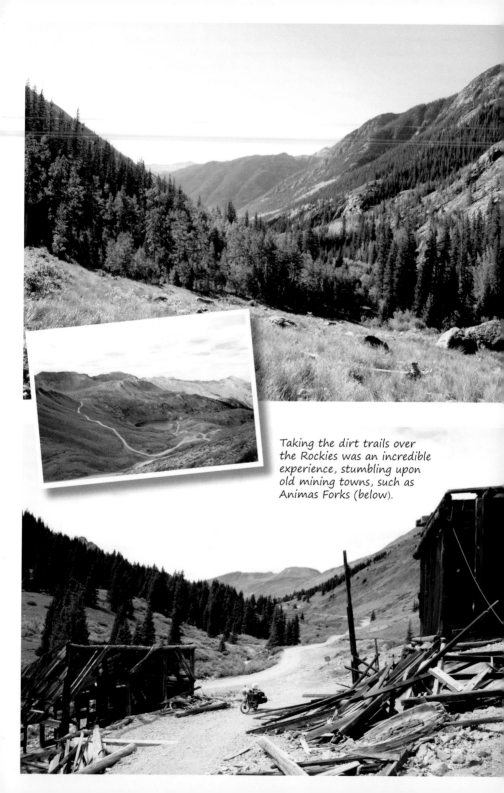

Taking the dirt trails over
the Rockies was an incredible
experience, stumbling upon
old mining towns, such as
Animas Forks (below).

naturally forming rock garden with a road running through the heart of it and a massive boulder perched on a ledge that people stop to photograph. There are also many hiking trails, and rock faces to climb. We didn't really do any of those things, just cruised through in the car, parking up a few times to take in the beauty of it all.

After that we drove up to look at where only a few months prior a savage bush fire had torched almost 300 homes, killing one person and turning the entire mountainside black and charred. It was unbelievable to see; the way in which the fire had rampaged down the mountain, destroying most of the houses, yet somehow leaving some completely untouched, almost as though it bore a grudge against some, but not against others. On one street the fire had even jumped the road and only burnt two or three homes on the opposite side, which for those residents must have been perplexing, wondering what they'd done to deserve it, whilst their neighbours still had an unscathed home.

We ate lunch in a great cafe, before pulling up at the gates of a private complex for wealthy Christian residents, with security cameras and an enclave of homes set well out of sight, at the foot of the mountains. Phil hinted at how there might be more of this to come – the wealthy living in private communities – especially with talk of privatising the police force in various parts of America and the implications that come with that.

Even back in New Jersey I'd read of a city district that had just sacked its entire police force as it simply couldn't afford to pay them, and this was a city – Camden – with one of the highest homicide rates in America. Equally in Detroit, the head of the Police Union had just declared that you enter Detroit at your own risk, with him citing his officers as being overworked and grossly understaffed to cope with the troubles there. A sense then of those with money being able to pay to privately protect themselves, and the rest no longer able to rely on the state to provide such fundamental things.

Then when you hear how the Government wishes to fly armed drones over the nation and possibly inject microchips into each citizen –

containing their medical information – you do begin to wonder if George Orwell's vision of 1984 may one day turn true.

One of the most troubling whispers I heard was about the privatisation of the prison service, and how there was profit to be made in putting people in jail, some even going as far as to suggest that the war on drugs is nothing more than a ploy to populate the prisons. To combine that with talk of privatising the police force really does make you stop and wonder just what the future holds for America if that's the game that is increasingly being played.

I always remember meeting a traveller back in India – at a coffee shop in Manali – who genuinely believed in the concept of the New World Order, and the power of the few, to rule and dominate the rest of us; the intention being to create a single world government. At the time I didn't agree with him, nor believe it to be possible, and in a way I still don't (I just don't believe in such passiveness of man to allow it to happen). But crossing America, you do get a sense of the murkiness that lies beneath the apparent order of the world, and how things are changing, and how this plateau of peace and civilisation we currently enjoy might not be as permanent as one would wish for.

Perhaps once more it may just have been down to me and my own mind. I mean, once you've been to a dark place, combined with the way that a trip such as this allows you to stand back and observe the 'traffic' rushing past, then possibly I was riddled with nihilism, and so looked out for signs of decline, rather than success. I really don't know. I just remember coming across America that first time – on that organised trip – and seeing or thinking none of these things. I was just on holiday, blown away by the brilliance of it all.

This time I was looking at things from a different angle, wondering what direction the world takes from here; worried as we all are at times about its future, yet equally being resigned to whatever does become of it, because to worry about things beyond your own control is to send yourself senseless. But with so many hours in the saddle to pass, you have to have something to think about. And these were the things I thought about.

**

As much as I was enjoying my time in Colorado Springs I knew that I had to keep moving, because to stay any longer I would have needed a real big push to get back on the road again. When you're on the road momentum keeps you going, but the moment you stop and start to feel comfortable in your environment the labours of the road suddenly don't seem so appealing. Why sit on the bike for fourteen hours a day and sleep in an undersized tent by night when you can stay here lounging on the sofa, drinking beer and watching TV? That's why I knew I needed to get going again.

To fix the faulty light we picked up a new battery from an auto parts store, it not making a blind bit of difference because in the end it turned out to be the bulb. As for the drop in performance, I'd not realised it at the time but all the way from St. Louis the road had been climbing, imperceptibly, for almost 1,000 miles, all the way from the Mississippi River, meaning that by the time I'd reached Colorado Springs I was at almost 7,000 feet. This is enough to mess up the air mixture and make a small carburettor-fed bike like this one really begin to struggle.

It was for this reason that I decided that rather than take the main tarmac roads up and over the mountains, I would take the dirt roads over the Rockies instead. Not only would this make for more enjoyment, but it would also keep me away from the traffic, which by now I was simply tired of; the traffic across Kansas particularly ferocious. It was the trucks squeezing me into the gutter that did it, making me wish at times for just a little bit more speed and engine power. I dreaded to think how the cyclists coped with it all.

Before leaving Colorado Springs I went through all of my luggage to dispose of any surplus weight. I threw out some T-shirts, pants, a few tools, reorganised my chargers and electrical equipment – this takes up much more space than you'd think – before facing a dilemma about which pair of shoes to ditch as I couldn't be bothered to carry two pairs any longer.

I'd barely worn the Converse high-tops, instead riding in the Australian workman boots almost the entire way. Sounds odd, but the boots made me feel quite manly and strong. It's what real men wear (at least that's what I told myself), whereas Converse is what the youth of today wears. And so perhaps I had to accept that this mindset didn't fit me any more. I'd grown up, moved on. And I never thought that moment would be so symbolically represented by a single pair of shoes. But whether I liked it or not, I didn't feel comfortable in Converse any more, leaving them – and my youth – beside the bin in Vermin's backyard. Perhaps in thirty years' time I'll come back for them so that I can dance the funky chicken.

Once again Phil said he was again going to ride with me, for half a day at least, but with little surprise, after no more than a few miles, just as the road started to steepen, he changed his mind and we pulled over on to a patch of gravel to say goodbye again. I didn't blame him, as travelling this slow can be quite miserable at times, especially if you're on a bike capable of going much faster. Regardless of this, he and his family had helped me no end on this journey across America. Without them I would have been lost out here and struggled to find a safe base at which to gather my breath. I hope to repay the favour some day. In the meantime, thank you.

***

Once more I was back alone, leaving Colorado Springs behind as the dirt trail made its way up the mountain, the Midwest fading beneath me and this new challenge ahead, of climbing mountains and finding my way down the other side.

This was a recreational road, nobody using it but those wishing to get off the beaten track in their 4x4s or off-road motorcycles. As the altitude climbed so did the fullness of the forests, currently on the cusp of switching to their autumn colours. It was all silver birch and an atmosphere of discovery, along what was known as Old Stage Road, not far from where the famous Pikes Peak hill-climb race takes place.

At various times the trail took the path of the old railway line, built up on the top of banks and bridging shallow valleys and ravines. These expanses proved a perfect place to stop and take a photo of the scenery. I barely saw another soul, only the occasional 4x4 travelling in the opposite direction; the rest of the time it was just me and a sea of a thousand trees.

Having circled around Sugarloaf Mountain and Knights Peak, the road spits you out an hour or so later at the old mining town of Victor. Victor was founded in 1891, back when this entire region was the biggest gold-mining district of the United States. The industry declined during the early years of the twentieth century, before closing completely by 1961. In recent years there have been efforts to kick-start gold mining in the area once again, with the Cripple Creek & Victor Gold Mining Company opening the Cresson mine in 1994, with its mine head visible from the town.

Victor wasn't a big place, just 440 residents, a couple of streets, a museum, a pizza diner and a police car that slowed to take a look at my number plate as I parked up in the street. If the town and the region reminded me of anything, it was the setting for the original *Rambo*, a small town with a local sheriff, and a place up in the mountains in which to hide.

Coincidently, in the pizza parlour on the main street, the toilet walls were scrawled with messages of support to, and from, American soldiers dating back as far as the Vietnam War. The owner was a tough female in the mould of Linda Hamilton from *The Terminator* movie, looking as though she might have served in the forces herself. Rambo would have been welcome here.

I stayed for a pizza, before taking a quick look around the town's museum. I discovered that in 1903, Victor was home of the Colorado Labor Wars, between the Unions and the mine companies, with bullet holes still visible in the town's union hall as that's just how they seemed to settle their disputes back then. Meanwhile, in a shop window on the main street of town, two old skeletons with animal skulls for heads sat at a table in their dungarees about to eat dinner. In a way this image summed up the town perfectly; a place with plenty of character, out of kilter with the modern world perhaps, but all the better for it.

Beyond Victor lay the bigger town of Cripple Creek, which was built at 9,554 feet, and alongside Victor became a prominent hub for gold mining back in the late nineteenth century. By the 1970s and 80s the town was nearly deserted, with only a few hundred residents remaining; some running cafés and restaurants for the steady flow of tourists passing through these parts.

Then, in 1991, gambling was legalised and from that moment on everything changed. The town prospered, with casinos, diners and restaurants all opening their doors. It wasn't quite Las Vegas – not in the visual sense – but the spirit was there. It was odd and somewhat bewildering to discover this casino town in the middle of the Colorado Rockies, many of the buildings the same timber style as they would have been back when the town was established. I didn't stay long, simply riding up and down the main strip in order to take stock of it all, before making haste towards the setting sun.

At the gas station at the top end of town I chatted with three late-teens filling their truck at the pump next to mine. They were Republicans and worried about what Obama was doing to their country: robbing it of jobs, killing the economy, infringing on personal freedoms. Politically, it seems this place is explosive; a chasm between the two parties, yet both leaning further – at least to my mind – to the right than Labour or the Conservatives here in England. I would say the Democrats in America sit more atop the Conservatives than they do Labour, with the Republicans even further to the right than that.

What that means in practice is that most people are more conservative than they would be in Europe. The divide in recent years has been between those that are financially conservative, and those that are religiously conservative. Those anti-abortion banners back in Kansas, for example, were a sign of the latter. There seems to be a growing faction in the right whereby God and Christian values are increasingly overlapping with politics (despite secularism at heart of the constitution) and perhaps linking back to what was said about Manifest Destiny and the backing of God.

From what I gather this is different from how it was in the eighties, when it was more about fiscal conservatism: balancing the books, running a good business. I wondered if such religious dogma entering politics to such an extent is due once more to that concept of fear; fear that the American Dream hasn't quite materialised, resorting back to religion (a form of anti-depressant or satnav perhaps?) for some kind of comfort blanket. Perhaps it's to do with racial tension and the fear of the dilution of the racial pallet. Fear of a new hegemony. Fear that things are changing. Fear that nothing stays the same and people aren't quite ready to move on just yet.

In a strange way, I couldn't help but feel a certain empathy with America as I journeyed across it. To me it seemed to be in the same place I was after that first trip from Sydney to London. It's been on a massive journey, trying to conquer something, in a way sort of succeeding (America becoming *the* global superpower), and now not quite sure what to make of it all, with the question of what happens now, what happens next? How do we sustain this, how do we move forward? The fear of losing all momentum and sliding all the way back down to the bottom, where the black dogs roam; it now a case of picking itself up and finding a new direction and horizon to aim towards. It will perhaps just take time, and lots of self-analysis.

As for me, I simply carried on riding this day. I was back on tarmac now, but this wasn't highway or those busy roads of Kansas; this was two-lane, meandering across the plains of Colorado, the biggest climbs behind me for the day. The yellow road markings down the centre of the road bringing extra colour to a world that was already vivid; mute green of the trees and the parched brown of the sunburnt grass. Then clouds, angry and vast. The sense of a storm ahead, creating an eerie mood as I rode beneath an ocean of tumultuous sky.

Then the clouds would scatter and blue sky would shine through. The world would light up. I'd sing, I'd think to myself, reflect on the past, ponder the future, still with my own questions of why am I doing this; where am I heading to; where will it end; what will it lead to?

A times, I imagined a crowd of thoughts chasing me, like monsters beneath the bed, and at the front I'm fleeing from them, like that reoccurring dream where no matter how fast you run you can't get away. Time to face, time to run. This time I felt like I was running towards something (even if I didn't necessarily know what it was), not running away from something as it had often felt on that first trip. I much preferred it this way. I certainly spent a lot less time looking over my shoulder to what I was leaving behind, focusing more instead on what lay ahead.

***

This night I was aiming for the town of Salida, but constant with most other best laid plans I didn't quite make it, arriving at a junction where the road I'd been travelling on rejoined Route 50, the Lonely Highway. This was the road I'd detoured from back in Pueblo, in order to go and visit Phil in Colorado Springs. To turn right now (to face west) would take me the seventy miles down into Salida, whereas turning left revealed that just along from the junction was a campsite which, for whatever reason, just seemed more appealing than another two hours on the road, especially as it would soon be nightfall.

My issue with stopping too early is knowing what to do with myself until it gets dark and I have to go to sleep. I have nothing to entertain or amuse myself whilst camping and the simple fact is that I generally find more amusement in riding, than I do in standing still. This is why I'd rather be riding until the cusp of darkness, at which point there isn't much left to do but put the tent up and go to bed. Stopping now was a touch too early, but it had been a long day, and the driveway down to the Royal View Campsite just seemed so appealing.

A sign gave instructions as to what you should do if you arrive after hours, which clearly it must have been as no one was around to check me in or take my money. The sign instructed that you take an available pitch from the slots on a board, go off and find it, then pay in the morning. The price of the pitch was $35, something I baulked at and was reluctant to pay, but I simply didn't have the heart to ride any further. It just seemed an awful lot of money to pitch a six-by-four tent for the night.

It was a decent site though, with its own picnic bench and firepit, surrounded by bushes and the branches of low lying trees. I could hear and faintly see the family on the pitch across the other side of the path. They were laughing and playing, the only sound in this still, silent valley, the air starting to cool and the orange glow of the sun slowly fading to nothing. I cooked up some instant noodles on the stove. I had some bread to dip in the juice, whilst to drink I had with me a litre of water.

Making the most of the last rays of sunlight I wrote some notes in my diary, even taking out my laptop and playing some quiet music through that. I was glad that I'd come to this early rest, sitting up well into darkness, slowly getting my things ready for bed and finally closing the zip on my tent.

The next morning I considered doing a runner to avoid the extortionate amount of money for the site. I figured that if I packed up and left early enough then no one would even know I'd been. I could get away with it and save myself some money. Annoyingly, my conscience got the better of me and wouldn't allow me to do this; it would have deemed it bad karma, and sometimes karma is all that counts on journeys such as these. I concluded instead that I would just have to pay the fee and grumble about it later.

Strangely, even at 7am there was still no one around to pay, which was frustrating as I needed to pay by card as I only had ten dollars in my wallet and, equally, I just wanted to get on the road and keep on trucking. The compromise I came to was to write a note, explaining my predicament, and putting it in an envelope, along with the last ten dollars I had (promising to send the rest by post at a later date), and sliding it under the door of reception. This, I felt, would appease my conscience and help retain some hard-fought karma. Annoyingly; five miles down the road, in the direction of Salida, I rode past a state-run campsite that I could have camped at for free. Karma indeed.

Chapter Ten
The Rockies

I rode down the valley towards Salida early this cold morning. The valley was cold as it hadn't received any direct sunlight yet. There was also vapour rising from the churning water of the Arkansas River as it flowed down the barrel of the valley, making this the coldest I'd been for quite some time. As a result I had everything on, even the fluorescent jacket and two pairs of gloves. The last time I was this cold on a bike was when riding into China over the Himalayas, through a wind-whipped valley, being chased by that blasted tourist bus.

Here in Colorado – some 8,000 miles of riding to the west of that border between China and Pakistan – I passed a little restaurant that had just opened for the morning. I ordered a coffee and some toast. The girl who served me was stunning; I was quite smitten, until a regular asked how she was doing at school and I felt quite repulsed with myself. This was just the state of my mind out here. Not really sure of anything any more, only that if I carried on riding west I would hit the coast eventually and hope that I was somewhere in the vicinity of San Francisco.

Beyond Salida that morning (a nice town, once prosperous through ranching, now through tourism) I turned left onto Route 285, then a little way along turned right off the tarmac and found myself at the start of another dirt trail. I had decided to take this route along the back road trails, as to take the tarmac would mean circling around many of the mountains, whereas these routes would take me right over the top of them.

At the start of this first trail was a notice board warning of bears in the area. It also said to inform someone of your intention to take this dirt trail in case anything happened to you. Good advice, but without a sim in my UK phone or anyone to call even if I had one, I skipped that part and set off into the wilderness alone.

The path was rocky and made its way through forest as it climbed over Mount Ouray, along County Road Xx32. I was nervous of this trail. It looked lonely, spearing right through the heart of the Colorado wilderness and far more isolated than the trail I took out of Colorado Springs.

I worried about bears and what to do if one suddenly jumped out of the forest. I was doubtful of being able to outrun it. After all, I only beat the wild dogs of Kyrgyzstan by the momentum of a downhill road. This trail however ran uphill, and so if it's true that bears can run at up to 40mph then I was done for. It was reassuring then to soon come across a lone cyclist heading in the same direction. He cast a lonely shadow out here, and I thought that if the bears are hungry this day then surely he will be first for dinner. I slowed to see if he was okay and ask if he needed any water. He was fine, so I carried on.

The question of what happens if you break down out here does occasionally fill your mind. If it was as simple as a puncture then I would fix it. If those spokes broke again – and I feared they might, given how rough the terrain was – I would try and fix them, as long as I had plenty of spares. If something serious happened with the engine or anything structural broke, like the frame snapped, then I suppose it would be a case of pushing out, or walking out and coming back with the cavalry. As for falling off and injuring yourself, at times like these you just make damn sure that you don't. 'Ride hard, but ride safe,' that was my motto.

The trail climbed through the sea of silver birch trees for a good hour or more. It was slow going but enjoyable, stopping every once in a while to stare out at the view; one of green carpeted hills that appeared to go on for ever and ever. To compare the empty vastness of here to the dense population of somewhere like New York or Chicago felt like going from an ant in a big nest to being the last man on earth. One country, and yet so much variety and change. This is what I did love about America; the land and the landscape. It was simply phenomenal, and the best views were still to come.

At the top of this summit I met five other motorcyclists admiring the view of the valley beyond. I was glad to see them, pulling to a frantic halt, climbing off and cheering 'hello,' to which they waved back. The men rode proper enduro bikes, with big wheels and knobbly tyres. They also wore heavy-duty motocross clothing, meaning big boots, body armour, elbow pads, full face helmets, goggles and colourful tops and trousers that belied their age, as most of them must have been in their fifties, some of them older.

They told me they were out riding for a few days, taking in the trails and generally spending a boy's weekend out on bikes. They asked about my bike, slightly puzzled as to what a foreigner on a small bike might be doing up here. I explained, them looking not quite convinced by my story, though I assured them it was true.

But would you believe it? You're at the top of the mountain in the middle of Colorado. A weird looking guy on a weird looking bike, with a weird foreign numberplate pulls up next to you, climbs off and explains that his journey began almost four years ago in Australia. That since then he'd covered almost 30,000 miles on a 105cc machine – smaller than most lawn-mowers – riding through such random places as Indonesia, East Timor, India, Nepal, Pakistan, China, Russia, Kazakhstan, and he's just ridden that same bike across America as well. I wouldn't believe him either.

Having chatted a while we agreed it was time to take the trail down the mountain. I invited them to go first as undoubtedly they would be faster than me and I would just get in the way. That was a big mistake, because as soon as they set off I took off a few minutes later in hot pursuit, determined for no real reason other than pride to try and catch them and keep up with them, despite them being on 400cc bikes and wearing all the proper protective gear. I was still in jeans and my flannel shirt, down on power, but with gravity now on my side.

I rode like an idiot that day. Flat out, both wheels skipping and drifting across the dust and gravel surface, minimal grip from my cheap road tyres, little suspension travel, all the weight of the saddle bags kicking around at the back, and my brakes not that great either. But I had venom in my eyes and it couldn't be stopped. I chased and chased, down the mountainside, the road snaking back on itself, tree lined and precarious in places, heavily stoned in others, opening out into a fast section at other times, my eyes behind those J-Lo glasses shining like emeralds. 'Slow down,' I said to myself. 'Get lost,' said the other me, intent on catching these old timers on their proper machines.

I almost did, blazing out from the end of the trail that just so happened to end right beside the gas station where the men were just about to start filling their fuel tanks. They couldn't believe it. They thought I'd be miles behind. But I was there. Dot was ticking from the flogging she'd just received and I was grateful to have made it down in one piece. It was stupid to have gotten carried away like that. But I was enjoying myself, and I'd not said that in a long while.

I ate lunch at the gas station diner with Pat and John, two other trail bike riders up on a trip from their homes in Texas. They were just deciding whether to ride the bikes back or rent a van and drive them back in that.

Good times these, I felt part of something, a real sense of camaraderie with the off-road riders of Colorado. It was certainly a beautiful place to be riding a motorcycle, with some of the riders doing what was called the Trans-America Trail. This is a completely off-road route, starting all the way back in the Appalachian Mountains and finishing 2,700 miles to the west, somewhere along the Pacific Coast. I had thought about taking this route across America myself, but figured I'd miss too much of the country's intrigue had I done so.

There were many places I'd have to miss and skip completely. I would have loved to have gone down and seen New Orleans, having visited it before on that organised trip and enjoying the spookiness of the place. Roswell too, and Nashville, and Memphis, and it would have been good to see Santa Fe again as well. But across America you can't see everything. It would take a lifetime to do so, meaning that the line you take across it is only one representation. It does not represent the whole.

***

A series of off-road trails continued this day, some as many as 70 miles long, right through the heart of nothingness. It was mind-blowing really, to find yourself on a dirt trail, the satnav no good out here, the paper map (picked up from Liz back at the start of Colorado) no good either as it had long since blown away in the wind, leaving me little choice but to take a guess on a direction and hope it brought me out in the right place, based on a vague visualisation I had of the map, moments before it blew away in the wind.

Fear washed over me as I found myself on a dirt trail, no one or nothing around for miles. Then quite by chance I met a friendly lady on horseback tending the cattle on her ranch, who assured me I was travelling in the right direction.

Occasionally the dirt trail would turf me out on to tarmac for a brief while, before another back road would present itself for me to take. On one stretch of tarmac I met a man named Doug, a larger than life Brian Blessed like character on a huge intergalactic BMW who pulled over to chat as I stopped to take a photograph.

He was a businessman, philanthropist and all-round good guy, who had even heard of Dorothy having read about our adventures on the internet. I never stopped being surprised by this. For this man, a strange man, to know of me, an Englishman, here in the middle of the Colorado hills. How completely random life can sometimes be.

Doug had a seat on Dorothy and I took a photograph of the pair. He told me to drop by his place just outside of San Francisco if I was ever passing through and gave me his business card. We shook hands, his massive engine roaring into life like a giant animated thruster, and away, Brian Blessed was gone.

For the rest of the day I found myself on narrow trails running through forests and across open dusty plains. At times the trail would open up and give plenty of space in which to breathe. Other times it would negotiate around trees and drop down gullies. I stopped at one point completely perplexed by a sign at a three way junction, not sure of which avenue to take. I took a moment, relying on instinct and intuition, letting go of conscious thought and just going with it. The trail turned more beautiful from here, passing remote cattle ranches with cows penned in by rustic log fences, and then a river, along the banks of which the trail roamed.

It wasn't long before finally, after what must have been three hours of riding almost completely alone along those dirt trails, I emerged on to bitumen, coming to a halt at a junction at which I could turn left or right.

The signpost told me that to the left was Creede, while to the right I'd find the town of Lake City. By this time I'd covered a lot of ground that day and just needed somewhere to fill the gas tanks and rest my head for the night. A car came up behind me (probably one of the campers I'd spotted down by the river), turning on to the road and taking off before I'd even had time to flag it down for directions.

The next car I wasn't letting pass so easily, frantically bringing it to a halt and having it stop at the point at which dirt road joined tarmac. The occupants – an elderly couple – seemed reluctant to help at first, or even wind their window down. I was after all a scruffy-looking stranger, flagging them down in the middle of nowhere, and if that were me, I would be apprehensive as well. But I was that high from the vapours of the road that day that they soon let go of their tension and we talked for a while. Their names were Jeanie and Gerald, a couple in retirement with a little yapping dog on Jeanie's lap.

'Where do you want to go?' they asked.

'I'm not sure. Should I go left or right?'

'Well, left takes you to Creede, right takes you to Lake City.'

'I just need somewhere to sleep for the night. Which is the best place to pitch a tent?'

'There are a few spots just outside Lake City, but there's a hostel in town. Why don't you stay there?'

I thought about it.

'We know the owners, Lucky and Amy-Jo. I'm sure they'll do you a good price.'

With that I was sold on the idea, Jeanie and Gerald giving me directions to the hostel, before taking off in that direction themselves.

The road from there was downhill, beautifully surfaced with fresh tarmac, running like a serpent through a density of trees. It was like a road you might expect to find in the Alps. After around ten miles it reached the bottom of the valley, where the river ran, and there, on the brink of evening, I rode into Lake City, which wasn't a city at all, just a great little town, all made from wood, nestled deep in the mountains of Colorado.

Jeanie and Gerald were waiting for me at the old-fashioned petrol pumps on the entrance into town.

'We thought we'd treat you to dinner tonight. Go and dump your stuff at the hostel and we'll meet you back here in ten minutes time…'

And later that evening, that's what the three of us did. Another surreal encounter of the road.

Chapter Eleven
Lake City

Jeanie and Gerald lived in Florida, but every year, to escape the ferocious summer sun, they would drive up to Lake City to spend three months in a caravan beside the river. Both were retired teachers, with Jeanie liking to make a fuss and be the life and soul of the party, while Gerald preferred to take a back seat, being the quiet one, perhaps learning over the years it was the easiest route to happiness. I couldn't have met a nicer couple that evening. Outside their caravan we had pre-meal drinks of red wine, served in plastic wine glasses that were battery operated and so changed colour, from red to blue to green to yellow, and then back again.

The caravan was on a site down by the river, along with around twenty other vans, all positioned in a circle, as though they were about to ward off an Indian attack. A bridge over the river took you into the main hub of the town; a quiet, sleepy little place, popular with nature-loving tourists, the shadowy mountain peaks – skiable in winter – looming all around. It was certainly calm and peaceful, and I could see how you could spend three months of the year here and not feel restless.

We ate in a pizza parlour called Poker Alice, a wooden cabin opposite the old gas station on the way into town. The staff were predominantly from Poland, working here for the summer before travelling around for a while and then flying home, much like I'd done with Camp America. A few of Gerald and Jeanie's friends joined us, and it was a night of sharing stories, elbows resting on the red and white plastic chequered tablecloth, plastic flowers in a vase in the centre, and great pizzas all around.

I could see one of the group – an elderly married man – was quiet but curious about my travels. It made me wonder if there's a part of every man and woman that has the simple desire to take off for a while, to escape the world, to leave it all behind and be free.

The man was keen to know what that feels like. I told him that it feels good, but that you have to accept that you can never leave it all behind, not completely. You can only take a break from it, with the problems you were escaping still there when you get back, only now more stubborn than ever. The solution perhaps is to deal with them first, and then go. Though if you did that you might never go at all.

We talked about the road ahead and how I would be taking the nearby Cinnamon Pass. They laughed at this, having seen the size of my bike, and explained that it's a tough, steep route, over the top of the mountain. While I thought I could do it in a morning they thought it would take me all day, if I made it at all. I get protective of the bike at such times, insisting she can do it, will do it, even if I have to push her we're going over that pass, because to not do so would involve a long detour, and that just sounded so tedious. But still they looked dubious at my mountainous proposition.

I planned on leaving the next morning, this being 12th September and I still had some faint hope of reaching Alaska by the end of the month. But I just didn't feel like leaving. I liked it here in Lake City, so stayed another night. The hostel was simply superb. Lucky, the owner, was an Irishman, early thirties I would have said, who seven years before had been hiking the Colorado Trail when he stopped off in Lake City to find a place to sleep for the night. By chance he met resident Amy-Jo, and the rest as they say is history. Lucky quit his walking trip, moved here permanently, and now they have kids and a trio of dogs.

Lucky built the hostel himself; a simple single-storey wooden structure in the back yard of their simple single-storey wooden house. The Raven's Rest, as it was called, was such a beautiful place, with double doors leading into the kitchen and living room area. The kitchen had a huge wooden table made from reclaimed wood; the lounge had comfy sofas; and beyond that were two doors into sleeping rooms with bunk beds to sleep four in each room. It had been done with such amazing attention to detail, out of local timbers, so rustic and charming. It was perhaps the best hostel I'd ever stayed in, and I'd stayed in a quite a few.

Despite being the only guest that first night, I was joined the next night by a motley crew of individuals. The first to arrive was Snow Cat, a lady who must have been in her sixties and walking the 500-mile Colorado Trail – from Denver to Durango – all on her own.

Snow Cat was her trail name, a tradition maintained by trail walkers, and not so different to why Phil goes by the name of Vermin whenever the bike is involved. I never did catch Snow Cat's real name, just sat bewildered by how it all works: walking for three days or more through the wilderness like the one I'd passed through, having to carry all your water, food and supplies to last for that time. Then, when you arrive at the next town, you collect a parcel that you posted ahead from the last town. In that parcel might be spare food, a sewing kit, shampoo, spare shoes, anything that couldn't be carried on a day-to-day basis, but with the right amount of forward planning could be continuously posted on to your next destination.

It was an astounding system, and Snow Cat an astounding woman. A tough lady, skin like leather from the sun, a peaceful soul behind all that, and still a fiery determination to explore the world and see it from the ground up. I sat and had a coffee with her in the rustic cafe next door to the hostel, listening to the stories of her travelling and living in Europe and Australia. She had a husband who just had to wait patiently while she went off on these adventures, such as this one, through bear territory, with no weapon of defence, no nothing.

The next arrival to the hostel was the Old Minister, another walker, this one even older, in her seventies at least, walking with poles to keep her going. The Old Minister was walking even further than Snow Cat!

I couldn't fathom these women. They were unstoppable and without fear, with terrific planning and forethought put into their routes. But then also with such a faith in the world, like Snow Cat who had arrived at the end of the same trail as I had (where I met Jeanie and Gerald), before hitch-hiking the ten miles down into town with a random man that pulled over and even offered to pick her up and take her back to the start of the trail once she was done in Lake City. What a story to be told. What a legacy to be leaving.

The last arrival of my stay was a man named Craig, travelling in a Jeep with his dog, and I think just coming out here to get away from it all. He had a brother in the Marines who'd served in Iraq, and around the solid wooden table we all talked one night. Conversation grew quite heated at times, Craig defensive about America's role in the Middle East and how it was there to do good, and he wasn't having any of it when we tried to argue otherwise. Jingoism, perhaps, but I don't think he was fooling himself. He genuinely believed that America was out to do good in the world and I accepted it wasn't my place or anybody else's to try and convince him otherwise. I admired his resolute defence, because that's genuinely what he believed.

On my final evening in Lake City I was given a blue rubber wristband to wear by Jeanie and Gerald, inscribed with the motif, 'God is big enough.' The words were a representation of their faith, Jeanie telling me that even right-wing Alaskan politician Sarah Palin wears one!

The wristband wasn't really to my taste, but it was sweet in a way and I promised to wear it on the rest of my journey across America (and did wear it, though I turned the words to face my wrist). I wore it because irrespective of my lack of belief in their faith, deep down I did believe in something, something bigger than this. That's not to say I believed in organised religion as such, but I certainly believed in faith, even if it's only faith in yourself, your fellow man, and in the world around you.

During my darkest days back in England I went and sat in the church in the centre of our local town of Malton. I don't know why I felt compelled to do this. Maybe it was simply to feel the power of being in a place born out of faith. I certainly didn't go to pray, or give my life to Jesus, I just found this quiet, peaceful church, at the heart of the town's commotion, a necessary place to retreat to, and be at peace for a moment, well away from the world and the screaming nature of my mind. I didn't feel the need to go back after that, one visit was enough. I just think it's hard pretending to be strong when you're actually weak, and when I think back, that was the moment I finally started to climb, having first had to admit defeat.

***

The day of riding Cinnamon Pass was signalled by a blue sky morning. Once more I left my temporary sanctuary behind, taking with me memories of a happy time there in Lake City. Jeanie and Gerald, Lucky and Amy-Jo, Snow Cat, the Old Reverend, and Craig who I had a coffee with before both of us hit the road. We bought it from a baker's that had suffered a spate of bear attacks, bears breaking in and stealing the food. That was a daunting thought for the journey ahead, as the road was only going to get wilder from here.

It was a cold morning so I wore most of my clothing. I wore those sturdy Australian boots, blue jeans (even some thermal leggings), a good few layers of tops and a jumper, not to mention the BigZoners jacket, then over all of that the fluorescent orange Royal Mail jacket, the beige gardening gloves which by now were well bedded in, the helmet, the neckerchief around my face – the bump from the wasp sting still there – and the J-Lo glasses, now covered with scratches and the frames a little bent.

The bike was also beginning to resemble a travelling gypsy. The bulbous sleeping bag in a grey sack was strapped fiercely to the tent rack on the front. The green tent and blue roll mat were strapped to the rack on the back, while a spare tyre – purchased from a helpful bike shop on the outskirts of St. Louis (Flying Tiger) – was wedged over the top of the left pannier. The yellow bell given to me by the BigZoners back in Indonesia was still on the handlebars, while on the opposite side of the bars I had tied with a piece of string a blue plastic cup bought from a cheap Chinese store in Toronto, back at the start of the trip when I went to visit Mandy. The cup had never been used and was just there as a strange, clattering inconvenience tied around my handlebars.

What surprised me most about the trail up to Cinnamon Pass was just how precarious it was, with huge drops by the side of the track and no guard rails or warning signs. It felt like being back in India on the road through the Himalayas, where there really is nothing to stop you just going over the edge. Thankfully, in being up so early in the morning I was the only one out here, for the time being at least, with a wave of 4x4s hunting me from behind as the day progressed.

The trail soon turned to switchbacks, the severity of the turns being just enough to sap all momentum, meaning that on the approach to the corner, just as my speed was slowing, I would have to leap off the bike, push like crazy up and around the corner, then, after momentum had been regained, hop back on and gas it all the way to the next corner, where I would do it again, and again, all the way up this mountain, at least fifteen turns in total, pushing through each and every one. I was completely shattered by the time I reached the top of Cinnamon Pass, but at least we'd made it.

I stood and shared the moment with a pair of fellow motorcyclists, plus a convoy of Jeeps, the passengers of which had all climbed out to take photos of the breathtaking mountain scenery all around. One lady was originally from England and we chatted a while about her time there in the seventies, before she moved permanently to America. The lady said she barely ever went back to her English homeland, which I always found strange, or admirable, the way some people are able to abandon the past like that, and start afresh. Unless the past was really unpleasant of course, in which case I could well understand it.

I followed their Jeep down the mountainside; a brutal, slippery descent, with curling corners and one or two buckaroo moments when the bike would try and shoot off in all manner of directions. At one point – due to my own carelessness and greed for speed – I ended up pointing back up the mountain, having completed a full 180-degree rotation, doing well not to fall off in the process. 'Slow down Nathan, slow down,' I said to myself insistently.

At the foot of this devil's tail of mountain trails were the ruins of what was once the town of Animas Forks, an old gold mining community, founded in 1877 and built at 11,600 feet. It boasted several general stores, a hotel and a saloon, but was prone to avalanches and was abandoned at the end of the nineteenth century. Since then the town has slowly been lost to nature, the timber buildings in slow decay, some of them crumbling and falling down, others almost completely intact and you able to go inside and look around, as though you are stepping right back in to the carcasses of the past.

What it must have been like to live up here. How bitterly cold in winter, how gorgeous in summer. And then when the gold was gone the community moved on, no time for sentiment or despair. I found that quite common in America; this ability to let go of the past and migrate to (hopefully) better times. Perhaps in a hundred years time people will do the same with Detroit; nothing but an abandonment along the prairie, for tourists to stop and take photographs of.

Beyond the remains of Animas Forks came the toughest task of them all. It was a steep valley, the dusty trail running right up the heart of it, culminating in what appeared at a distance to be an impenetrable slope, though I was guaranteed the trail did go up there.

After a mile or so of winding trail, it soon arced to the right before turning a sharp left on itself, the incline increasing with every metre of travel. Even down in first gear it was too much for the bike which threatened to stall at any moment; just not enough power in that little engine to sustain sufficient forward thrust, not at this altitude, with the lack of air robbing the carburettor and therefore the engine of all its power.

I dismounted and ran alongside the bike, pushing it with all my might. I made it to a corner, a tight right one, which led on to a part of the trail I knew for certain I couldn't ride up, and would even struggle to push up, especially now at over 12,000 feet. At that moment I spotted an off-road super-powered golf buggy that seemed popular in these parts. It was travelling in the same direction as me and I thought if I could ask the driver to carry my panniers and thus lighten the load, I might just be able to shove the old bike to the summit.

I watched as the vehicle came closer and closer. Perhaps it was my mistake, but I assumed it would just stop or at least acknowledge the breathless traveller at the bottom of this steep climb, alone in this wilderness, with the day fast losing light. Instead, the two occupants didn't even acknowledge me. They just drove past, and I could have killed them both right there and then had I been given the chance, such was my rage.

As it was, I filled my lungs as best I could, dug my heels into the dirt, eyed up the long steep slope leading to a corner, before another long steep slope, gunned the throttle, flat out in first, the bike barely able to haul its own weight, me leaning into the handlebars, no helmet on, every muscle straining, the mountain fighting against us, and in that moment I let out the loudest, fiercest primal scream I could muster. I was pushing that bike to the top of that mountain even if it killed me, and it almost did.

I screamed, and I screamed, and I shoved, and I shoved. My legs burnt like flames as my heels pushed against the dirt, those sturdy Australian boots being squeezed into the earth, step after step after step. It was a brutal rush to the summit, thinking that I was never going to get there.

I made it to the top and collapsed, taking an age to catch my breath. A little later I came across a couple in a 4x4 who said they'd heard screaming from over the other side of the mountain and I had to confess to it being me, and how I'd almost shouted the mountain down in my determination to get over it. As tired as I was, I wasn't going to be beaten that day, I'd come too far to allow it.

From that point on, it looked as though I was going to have to push up and over yet another mountain. Thankfully, just as I did finally hit my brick wall and concede that I might need to camp out here on the mountain overnight, a local guide on a quad bike, leading a group of two others, came down the hill towards me, telling me that if I turned around and took a right turn back at the 'junction' I'd just passed, the trail would lead me all the way down into Silverton, the town I'd planned on reaching that evening.

I followed the guide's instructions, turning around, putting my whole world into neutral and gliding down the hill into Silverton, camping that night beside the railway line on the outskirts of town, where the next morning I was told about the bear.

Chapter Twelve
Silverton

The bear had been spotted wandering the town that night, no doubt looking for an Englishman to eat. I was told about this by the staff in the Avalanche Café, one of them a beautiful girl named Stacey who spent the summer months living in a tent on the outskirts of town, sleeping with a gun beneath her pillow. A couple of other bikers in the cafe that morning, Bill and Graeme, suggested I try and sleep in Stacey's tent for protection next time. It would take a braver man than me to attempt such a thing.

It was a nice atmosphere in the café that morning; Silverton itself a very friendly and inviting town, built on what was probably the only flat piece of land for miles around, the mountains rising high on either side of it. The main street was wide and lined with old-fashioned wooden buildings. You could almost imagine a time when the road was made of dirt, not tarmac, horses tethered up outside rowdy bars, and men with long moustaches and ten gallon hats. Colorado in fact still had many men with long silvery moustaches; it's what seemed to set the men apart from those found in the rest of America.

I had thought about staying at the town's hostel, arriving in the evening, and enquiring about the cost, which at around $25 wasn't so bad. For whatever reason though I just didn't feel in the mood, heading instead to the Avalanche Café for some supper and use of their free Wi-Fi.

As it was about to close for the evening I rode briefly out of town, beyond the fringe of the residential streets, finding the abandoned railway line and setting up the tent in the dark, careful not to draw any attention to myself. It was only the next morning, when I went back into the Avalanche Café for a hot cup of coffee, that Stacey told me about the bear, though around these parts it would have been a black bear rather than the more dangerous grizzly.

From Silverton it was a case of taking the road down to Durango, perhaps only forty miles from here. The road's nickname; the Million Dollar Highway, was said to have been given for one of two reasons. The first, as some claim, is because it cost a million dollars to build. The other explanation is because the views it offers whilst driving along it are said to be worth a million dollars. I preferred the latter, although it's a shame that in joining it on the outskirts of Silverton, I'd already missed the best part of it, that being the stretch of road running north, from here to the town of Ouray.

This was still a beautiful section though, and it was actually a relief to have tarmac beneath the tyres instead of more rock and dirt. That passage over the Rockies had been one hell of an adventure. I'd enjoyed it immensely and in a way was quite sad that this road down into Durango, and then west from there, would effectively signal the end of the Rockies, and the end of Colorado, as it had been my favourite part of the journey to this point. I was glad to have come this way rather dipping down beneath the Rockies, which is where that route through Sante Fe would have taken me.

Durango was also worth visiting, the town named after Durango in Mexico, which itself is named after Durango in Spain, the word Durango originating from the Basque word 'urango,' meaning 'water town.' The Million Dollar Highway indeed runs downhill in the direction of Durango, shedding almost three-thousand feet of altitude in the space of just those forty short miles.

While in town I called in at a Honda dealer to pick up a new headlight bulb and to change the oil as Dorothy had taken a battering coming over the Rockies. She was now fast approaching 90,000 kilometres, still running original engine, and generally that's unheard of for a bike of this size, especially one put through such rigorous testing. Far from being paranoid about her longevity though, as I was on that first trip, I was more of the opinion that we'll simply ride as far as we can, and if she packs up, then we'll fix her, and then ride some more. It really was that straight-forward.

I also met a young man in Durango who had recently been reading about me and Dorothy on the internet. It was an old ride report for ADVRider I'd written about that trip from Sydney to London, which by now had received almost 1.5 million views. Perhaps it was the spontaneity of it all; riding out of Sydney after just two days of planning, on the bike and in the kit I already owned, and having no real clue whether I was going to make it to England or not. It was then the opposite of how it's usually done. I sat and had my lunch with the young man, chatting about bikes and other things.

In a way I felt the a certain pressure from all this, as when you do a big trip, and write a book about it, the only question people have of you is, 'When's the next trip?' or, 'Where are you going next?' These words alone, and the repetition of them, is enough to sow enough seeds in your own mind, possibly because a part of you thinks you have to live up to their expectations (let alone your own expectations), and largely because you get sick of saying, 'not sure, maybe America.' That's why doing a big trip completely in silence, is arguably the best way of doing it. Why write a book then? To help make sense of things and get stuff off your chest I suppose.

***

West from here was now a case of following the Navajo Trail, a name that perhaps makes it sound more glamorous and triumphant than it actually is. It was just a road, running down from the remnants of the Rockies and out across the sandy floor of the encroaching desert. Ahead lay Utah and Nevada; Las Vegas not much more than 500 miles away, the Grand Canyon a few hundred less than that. I'd been to some of those places before on that organised trip I took after summer camp. I remembered them well and was really looking forward to seeing them again.

I also realised that by taking this route I would soon pass right by Mesa Verde National Park, a place that Elizabeth, back in the tourist information centre in Colorado, had told me about, insisting that I go and see it if I got the chance. These are a series of cave dwellings built into thin lips of rock and said to have been abandoned by the Ancestral Puebloan Indians that lived there way back in 1300AD.

Having been discovered, photographed and explored in the late nineteenth century, the cave dwellings were slowly vandalised and stripped bare of much that made them fascinating – walls being torn down to let in more light, beams of roofing timber burnt as fire wood, floors dug and graves disturbed. It was only in 1906, when Theodore Roosevelt declared Mesa Verde a US National Park, that it was finally preserved in its current state.

Some assume that the Ancient Pueblo Indians were primitive, but even back then they were building homes out of rock, using a form of cement. The homes were built to a blueprint, as much as they could be, given that they had to embrace the contours of the cliff walls. It's been suggested that the indigenous people of America, before the Europeans arrived, were quite advanced, culturally, socially and mechanically, but that a great plague decreased their numbers to such an extent that the arrival and subsequent expansion west of the early European settlers was met with such modest resistance. We'll never know.

Having left the main road and entered the park via a steep twisting road, I took a walk around the ruins of Mesa Verde, climbing a ladder down into a circular pit, once used as a larder with the air much cooler than it was up above. From the cliff top I then made a photograph of the eagle that hovered overhead. It was such a hot day, the eagle easy to spot against the cloudless blue sky. I didn't linger long however, soon running out of excuses for not being on the road, returning to the bike and riding away from the cliff tops of Mesa Verde.

I didn't get very far however, as I simply couldn't be bothered. I was hot, sweaty, tired and content to instead simply pull into the campsite at the base of the National Park and pay too much to pitch the tent for the night. It was expensive but I'm glad I paid it, as the following morning I woke to find my tent surrounded by wild deer, tame enough to allow me to take their photograph as they meandered past and into the trees beyond. The simple joy of nature passing.

Later, in the next town of Cortez (the last in Colorado), I met a bus load of Australian tourists on a guided tour of the region, a few from the group spotting the Aussie post bike and coming over to have a chat.

I liked other tourists. It created a sense of community and camaraderie. After all, we were all out of our comfort zones, even if they got to sit on air-conditioned buses, while I sat on a well worn saddle. We chatted a while before they marched inside to stock up on maps and leaflets about all the things they intended to see whilst they were here, leaving me to push west alone.

***

From Cortez I travelling briefly along Route 441, in the direction of the town's airport, before taking a turn on to County Road G. This was a back road, and a route that sadly would bypass Four Corners (the point at which the states of New Mexico, Colorado, Utah and Arizona meet), something I wasn't aware of at the time, realising only once it was too late and I'd ridden well past it. Again, on a journey across America, you can't possibly see everything.

What I saw instead was a very strange road. It ran at times through isolated countryside, road signs along it shot through with bullets, the verge littered with the endless remains of beer bottles – some smashed, some intact – shards of glass twinkling in the sunlight. So too were there empty cardboard boxes of beer, cans of lager, bottles of rum and whiskey. It seemed like someone had been having a party the entire length of the road, for mile after mile, leaving a trail of destruction, as well as an air of intimidation for people such as me who wondered what vermin lived around these parts. I wouldn't want to have ridden this road at night, when the bottles are being tossed, and the signposts being shot at.

I later learned that the road was used by local native Americans who aren't permitted to drink alcohol on their reservations, and so drive into Cortez to pick up beer, and drink it on the way back, tossing the bottles into the scrub so as not to incriminate themselves when they return to their reservation. I wish I'd have known this at time, as that explanation didn't intimidate me as much as others might have done, because they had vague justification, or you could at least trace back the mental process, whereas if it had just been hillbillies, with no real reason, then that would have been more intimidating.

More attractive were the wild horses that roamed these parts. I came across a gathering of them on the road, half a dozen in total; some black, some grey, some white, some brown. They didn't shift as I approached, simply staying put in the road, staring at me as I passed, chewing on grass. I'm sure they said 'hello', and I said 'hello' back. Because it was just me and the horses out here, and the broken beer bottles, twinkling in the grass.

Beyond this lay the small town of Bluff, just over the border in Utah. The town was overlooked by a fabulous rock formation; layers of sandy rock, almost like a flaky pastry, with huge chunks of beef – or rocks – sat on top. I parked up and stared at it for a while. It was so beautiful and elegant, carved over how many millions of years by the hands of nature, and now with a cafe built at the foot of it, popular it seemed with those on Harley Davidsons who roamed these parts, like two-wheeled flocks of those wild horses.

This makes them sound like a band of outlaws, when in fact, most were German and French tourists on rented bikes out of Vegas or LA. It was always amusing to park next to them, and watch them as they looked down on me, and in return, if that was the case, I would look down on them.

I sat and drank a coffee and ate some deep fried doughnut bread on the veranda of the cafe, watching the bikers and the motorhome drivers come and go, those big lumps of rock towering above us, casting shadows on us like ants scurrying about below. I think finally I felt sure-footed of my position, and of my intention. I drank my coffee as cool as I could, before paying the bill, returning to my bike, and roaring off at a GPS-verified 37mph with the target helmet and my gardening gloves on. What a seriously weird guy I must have looked that day.

***

Beyond Bluff I turned off the main highway and into the Valley of the Gods, a circular loop of dirt road, approximately seventeen miles in length, taking you right through the heart of the Utah landscape. Regular cars can drive along it, but it's sandy, and in places the trail dips down into dried-up riverbeds requiring a careful bit of acceleration to climb out the other side. There were a few cars on the trail this day, but for the rest of the time, I was completely alone in this blazing-saddle landscape, the desert floor before me dotted with plants and scrub, rock towers rising from the earth, and beyond that a wall of vast stone formations, having you wonder just where the road is going to take you.

The Valley of the Gods finally spits you out at the foot of the Moki Dugway; a series of switchbacks cut into what looks to be an almost vertical wall of rock, the road climbing 1,100 feet in less than three miles. It was built in 1958 by Texas Zinc, a mining company, to transport uranium ore from the 'Happy Jack' mine in Fry Canyon, Utah, to the processing mill in Mexican Hat, just south of here. It was a stunning piece of road, the pictures not doing justice to how fierce the battle must have been between the mountainside and the workmen that built it.

When you stop at the top and look back out across the flat plain beneath you, it gives the impression of riding a massive rock wave, about to tear across the landscape and swamp it like a giant tsunami.

I imagined everyone I met on my travels standing up here with me; Joe from the bike shop, Denise and her fairies from Mount Isa, Rita from East Timor, the cyclists from Germany, BigZoners from Indonesia, Tobias and Manus, the backpackers I hung out with in Bangkok, the people of India I met, those travellers in the Internet Guesthouse in Lahore, Daniel Sprague, Michel on his BMW, Andrew and Amelia in their Land Rover Discovery. Abdul the Chinese guide, Claudia and Andreas who I rode with across Kazakhstan, Bartek the Polish mechanic who tuned the engine on the last stretch. Then everyone so far from America: John, Vermin, his family, Jeanie and Gerald, Stacey from Silverton with her gun under her pillow. All of us stood at the top of Moki Dugway this day, all staring out; a journey of so many different faces, very few of which I'll ever see again (Sonder).

***

For now, I was riding along the road on which Forrest Gump famously stops running, uttering the words as he does so; 'You've got to put the past behind you before you can move on.' If I'm honest, the landscape in real life doesn't quite match the drama as it appears on the screen, but the feeling of being here, at another one of those iconic Hollywood sights, is electrifying and utterly surreal, as though you can't possibly be there. I'm dreaming it.

It was here, having stopped to take a photograph, that I met a motorcycle tour guide from England who explained the mystery of the broken bottles by the roadside back near Cortez. He was on a Harley Davidson, leading a tour group of fellow Brits with his wife. Not a bad place to call your office.

For me, the excitement came in knowing that Monument Valley lay just beyond the horizon. For whatever reason this location had represented something of a milestone on this journey, the one place I needed to reach, and see again, having visited it on that first trip across America and fallen in love with the place.

You might recognise it from a thousand western movies, the towering pillars of rock rising from the earth, as a cowboy rides past on his horse, in pursuit, or being pursued, by Indians.

It had changed little when I finally landed there. The road to the visitor centre was now tarmac, not dirt. The car park was much bigger, and the viewing area now a tarmac floor. The building housing the cafe and gift store had been rebuilt and redesigned, removing some of the rustic charm of the place. But the view was still the same; the famous Three Mittens, like giant rock hands pointing upwards from the ground.

I sat there for a while, enjoying the view and the sudden moment of calm that had flooded over me; Dorothy parked behind, on the kerbside, caked in the dirt of almost four thousand miles of riding, still with all my gear dangling off the back like she was the transport of an old rag-and-bone man. I spoke with several people who came asking about the bike and the UK plate. This gave me two emotions.

The first was one of gratitude, that I was seeing this on my own schedule, riding my own bike, no one telling me what to do or where to be (the people I spoke to on the other hand all had jobs to get back to, or rental cars to return, or hotel reservations that night that meant they had to move on).

The second emotion was envy; that they had other people with them to share this moment with. To look across to the wife and point and say, 'Look at that.' Whereas Dorothy just wasn't interested, and so I sat on my own and stared out at the scenery for what seemed like an eternity, a mind of racing thoughts and distant dreaming.

With no particular place to stay this night I sauntered back down the five-mile access road, realising there to be a holiday resort named Goulding's, with a hotel, campsite, shop and swimming pool, just over the other side of the main road. I inquired about the price to pitch a tent and paid the $25 begrudgingly.

I was glad I made that decision, as the campsite was pleasant, surrounded as it was by red cliffs, the site full of travellers, those next to me on an organised walking tour for French people, run by French people.

Having put my tent up and unloaded my things I spoke with the French lady left behind after all the others had suddenly disappeared.

'Where have they gone?' I asked.

'They've gone to watch the sunset over Monument Valley, aren't you going?'

'When is it?'

'In about fifteen minutes' time.'

I looked at Dorothy, now lightened of her load. I considered the five or so miles it was back down to the visitor centre and the plateau looking out across the Three Mittens. And in that moment my eyes lit with flames at the thought of a race against the sun. I jumped on the bike, just my jeans, T-shirt, like Maverick in *Top Gun*, chasing after Kelly McGillis, but with a helmet on, blasting out of the campsite and roaring off along the road towards the sunset splendour.

Forty-five miles per hour (flat out) never felt so fast, the remnants of the sun glaring over my shoulder, stabbing me with its final shards of light, threatening to dip beneath the horizon before I made it there in time. The lady on the toll booth recognised me from earlier and let me through, roaring away and screeching to a halt in the car park, racing to the edge and looking out just in time to see the final shafts of natural daylight slither down the Mittens and creep along the ground, until all that was left was dusk.

I rode down the tourist trail to take a picture, before returning to the top and making the most of this evening, sat on a rock, still at peace with the world, then finally riding back to the campsite, crawling into my tent, and going to sleep, beneath a blanket of warm content.

I woke the next morning to see the sun rise above the red scorched land. This was what travelling was all about. These moments. These memories. You have to fight hard for them. They don't come easy. They don't last long. But when they happen, everything you've gone through suddenly all seems worthwhile. I treasured this day, and just wish you could have been there.

Chapter Thirteen
Zion

That morning I passed through Kayenta, the largest Navajo town in the area. It looked and felt just like any other town; it even had a McDonald's at which I stopped for breakfast. A cheerful Indian man named George approached me as I parked. He was wearing a wide-brimmed cowboy hat and clothes he'd probably slept in the night before. We chatted a while before he asked if I had any spare change so that he could buy himself a coffee. I handed him all the coins in my pocket, which must have totalled $5 or more. George thanked me, walked straight past the entrance of McDonald's and off into the distance, possibly to buy bottles that would soon end up smashed by the side of the road.

On journeys such as these you do get used to being approached by beggars and homeless people, especially in India and Nepal where in the cities there can be so many. I'll always remember from the streets of Delhi one young boy who approached me whilst clutching his head, stemming the flow of blood from a nasty open wound right on his scalp. He was crying violently, tears running down his filthy face, all the while holding out the other hand motioning for money. You hear stories of how a boy like this might cut themselves deliberately, in order to elicit more sympathy, but this was just horrific, and you stand there not knowing what to do, because half of you wants to help the kid, and the other half is just repulsed and wants to tell them to go away and bother someone else. It's a horrible internal contradiction.

The Navajo have also encountered bloodshed over the years. In the nineteenth century this entire western flank of America was home to a wide variety of tribes all in competition for supremacy. Along with the Navajo, there were the Comanche, the Apache, the Mexicans, the Spanish and after 1846, the new white tribe of settlers joining the melee as well. A power struggle took place. Groups would go on raids, steal horses and take prisoners as slaves. Power rose to the top.

The Navajo were said to have been without strong leadership and a united government and so lost out to other tribes. They also caused trouble for themselves, rustling cattle and not obeying the laws of the land. The dominant white settlers grew tired of this disobedience, and so at gunpoint in 1864 forced between 8,000 to 9,000 Navajo to walk 450 miles from their homeland in Arizona to Fort Sumner in the Bosque Redondo area of New Mexico, two hundred of them dying along the way. They were forced to live in camps, with the ordeal later described as the Long Walk of the Navajo.

Two years later, with a change of heart, or recognition of failure, the US government disbanded the camp and relocated the Navajo back to their homeland here in Arizona, a vast area, much bigger than I'd imagined, spanning around 27,000 square miles, covering parts of Colorado, Utah, Mexico and Arizona. The Navajo Nation now has its own laws, its own courts, police departments, hospitals, schools and, unlike the rest of America, free health care for all. The rate of tax is also very low; there is no property tax, and while voting for their own government, they also get to vote in the national elections as well. Almost like a country within a country.

For a long time the Navajo Nation – unlike other tribes – rejected a vote to allow gambling, which would have led to casinos being built. There were concerns over the effect it would have had on the Navajo people who, for a long time, had been against the principles of gambling. But power, money, and the need for financial survival finally changed their minds, with the decision being revoked in recent years and the casinos being built. From tribal Indians to members of a modern economy, new-found followers of the American Dream.

Compare and contrast with the native Aboriginals of Australia, who seem to have no purpose or place in Australian society at all. They are completely on the fringe, isolated and treated with indignation by so many they now share their country with. They exist almost as ghosts in a society that doesn't really want them there. They have no casinos, no forward thrust or seemingly any purpose in life. Instead they are static, arguably decaying, memories of the Stolen Generations still lingering above them (when babies were removed from Aboriginal parents and relocated to white families in the city).

And then the Indonesian BigZoners I met on my first trip in Sumatra, seemingly desperate to have the same trappings as the western nations, keen for their own country to emulate ours, at least in terms of economic success. I'm not sure what all this means; perhaps just that there are those who have and those who have not, and those who want and those who are able to get. Ultimately it would seem however that all people are the same the world over; they just want to be prosperous; whichever way they choose to personally measure that prosperity. But always, it seems, such things must start with a clearly defined purpose and direction. Without it, all of us seemingly are lost.

***

The path now lead in the direction of Zion, a national park some 216 miles to the north-west of Kayenta. Zion wasn't on my way to San Francisco – it would take a long detour of at least two days to get there – but I felt I had to go because, on that previous occasion crossing America on the organised tour, we came to Zion to climb a trail called Angels Landing and, at the time, due to my fear of heights, I dared not even attempt it. I wouldn't say it haunted me, but it was just one of those moments in life when you're disappointed with yourself, and wish you could do things better. I felt that now, with the wind in my sails, it was time to try and rectify that.

Twenty miles out of Kayenta I turned right on to Route 98, heading in the direction of Page. It was a world of clouds out here. It's amazing just how fascinated you can be by nothingness. I never grew tired of it, or wished for more attractions to stop and see, the sensation perhaps born out of that desire we all have at times to feel like we've disappeared off the face of the planet.

After all, no one knew I was here, only the occasional blur of traffic as it passed me by, but they wouldn't have cared. They would have been too lost in their own worlds to notice. And I think it is this that attracts me to the road; the feeling of disappearance, and having no one to answer to, the cruel irony being that the more you get used to this, the harder it is to go back and live in the real world.

I think that's my problem, I don't like the real world very much. I'm not sure we were born or built to operate like that. Being shut away in factories or offices, chained to a routine, programmed to worship money, penned in by the system to conform, the suppression of anger and aggression, both things eventually forced to spill out in unpleasant ways. We're still wild at heart, and without the daily challenge of survival we sometimes struggle to find meaning amongst it all. I mean, what is the point of getting up every day? Sometimes it seems like there is no point at all.

In the distance you begin to notice the chimney stacks of the Navajo Generating Station, a coal-fired plant, supplying power to California, Arizona and Nevada. It's an ugly thing; three chimney stacks puffing clouds of smoke, or steam, high into the sky. It sits incongruous with the surroundings of vast desert expanse; a carbuncle on the land. Lake Powell sits behind it; a man-made reservoir created by the flooding of Glen

Canyon and the building of the Glen Canyon Dam, the work beginning in 1956, completed seven years later having claimed 18 lives in the process.

The man who commissioned the dam, Floyd Dominy, said at the time: 'Now I admit that nature can't improve upon man. We're probably the supreme being.' And you could forgive Floyd his arrogance when you stand up on that bridge and look out across this endless sprawl of water, 560 feet deep in places, 186 miles in length, 5,370,000 cubic yards of water when full, and all of that held back by a sixty-year-old concrete wall built by the fallible mind of man. It was an amazing spectacle, and Lake Powell an amazing sight, serving as a vast oasis in the desert.

In Page – the town built on its shores – I noticed a bolt was missing from the bike's cam-chain tensioner screw, having adjusted it a few days earlier and forgotten to re-tighten the locking nut. It wasn't a disaster, just hinting at the general abuse and wear and tear she was receiving. The red dust and dirt of Colorado was still caked upon her. Her chain was dry and stiff after I lost the can of chain lube coming over Cinnamon Pass. I needed to buy some replacement, dabbing the chain with engine oil in the meantime to keep it moist. The spokes in the rear wheel also required regular attention, at least three times a day, feeling for the loose ones and tightening them up with an adjustable spanner I kept in the tank bag. I still changed the oil as often as I needed to, but the engine wasn't running that great; she was just beginning to feel her age.

I was battered as well: tired, dirty, a little sunburnt and not so well nourished, not from my diet of coffee and 99 cent burgers from McDonald's. If anything I'd lost weight, not gained it. Eating, or sleeping for that matter, just doesn't seem so important when you're on the road, not until you look in the mirror and see the state of yourself.

For the rest of the day I simply meandered along the road between Page and Zion, passing through the town of Kanab, where a man I met outside a gas station gave me a decent map of the area, as he worked for the land agency and had a box full of them. On the way through to Kanab I crossed the state border line from Nevada into Utah, pulling over to take a picture of the sign; brightly coloured – orange and blue – with an illustration of Lake Powell in the background and the words 'Life Elevated' written at the front.

If you ever get the chance to travel this part of America, be it in a rental car, a motorhome, a motorbike, or even on a pushbike, then you really must come and see it. If there's a group of you it's not even that expensive, especially in a motorhome, staying on campsites and cooking in the van. A manageable road trip for anybody, and you'll never stop being enchanted by the desert.

**

I arrived on the outskirts of Zion National Park just as daylight began leaving the sky, finding a campsite half an hour's ride from the centre of the park, before you begin the descent into it. Across from the campsite was a souvenir shop and cafe, where I bought a few slices of cheap left over pizza and talked to a young girl in the shop about her dreams of taking off and travelling; to London, to Australia, to anywhere but her home of Zion National Park. You could see she'd got that bug, that desire to go, even if she didn't at the moment have the time or the money to do so. But she would find it someday, and no doubt finally come back to Zion, with many stories to tell.

I also met a group of Christian tourists, of senior age and travelling by minibus, keen to hear where I'd come from and pose for a group photograph. I showed them my Sarah Palin bracelet, which they applauded, before wishing me well and heading off in the direction of their hotel somewhere, while I bunked down in my $18 tent that was still doing me proud; a real life home from home.

The following morning I made my descent into Zion, entering via a long winding road cut through the heart of soft-red sandstone. It was a different world to any I'd passed through until this point. The colours were mute and pastel, the rock faces smooth and less violent than anywhere else. Tufts of grass and shoots of trees grew out from the rock in haphazard style. The road was a burgundy red, swooping along the shallow valley, a yellow centre line dividing the lines of traffic passing through the park on that busy day, throngs of tourists in rental cars heading in the same direction. I met a German couple just married in Vegas, and honeymooning in Zion. We were all in the midst of new adventures that day.

The road passed through a long black tunnel, too dark for my headlight, forcing me to hang off the bumper of the car in front, using its headlights to see the road ahead. Then suddenly, from darkness into bright light, the tunnel spits you out into the Zion Canyon. You appear to be halfway from the bottom (and halfway from the top), riding along a ridge, looking out over a paradise that is beneath, above and all around you. It is a startling realisation of scale, as you feel so tiny. Zion Canyon is fifteen miles long and half a mile deep. And I am just a speck.

The first human settlements here date back 8,000 years, to a small family group of semi-nomadic Native Americans known as Basketmaker Anasazi. The Parowan Fremont followed, then the Parrusits, and finally, in 1858, came the Mormons. The park was originally named Mukuntuweap National Monument in 1909, then renamed in 1918 as Zion, as it was thought a more appealing name to those who may wish to visit; Zion often used as a synonym for Jerusalem.

Down at the bottom of the valley, right in the heart of Zion, lies the small town of Springdale, not to mention the visitor centre and state-operated campsite, where a pitch cost $16, regardless of whether you're on a 105cc motorbike or in an eight-berth motorhome. A warden patrols in a golf buggy, making sure people have paid, and that they obey the one way system that wraps itself around this cluster of trees.

Like all the other National Parks that I would visit, Zion is incredibly well organised and preserved. Vehicles are only allowed along the main route. To get to the start of trails you must use the scheduled shuttle bus service, running at regular intervals, each bus at this time of year loaded with eager hikers and walkers, keen to get out and meander through the valley, which is like no other valley I've seen before. To have stumbled upon it, back when this land was first being discovered, must have taken breaths away, and left those people speechless, just as it continues to do to this day.

I set up camp, and unloaded most of my gear into the tent, including the panniers and everything else strapped to the bike. I never worry about things being stolen. It doesn't pay to. I put on a pair of shorts, T-shirt, and those sturdy boots I'd now been wearing all the way from New York. I filled one of the red water bottles that had been holstered in racks on Dot's frame, and secured it to my belt buckle. To cover my head from the sun I wore the One Ten Motorcycles cap given to me by Joe, back when I saw him in Australia last.

After catching the shuttle bus and hiking a mile or so up the valley, I reached a section called Walter's Wiggles, a series of man-made switchbacks stacked right on top of one another, elevating you a good ten floors or so in the space of only a few minutes. With every step taken I could almost hear the beat of a ceremonial drum, like the one in old movies when colonialists are about to be burned alive over a wild tribe's fire. I was nervous and scared; I didn't really want to do it, but knew that I couldn't chicken out either. It was simply the altitude I was scared of, having never been very good with heights. Then, with a few more steps, you emerge, on a ridge overlooking the canyon of Zion.

The canyon trails off to the left and to the right, but strutting out across the canyon floor right in front of you is the towering rocky ridge that is Angels Landing. A half mile trail, running across the top of this razor's edge, leads to a point at which all you can do is turn around and walk back again, because to take another step would lead you off the end. It is then like a pier into the sea, but one that runs out into a valley rather than a sea; the challenge being to walk to the far end of it, before turning around and coming back again.

The ridge is 1,488 feet high, with chain rails to hold on to. A warning sign states the number of people to have died on the ridge, with six in the last eight years. I doubt this route would be allowed in England. It would be fenced off completely or regulated by the State. I like how in America responsibility is still left in the hands of the individual. It is your life, to do with as you wish (which perhaps explains why so many are against universal healthcare, as self-determinism is valued highly here in America). The only advice is that you wear appropriate footwear and don't tackle it in bad weather. But if you slip, fall and die, then that's your choice to walk out on the ledge that day; don't blame anyone else.

The last time I was here I didn't get much further than this. While most of the others in the group went off and tackled Angels Landing, I waited for them at the bottom. Now I was here to attempt it again, twelve extra years of knowledge, wisdom and experience with which to propel myself. In a weird way, I perhaps saw this as an opportunity to quantify just how far I'd come in life. A measure of my advance. In reality, I was petrified.

Stepping out, I grabbed hold of the chain and began to scramble. I leaned into the rock, almost embracing it, as over my shoulder the ground gradually gave way to a very long drop, with an even steeper drop on the other side, almost as though you're walking along the blade of a knife, or as it looks in the pictures afterwards, the trunk of an elephant. It was no use though. I'm not brave enough for this, coming to a frozen halt at the point at which the first set of hand-chain ends and there's a small ledge to rest upon.

Other hikers passed me by. Some were completely unfazed by the trail ahead; they walked it as though it was the pavement on the way to the shops. Others battled their demons; one man equally as terrified as I was, resting at the same spot and gently coaxing himself to go on. He didn't want to, but needed to, if only for himself. And I can well understand the awkwardness of that.

A girl by the name of Lisa passed by with her friend. She too was nervous. We chatted for a while. Lisa lived in Seattle, but for the last ten days had been travelling across America on her own, living in the back of her pickup truck with a canopy on the back, the simple task of getting away from the world for a while. She was slim and pretty, with dark brown hair and a smile that made you smile. Her friend Sam had flown down to Las Vegas and for the next few days they were exploring Zion together. I admired Lisa's spirit; she had plenty of it, and having composed herself, she took off up the trail, leaving me to watch in awe.

The man I'd talked to on his way up now came back down. He looked pale and troubled. 'Not today,' he said on the way past, explaining briefly how he'd reached the middle plateau – a third of the way along the trail – but couldn't go any further, as the path gets much narrower from there to the end. He was disappointed with himself, though he shouldn't have been as he'd done all right. I on the other hand couldn't go any further. It was that hypnotic urge to leap off the edge that was doing it for me.

I think when you've had death on your mind, as I had done for a while, you can't help but see that cliff as a shortcut to the end. And from that comes the fear that part of you is still in desire of it. To have that part of you that just wants to throw your whole body off feels like a relentless internal battle to stop yourself from doing such a thing. I wondered if it's perhaps because it represents an opportunity to skip all that fear of failure and endless worry that you hope won't dominate the rest of your life.

A shortcut to your own final solution perhaps, which sounds macabre, but I think when you find yourself with no meaning or purpose in life – and you don't know how to do anything about that – then what is the point? To prolong it? To endure it some more? Or to just be done with it, because your fear is that things are never going to change, because you are not going to change, so why would you want to live a life of that? Thankfully I wasn't at that point anymore, though I still don't think I would have had the bravery to take that final step. A coward caught in the middle, trying to take a step back from the edge.

I scaled the chains back down to safety, disappointed with myself. I'd only made it a few more paces than the first time. I sat on a rock and fed the chipmunks with the scraps of food that I carried. Time passed by in the shade. I listened to my thoughts and to my feelings. They didn't betray me this day; they weren't defeated just yet. If they had been then I'd be back down that trail already, heading back to camp. Instead I just sat there on the shaded rock, churning, letting the water slowly simmer until it reached boiling point, causing me to force my legs into the ground and stand up; bracing my arms against the bars and taking steps back in the direction of the start of Angels Landing.

I scrambled back up the chains to the point at which I was previously at. I looked once more at the reality of my situation – a long way from the earth – then down at my feet, and for once I put faith in them, staring at my boots, grabbing hold of the chain, and ignoring the sliver of rock and the vertical slope on either side. I took strong short steps, staring at my feet, clinging to the chain, trying to shut everything down but my feet. Trust them. 'Believe in your feet.'

I don't think I've ever walked with such fire burning through my legs; strong and firm, clinging on with my left hand as I traversed the slope, the ground rolling away to my right. 'Don't look down, don't look down. It doesn't exist. It's just a path. There is no drop. Trust your feet, they won't let you fall.'

I arrived at a point around halfway up the elephant's trunk; the ground now flat and stable here. I assumed this was the same place the other man had reached. I looked up at the trail as it continued along and above the precipice, perhaps another quarter of a mile to go before the end point. For whatever reason – perhaps the fear of carrying on, or the satisfaction of getting this far – I felt contentment in how far I'd come and didn't feel any urge to go any further. I'd beaten my demon that day. Perhaps I'd beaten myself, and if anything it just reminded me that when faced with hurdles you don't think you can tackle, sometimes it's just a case of taking that first step. And from there, come the rest.

Chapter Fourteen
Grand Canyon

The next morning I headed out of Zion in the rain. I was aiming for Las Vegas, detouring via the Grand Canyon and hoping to be in the Sin City the following evening, just in time to hit the strip and gamble everything I owned on red, which I suppose I already had. For a short distance this day I would have to retrace my steps, back to the town of Kanab; then on from there, past the entrance to the north rim of the Grand Canyon, then all the way around its eastern edge until I was able to turn back west in order to stop off at the southern rim of the park.

The north rim is said to be much quieter than the south, but for me, in leaving Zion that morning, the southern rim represented the perfect riding distance that day of around 250 miles. In fact, this turned out to be one of my favourite days on the road. There was one stretch, between Kanab and Jacob Lake, where the road meandered through a vast open valley, a river running along the bottom of it, strong iron bridges built across it, and Navajo people selling their wares on the other side.

At times such as these I would just cruise on through, my hand lightly on the throttle, maintaining that constant speed of 37mph, doing my best to take it all in, feeling the warm breeze on my face, looking up at the sun

169

and across at the other vehicles that trickled past me throughout the day. I passed isolated farms, stopped at lonely outposts for gas, and met other travellers, most of whom had hired motorhomes and were doing it as a couple, or with their kids.

Later that day my mood changed and I started to feel quite lonely. This can happen at times and there isn't that much you can do about it, only hope that it will soon pass. I think it's the realisation that you're out here on your own, the mind suddenly skipping from seeing that as a good thing, to seeing it as a bad thing, because what if something goes wrong or you suddenly lost the ability to live like this? What happens then? How do you find your way out? Just keep on riding; that seems to be the only answer, much like life itself.

I turned off the main highway and along the fifty-mile access road that would lead me to the edge of the Grand Canyon. The first time you see the canyon you can't believe it's real, because it's on a scale that can't possibly be real. Not only is it deep, but it's also massively wide, and your expectation is of vertical walls, with a flat bottom. But it's not like that at all; instead there are fingers of outcrops dancing out into the canyon with the chaos of lightening strikes. Ridges of rock and dirt zigzag towards you, the other side of the canyon ten miles away, with that space in between filled with crevices and cracks, long plateaus and the Colorado River raging at the bottom. It is impossible to take in the complexities of what you're looking at.

We'd passed through this way on that organised trip, doing a day-long hike down to the mid-way point, arriving at the end of the Plateau Point Trail; an outcrop of earth that seems to have you hovering right in the heart of the canyon, it still another day's hike all the way down to the bottom. I wouldn't be doing any hiking this time, just passing through, with the plan being to spend the night at the Grand Canyon campsite and continue on the next morning. Money and momentum were both urging me along.

I stopped at several more lookout points along the roadside; parking up and wandering over to the railings, to lean against and look out at this big scar in the earth, bathed in tranquil fading light as it now was. I tried to photograph the spectacle but didn't get very good results. I think even my camera was overwhelmed by it all.

From there, the road leads to the main visitor centre. A short distance from this visitor centre I came across a lone female rider standing beside her motorcycle in a pull-in on the left hand side of the road. She looked out of place, there on her own, and so I stopped to see if she was all right and needed any help.

Naomi was waiting for a friend; the two of them from Los Angeles and soon to make their way back there having spent the past ten weeks covering 12,000 miles on a tour of the southern states of America. She rode a Moto Guzzi, an unusual choice in a way, being a slightly temperamental brand of Italian motorcycle. It may or may not be relevant, but she was of African American descent, and female, unique amongst the other riders I'd met so far.

Naomi explained how the previous night she and her friend had ridden into the Grand Canyon National Park in the midst of a rain storm, her friend reaching the gate house at the entrance and deciding she'd just had enough, parking up her bike and sleeping in the gutter, beneath the canopy of the gate house, much to the annoyance of the gate house staff. Naomi rode on the extra twenty miles or so until she was at the hotel she'd pre-booked for the night. Having chatted a while, Naomi said that if I was ever to make it to LA then I was to give her a call and I could hang out with her for a while, her apartment overlooking the Hollywood sign.

At this stage I wasn't sure if I was going to pass through LA or not. I had thought about it, but hadn't yet decided. I was waiting for an email from a man who lived near LA, who was storing a motorcycle that I was keen to go and see, and if I was able to go and see it, then I was going to detour that way. It's a strange story really, one that captures the bittersweet nature of life perhaps more than any other;

Some eight months prior, when I was dealing with my own demons back in England, I received an email out of the blue from a gentleman in

171

America who had a friend with terminal cancer. His friend's name was Mike. One of Mike's wishes before he died was to ride from his home in Louisiana – not far from New Orleans – down to Florida, and also across to California to visit his dad.

At the time, Mike didn't own a motorbike to do the trip on, and couldn't afford one either because of his illness. To rectify this, Mike's friend – the one who had emailed me – posted on ADVRider.com (the same site that had helped me many times already), wondering if people would be willing to have a whip around to raise enough money to buy Mike a bike for him to do his final journey on. The donations came flooding in.

With the money raised a bike was bought; a second-hand Honda cruiser, styled like a Harley Davidson. Mike was still weak from the chemotherapy and so was only able to muster ten minutes a day on it, hoping to build up his strength in order to embark on these trips he had planned. Sadly, Mike died before he ever got to go on them, and so this bike, bought for Mike's adventure, had no one to ride it.

The email I received was an invitation to come and do just that; take Mike's bike on an adventure, something I felt incredibly privileged to be offered. Sadly, at the time, I was still in the midst of my own battle, and didn't feel I could do it justice, so had to let them down, though it was a very hard decision to make. The bike had since been sent to another friend's house in LA and kept in storage there. I thought now, if I was passing through, then I would like to go and see Mike's bike and pay my respects to it. I was just waiting to hear if it was going to be convenient for me to stop by on my way through or not.

**

I camped that night on the official Grand Canyon campsite, beneath a sea of stars, and besides a friendly German couple who fed and watered me from the massive motorhome they'd rented for the fortnight. The next morning I rode in the direction of Williams, seventy miles to the south of the canyon. Here I intended to turn right, to point west, and from there carry on in the direction of Las Vegas, which I hoped to reach by that evening.

Having reached Williams I hit a snag, as the only road west from there was the I-40 interstate (the one that had replaced Route 66), and whether legal or otherwise on such a small bike, the thought of doing battle with all those massive trucks just didn't seem so appealing. I had done such things before, on the German Autobahn and the busy motorways of Poland and Belgium, but on those occasions I was so desperate to reach England that I would have gone through any danger to make it. Now, in America, with far less desperation in reaching San Francisco, I accepted that I would just have to find another way around.

Fortunately, the owner of a motorcycle shop in Williams was able to give me directions along a dirt trail running parallel to the interstate for some forty miles, at which point the interstate would have ended and I would be able to rejoin the tarmac road, rejoining old Route 66 in fact.

Having found the start of the trail beyond the town's golf course, it was then a case of following it through the forest and alongside the railway tracks. At times I would encounter campers tucked away in the forest, families enjoying their weekends closer to nature. I waved at them as I passed, and in return, they would wave back.

The trail finally spat me out in the small town of Ash Fork, a dilapidated little place, broken and ruined, right by the side of old Route 66. Had I stayed on Mother Road, rather than leave it in St. Louis, I would have come down through Oklahoma and Albuquerque, missing out the Rockies, Monument Valley and Zion, something I didn't regret.

As for Ash Fork, I read later how the town was originally built as a siding of the Atlantic and Pacific Railroad in 1882, back when the first settlers were flooding west in search of unclaimed land. Fire gutted the entire town a decade later, with it rebuilt on the opposite side of the tracks.

The town's prosperity improved in the 1950s, thanks to the increased traffic along Route 66, though it wasn't to last; the Santa Fe railroad deciding in the 1960s to move its main line north and away from the town, resulting in half the town's population moving out overnight.

Another fire destroyed most of downtown in 1977, before completion of the I-40 meant that trans-continental traffic – the only thing keeping the place alive – now bypassed the town completely. Finally, a third fire gutted almost everything that remained in 1987, and from the looks of things, not much work had been done since.

I couldn't help but feel sorry for the place; it had fought, lost, and been battered severely by the winds of change. It now looked to have accepted its fate, even being used as a backdrop for the 1992 movie *Universal Soldier* as the land was cheap and the misery of the town just what the director needed.

It was then with some surprise that in the museum on the outskirts of town I should meet a girl who claimed to have finished fifth in a recent series of *America's Next Top Model*. I could well believe it: a face like Denise Richards from *Starship Troopers*, legs all the way to the ceiling, short skirt and cowboy boots. *Yeehaa!*

Her name was Hannah, from Texas, driving across the country with her mum and all her gear, hoping to find fame and fortune in Los Angeles. They didn't seem rich and were completely down to earth. I admired that Hannah had this dream. Her mum was behind her all the way, they were going to LA, and she was going to make it as a movie star or model or whatever she chose. She was on a mission; running towards her own light, you could sense that.

Hannah said that if I was passing through LA, I should stop by and visit her. I must admit, the idea of spending the weekend hanging out with one of America's next top models in LA did sound a little surreal. After all, what would I do with Dorothy, and what would I wear? I've been wearing the same red flannel shirt all the way across America. I couldn't hang out in LA dressed like that. I'd have to buy new shoes, and a shirt, and cut my hair and use deodorant, and I was too old and sour for her. But maybe I could go to a photo shoot and watch. I don't know. Her mum was hot though; a real MILF.

We exchanged details in the car park, before I strapped on my crap helmet, pulled on those daft gardening gloves, fired the old bike into life and, as cool as I possibly could, rode off at my usual miles per hour, making sure they went ahead of me, so I didn't have that embarrassing moment where they would come streaming past, tooting their horn, and I would turn bright crimson, and return their signal with a half-cocked wave. Girls; the things they make you do.

***

I continued on along old Route 66, it now just a threadbare road across the prairie, the interstate over in the distance, and a train line in-between, on which a long blue freight train chugged along, causing me and Dorothy to try and race it. Naturally, we lost that one, and after a while the road brought me to the next town of Seligman, a place that served as inspiration for Radiator Springs, the fictional town in which the Pixar movie *Cars* was set.

Seligman is one of the few towns along old Route 66 that has managed to survive out here, becoming a tourist attraction in its own right. There isn't that much to see; a single strip of old burger joints, novelty gift shops and all manner of kitsch, bringing bus-loads of day trippers from Las Vegas and beyond, when in truth, they'd perhaps be better off carrying on to Ash Fork; arguably offering, as it does, a more accurate representation of the state of modern day Route 66.

I hung around for a while, taking some pictures and observing the way hordes of coach-trippers would disembark from their vehicles, race around with cameras and buy souvenirs, before being scooped back up and returned to Las Vegas. When one coach left another seemed to arrive. It was smash and grab tourism, but as long as it keeps the town afloat I suppose there's nothing wrong with that, and not everyone can afford the time and opportunity that I was enjoying on this trip.

Wandering to the end of the short little strip I came to the last souvenir shop of the row. It looked to be an old converted home, seeming quite lonely on the end. In the front garden was a collection of motorcycles, four of which were bikes just like mine, or at least the American version, and a few decades older so of slightly different design. I was intrigued by this and felt that I had to meet the owner.

I was told by his wife that he was out doing some shopping all the way back in Williams and wouldn't be back for an hour or more. I decided to sit and wait.

Two hours later a grumpy old man showed up. He had a wooden leg, from the knee down, but still rode bikes. I never did catch his name. He explained that he just loved the old Honda bikes, and that was that, no more explanation or small talk. I asked if he had a socket that would fit Dot's engine oil bolt as I'd left mine at Vermin's by mistake. The man had just the thing, suggesting I keep it for the oil changes ahead. He was a kind-hearted man really, just didn't know much how to show it.

By this time it was falling dark (it always seemed to be falling dark), making the final 175 miles to Las Vegas seem less than appealing, despite having a reservation in a hostel there that apparently had a scene from *The Hangover* filmed in it.

Instead, two precocious boys on pushbikes – who both dreamed of leaving Seligman behind – told me about a campsite on the outskirts of town, and I considered heading there, before looking longingly at the motels across the street, their neon signs twinkling in the early evening sky.

I'd not yet stayed in a proper American motel, and regardless of budget, which was now very much thin on the ground, I decided to bite the bullet and go and inquire about the cost of a room for the night. The two boys told me to try the Romney Inn, as that was alright, although they did tell me it often smells a little funny.

I wondered what they meant by this, but in passing through the front door of reception could immediately understand. The motel was owned by an Indian couple, and the fabulous smell was that of authentic Indian cuisine. All of a sudden I found myself back in Delhi again.

I was offered a room for $45 in the old style motel, built in the shape of a horseshoe, with parking outside each room. Having paid, we chatted a while about the various paths we'd taken to be in that same reception room that night. The couple told me how they'd previously lived in LA, buying the motel in recent years and completely refurbishing it.

I asked them how they'd been received by the locals, and the customers for that matter. They'd said they'd had no troubles, certainly not from the customers, just the usual hassle you get from some members of a small community when 'outsiders' – of whichever race or religion – move in. They were enjoying it, which was good to hear, although it did look a difficult business to sustain. In winter barely anyone passes through Seligman, at which point they move back to LA to earn a crust.

Helping the Indian couple to run the motel was a man named John, who also owned a ramshackle grocery store across the road. John was originally from Macedonia and had travelled the world through various means and for various different reasons.

John talked about retirement having previously lived in Las Vegas, buying the grocery store and moving out here for a quieter life. It was a wish he looked to have been granted, spending his evenings hanging out with the Indian couple, and the waifs and strays that passed on through this sleepy little town, which, when all the tourist buses had departed, was actually quite pleasant and charming; definitely the best time to see it.

John explained how he hoped to move back to Macedonia in the next few years and use his American pension to live on. He told me that he missed home; the dark rings beneath his eyes hinting at a hard and difficult life. But a nicer man you couldn't wish to meet.

Having chatted for a while in reception, John offered to make me a sandwich over at his shop. I joined him there, chatting for ages as he sliced a mound of ham and cheese, salad and pickle, handing me the biggest sandwich I'd ever seen, along with bags of crisps and chocolate bars to go with it. In return he wouldn't accept a dollar, so I forced ten of them into his collection jar that he had on his counter, money going towards people in need in the community.

John was definitely one of those people you meet that make it all worthwhile. It's almost as though you are meant to meet them, because they might say something, or explain something, that makes you stop and think, and reflect on how you're living your own life. John was a religious man, believing in God and in faith. I think most of all he believed in kindness and in the goodness of people. He had a warm heart, and his sandwiches were simply divine.

I often felt guilty meeting people such as John. They seemed to give so much to me, and I felt like I gave so little in return. It would make me feel embarrassed and extremely humble. There are so many good people in this world. They are literally everywhere, and I think it would do us some good to remind ourselves of this from time to time.

Before hitting the road the next morning John loaded me up with more sandwiches and all sorts of cakes, crisps and biscuits. In return I wished him well on his future adventures in Macedonia. I hope he's found himself there by now, or at least is on his way. Godspeed John.

**

It took me a long time to reach Las Vegas that day, simply because I didn't feel like I was in any hurry to get there. I stopped in the big town of Kingman for a McDonald's and some time spent on the Wi-Fi, uploading photos and confirming to my parents that I was still alive. I also passed Hoover Dam and stopped for a look around. To my eyes it wasn't half as impressive as the dam at Lake Powell, though I did meet a lady named Mia, a glamorous black lady, originally from Gary, Indiana – the place I'd passed through on my way into Chicago – who was interested to hear my experiences, as she ran a youth education programme for kids from the poor areas I'd been witness to.

This all meant that I didn't get to Las Vegas until dusk, the casino towers rising from the desert earth amidst a haze of dust and fading light. It really is just plonked here in the middle of nowhere, a city on the fringe of the Mojave Desert.

Las Vegas first sprang up in 1905, starting out as a place where steam locomotives stopped to fill their water tanks. The building of the Hoover Dam between 1929 and 1935 brought thousands of well paid employees to the area, and in 1931 gambling was legalised, when across the rest of America it was still considered a crime and a sin. The gambling in Las Vegas was said to have grown off the back of mob money, formalised casino gambling being a type of 'grifting', something that the mob excelled at. The new interstate and the invention of air-conditioning made the city popular with outsiders, while laws banning publicly held companies from owning casinos were eventually scrapped, giving rise to the corporate gambling mecca that rises from the desert today.

In recent years Las Vegas has been hit hard by the economic downturn, it dependent totally on the tourists coming to town, and if the tourist has no money, then neither does the town. I'd read before of homeless people living in the sewers beneath the city and it has one of the highest unemployment rates in America.

In a way I wish I'd been one of the millions of tourists flying into the airport, taking a taxi to one of the massive casino-hotel complexes, spending the week getting drunk and dining on all you can eat buffet, not caring what was happening out the window, because to see Vegas like that must be paradise. A real fun loving town.

But riding through the scruffy downbeat suburbs on a tiny motorbike, booked in to a cheap hostel on the wrong end of the strip, having no money with which to enjoy myself or dull my senses with booze, I was always bound to see a different side of things, and to be honest, Vegas this time was probably my least favourite place in America. Instead of the grand casinos I saw the discomfort of the promo girl outside the bar, with the surgically enhanced breasts, having to smile for the lecherous bastard who wished to have his photo taken with her.

Or I saw how seething the street performers, dressed up in various costumes as they were, became when tourists would take their photo and not offer the obligatory tip in exchange. Beneath the crass veneer was a place of utter shit, people doing the things they despise, simply to stay alive, in order to … I was going to say, in order to live the American Dream, but I think the word is survive. They do this to survive.

It was then just not a place for me, though I appreciate others thrive in this town, and find their amusement. I on the other hand, was much happier two days later, as I passed through the wonderful Death Valley.

Chapter Fifteen
Death Valley

It was around this point – between Las Vegas and Death Valley – that I lost the diary I'd been writing my notes in, assuming it must have fallen from my tank bag during the 121 mile ride between the two places.

I considered turning back and tracing my steps, but in a way, I was quite relieved. A diary (much like a book) can chain you to the past, and while it would have been handy for remembering the names of more people when writing this book, I learnt from the first book that sometimes it's easier to start with a blank page and write down the things that you remember, in the way that you remember them, rather than attempting to stitch together old sentences and thoughts written in various moods of the past.

What I remember most about this relatively short journey between Las Vegas and Death Valley was the colour of the sky. I'd not taken to the road until late in the day, so as I passed through the desert the sky ahead of me was a sea of crimson red and deep burnt orange. It was one of those irreplaceable moments, a warm breeze on your face, the familiar sound of the engine ticking along beneath you, still hanging in there, mile after mile, hour after hour, even chuckling at the roadside billboards encouraging people to vote in the next local elections for a lady with the unfortunate name of 'Judge Kim Wanker.' How many people would stop to take a photo of that? I know I did.

I happened upon the town of Pahrump, trying desperately to find somewhere to park up and sleep for the night. The onset of darkness didn't help, with it not looking like there was a campsite for tents, only for motorhomes and statics. There didn't seem to be any lanes or paths to dive down either. It was just one of those miserable evenings where you find yourself frantic, trying desperately to get off the road and shut down for a while.

Finally I found a building site at the top end of town, taking the access road and parking up behind a mound of dirt, laying the bike on its side and folding down the wing mirrors so no reflections could be seen by anyone on the road. I put up the tent in the dirt, drank some water from a bottle I'd been carrying, using the rest of it to brush my teeth, getting into bed, completely clothed, with the knife beside me, and then nervously trying to get some sleep. It was one of the worst night's sleep of the trip; the occasional passing car casting beams of light from the road, which made me think I was going to be detected at any time.

I rose early, packed away the tent under the cover of darkness and made my way down to the town's McDonald's for a routine cup of hot coffee. I must have stopped in most McDonald's between here and New York. I stopped at quite a few between Sydney and London as well. It would have been nice to have used more local cafés and diners, but it would have cost far more, and meant that at each stop I would have had to engage in conversation, whereas in McDonald's I can find a quiet corner and keep myself to myself, as I did this morning, using my laptop to check online while I drank my coffee and ate my muffin.

Around 6.30am, as I was back outside in the carpark prepping the bike for the journey into Death Valley, I met a mysterious man returning from the Californian mountains, after a futile search for gold.

The man was a tramp, or at least had the appearance of one (we both did). His clothes were tattered and his hair was long. He was perhaps sixty years of age, possibly more, and travelling on a beaten up old bicycle with a chain that slipped, which he told me he was trying to fix. Scattered on and around this battered old bike were all of the man's belongings, stored in white cylindrical plastic buckets hanging from the handlebars. Other bags and containers were strapped to a rack on the back and, best of all, he had a dog with him, tethered to the bike by a bedraggled piece of string.

The man told me that he lived down in Texas, sharing a caravan with his long suffering wife, but having heard whisper of this gold up in the Californian mountains, had set off on his bicycle, his dog trotting alongside on what must have been a 1,500-mile odyssey in either direction. Sadly, the man told me how he never did strike gold, despite panning the entire hill side for the summer, and was now on his way back to Texas, empty-handed, in need of appeasing his wife, and still with so many miles left to go.

The man told me how he would push the bike some of the way, simply because of all the weight, and the difficulty he had in pedalling it. Other times he'd take lifts, or the police would pick him up and drop him off at the next town. He lived on nothing. I don't know how he lived. I don't know how he survived. He was a man completely at odds with the modern world; far more off grid than I ever was.

As inspired as I was by this, deep down I remained hopeful that it wasn't a premonition of my future; a life on the road, searching far and wide for this piece of 'gold,' and still not being able to find it. Perhaps this man will return home and realise it was there all along, right under his nose. Or just maybe he was having me on, and instead of returning empty-handed he had actually struck upon a massive bounty, and in one of those buckets, or in one of those plastic bags on the back of the bike, was a bar of gold so vast it would set him up for the rest of his life. His wife could have a new caravan. He could have a new bike. And his dog could have had a new lead. No one deserved to find gold more than that man, whose name I never could quite remember. I probably had it written down in the pages of that blasted diary.

***

From Pahrump I took the old Charles Brown Highway, crossing the border into California not far out of town. San Francisco was still some 500 miles away, but it felt much closer now, being in the same state and all. It looked unlikely that I was going to divert down to LA to check out Mike's bike, or see Hannah, or Naomi, as the current keepers of Mike's bike hadn't got back to me yet. Also, the desire to see Death Valley would take me a little too far north to drop back down to LA. Some other time, that's what I reasoned to myself.

For now, the road dropped me down to the small community of Shoshone, the name of an Indian tribe that still live in these parts; their main reservation down at Furnace Creek, deep in the heart of Death Valley. In Shoshone there is nothing more than a gas station, convenience store, campsite, small museum and a few other bits and bobs, the town surviving as a jumping-off point for people heading into Death Valley.

The price of petrol reflected this, proving more expensive than anywhere else at $5.60 per gallon. Across the rest of America it had cost me around $4 a gallon, and in needing roughly three gallons to fill the bike, I could travel approximately 250 miles on twelve dollars (about £8). That's really how I'd managed to afford all this.

The lady inside the gas station told me that it was approximately ninety miles to the next pump at the visitor centre at Furnace Creek, which was well within range. The only time I'd had to carry extra fuel was when riding over the Himalayas in India, from Manali to Leh, where the biggest distance without anywhere to get gas was over 400 kilometres, though there's always someone with fuel if you get stuck.

Water was more of an issue out here, feeling the need to buy a four-litre drum from the gas station, along with a bunch of bananas, biscuits and a few other snacks that I strapped haphazardly to the back of the bike. I had spare inner tubes, my pump, necessary tools, still no mobile phone, but that was okay because I figured if I broke down in the middle of nowhere I'd just walk at night and take shelter by day.

The hottest temperature in the world was recorded in Death Valley, reaching 134 degrees Fahrenheit on the 10th July 1913 (about 56 degrees Celsius); though this being mid-September it was unlikely to get that hot. To prepare the bike for the heat I was already running a thicker grade of oil in the engine, hoping to counteract the way oil thins and loses effectiveness during really hot temperatures. Anything to keep this bike in good health, though she was certainly starting to feel her age.

Pretty much since St. Louis she'd not been running or sounding in great health. This hadn't really effected the speed, as it wasn't too great to begin with, but being so in-tune with the bike as I was I couldn't help but hear the rumbles and the slight ticking from the engine within, and when you're alone out here, the smallest of noises becomes an avalanche of fear that it will lead to something catastrophic. The heat of the impending desert definitely wasn't going to help from here.

Beyond Shoshone I turned left on to Jubilee Pass Road, stopping to take a photograph of the brightly coloured sign marking the entrance to Death Valley National Park. From here the road begins its long and winding descent towards the valley floor, seemingly getting hotter and hotter with every step.

Death Valley got its name from a time in 1849 when a group of pioneers got lost out here, one of the men apparently dying (though some accounts claim that not to be true), and, as the others eventually climbed out to salvation, one turned around and was reported to have said, 'Goodbye, death valley.' And from there stuck the name.

At the bottom of this long descent the road turns to the right, and there before you stretches the vast expanse of the valley floor. It is completely flat at the bottom, and wide, with steep rock slopes on either side, like being at the bottom of a bath tub with a road running through it. The colour of the rock is the most amazing sight. It is so fiery and red, like the colours you see when volcanoes erupt. Second to that is the absence of anything on the valley floor. It is flat and featureless. Scant plant life exists out here, just shoots of bushes and grasses. The rest is salt flats, white and hazy, the road hugging the safest part, where the salt flats meet the red rock walls of the valley.

This being early morning I was the only one out here, which perhaps led me to experience so much enchantment. Had there been a steady procession of rental cars, as there was during my passage through Zion, then my passion for it would have been less strong. As it was, I was alone and free, in the valley of the heat, sauntering along with all my skin covered, as patterns of sand and dust skipped across the worn tarmac ahead of me. When I stopped to take a photograph I removed my helmet, surprised not to hear a single sound. The whole world was at peace. Until a Ford Mustang V8 shot by with its roof down, and I remembered where I was again.

Around the next corner lay Badwater Basin, officially the lowest point in America at 282 feet below sea level, something made possible by the sheer heat of the valley, plus the impenetrability of its walls, preventing fresh water from entering. The salt plains are a remnant of the sea, back when this part of the world was under water.

The appeal of Badwater Basin is that you can park your car beneath the shadow of the rock, use the recently built toilets if need be, then proceed to walk out across salt flats on to what resembles a large white catwalk, stretching out for a couple of hundred metres or more into the heart of Death Valley. The ground underfoot is solid salt, while either side is a bubbling cauldron of salt-contaminated water, the taste of which lends the place its name, 'Badwater'.

What I enjoyed most about Death Valley was that you were completely immersed in it. You weren't looking at it from a distance, as you are at the Grand Canyon, parked up on the rim. Here you were actually in the heart of it, riding through it, and for me, travelling by motorcycle, and being able to ride that same motorcycle through here just made it that perfect experience. By far it was my favourite place in the whole of America.

Morning turned to afternoon, and in the full heat of the day I stopped to take in the Devil's Golf Course. This is an area at the heart of the flat of the valley resembling a carpet of tremendous white golf balls, each as big as washing machine drums and closely packed together. They're made from crystalised salt, and you can hop from one to another, the carpet of them stretching out for almost as far as the ground you can see. They took their name from when one of the first European settles came upon them and declared, 'only the devil would play golf on these.'

Not far from the Devil's Golf Course I took a ride along what's known as Artist's Drive. This is a narrow, one way road, running through a shallow side valley of beautifully coloured rocks, made that way by the metal in them that had oxidised over the years, turning them various shades of blue, red and green.

I leap-frogged a couple of travellers in a rental car throughout all this. It turned out that they were on a fortnight break from their home in Philadelphia; the guy originally from Germany, the girl from Chile, the couple now living in America together. We agreed to camp together that evening on a campsite at the far end of the valley, carrying on at our own pace until then.

I stopped at the Furnace Creek visitor centre to take on fluid and shade, finding it an enclave of activity in this vast empty valley. Coach loads of day-trippers, again from Vegas, were unloading and re-loading, having spent their dollars in the canteen or in the souvenir shop. Many posed with the thermometer, which at its peak this day hit almost 120 degrees Fahrenheit, or 48 degrees Celsius. This was as hot as it had been when coming across India, but in that country, with all its commotion, traffic, dust, noise and trickery, the heat just feels that little bit more intense, though it certainly took your breath here in Death Valley as well.

Beyond Furnace Creek I met another cyclist. I passed him by, heading in the opposite direction, before turning round and going back to check if he needed any water. He was a handsome man, tall and strong, wearing Lycra, and cycling with no luggage or bags, and barely any water, just a litre bottle in a pocket stitched to the back of his shirt. His destination was Las Vegas, riding there for a cycle-expo he was attending as he owned a bike shop and had a stall selling cycling equipment that he'd sent there in a container.

Rather than fly or drive, he'd decided instead to cycle the three-hundred miles from his home on the far west side of Death Valley to Las Vegas. He hoped to cover the distance in less than two days, and judging by the size of his thighs I wouldn't bet against it. He told me he had a wife and kids, but lived for adventure, keen whenever he could to get out and do something strenuous.

We talked for a long time, finding equal fascination in one another's adventures. Richard (I believe that was his name) hoped to take in Asia at some time, and possibly Australia as well. He was fascinated to hear about Pakistan, thinking it would be too dangerous to travel through at the moment, but I told him about the Austrian girl I'd met in Gilgit, only in her twenties and cycling the length of the country all by herself. Richard looked quite amazed by this, and I think, quite faintly, you could see his eyes light up, as the scope for his adventures had just doubled, tripled perhaps, because previously he'd imagined them extending no further than North America. Now he saw the world, and it was my pleasure to have given him that.

∗∗∗

That evening, rather than push any further, I found a lonely little campsite just on the rise out the other side of Death Valley. There was only space for half a dozen vehicles, wooden log dividers between the pitches, and each pitch with a pebble floor, picnic table and firepit. It was the only sign of civilisation for miles around, with the view back across Death Valley a simple brilliance of nothingness, with a wispy pink sky and stars that would start to dazzle brighter the darker it became.

I only intended to rest there for an hour or so, before pushing on to where the couple from Philadelphia were camped, but there was just something about this campsite, as low key as it was, that made me stay there for far longer, laying back on the wooden picnic bench and drifting off to sleep from around 5pm to 7pm, waking just as evening was beginning to set, and the last wave of tourists and travellers were making haste out of Death Valley for the night, leaving me alone on this little stone pitch, an ocean of dry sand and rock all around.

Other campers eventually joined me for the night. The first were a couple of old Czech men travelling by people carrier, out here to do some climbing, one of them bragging that he was on incapacity benefit but still able to climb. A lone woman sleeping on the seats of her rental car followed, somehow managing to unbolt and position them on the ground beside her vehicle. Lastly came a two-car convoy of young campers, arriving in darkness, cooking their food and heading straight to bed.

I lay on my back and looked up at the stars overhead. I thought about so many things, finding it hard to believe that it was only just over a month ago that I'd been in England, putting this bike on a plane, not sure what I was to encounter, wondering how things would turn out.

From there to here, lying back on a bench in the midst of Death Valley, made me realise just how far I'd travelled in that time. I was glad I'd put my faith in the road and not those tablets, or anything else prescribed by others, who I realise were only trying to help. But I'd always known deep down what it was that I needed to do, it just took me longer than expected to muster the courage and conviction - and clarity - to go ahead and do it.

One person told me that at such times you just have to make a decision, jump in with both feet, and stick with it, but I'm not so sure. To me, if you're stood in the middle of a cross-roads, not knowing which way to turn, then sometimes it's better to sit it out, to feel the emotions and feelings seep through you, standing firm on the spot and pushing back against the wind until the moment at which everything becomes clear, and you can now take that path, simply because you know with all your heart it's the right one to take. Patience, not haste; that seems to be the remedy to such periods of despair.

I got up the next morning, packed away the tent and left before any of the other campers had even woken. The sun was just beginning to rise, casting long warm shadows across the dusty earth, the road climbing to the top of the valley and dropping back down the other side. I pulled over by a side road, on a patch of gravel with a view of red-hot valley beyond. I killed the engine, took off my helmet and just sat there for a while, enjoying the silence that had enveloped me.

For so many years – pretty much for as long as I can remember – I've always had a mind of competing voices. Some wanting me to go one way, other voices wanting me to go another, feeling as though I'm being pulled in every direction and leaving me stranded on the spot, as I've just explained. But on this morning, finally, I didn't hear a single thing. The competing voices had been silenced, or perhaps had learnt to get along, because every single one of us wished to be nowhere but here, on a plateau overlooking the magnificence of Death Valley. The sensation was overwhelming and I hoped my mind would remain this way forever. Of course it wouldn't, but for this brief moment it did so. Nirvana.

Chapter Sixteen
California

A mission now lay ahead of me; aiming to be paddling in the waves of the Pacific Ocean by the end of the day, signalling that my journey across America would be over. It had been just over five weeks from landing in New York to here. In that time I had covered almost 5,000 miles, my funds were sorely depleted and the bike was beginning to fight against the onslaught of old age, the tripometer now ticking ever closer to 100,000 kilometres. Thirty thousand kilometres as a postal bike, ten thousand in the hands of Colin – the man who gave her the name – and almost 50,000 kilometres in my wicked hands.

No way would I make it to Alaska now, and besides, I no longer wanted to. I'd seen and ridden enough coming across America and I think I'd got out of it what I needed to get out of it: a cleansing of the soul, to leave something behind and have a new story to tell. I didn't need to ride up to Alaska to gain any more of that, San Francisco would be just far enough, my plan being to be there in two days, just in time to give a talk at a bike club in the neighbouring city of Oakland. I'd been invited there by a lady who had followed my travels on Facebook and happened to be a member of the Oakland Motorcycle Club. It was good to have this presentation booked in place, as it would provide the necessary pull to get me over the finishing line.

For now I was leaving Death Valley behind, making my way out on to Route 395, a long straight boring road, the opposite of what I'd just passed through. The trucks and lorries had returned, so I was once more riding with one eye on the rear view mirror and tucked well into the gutter. These are the times when you wish for just that little bit more power, when 37mph just feels so painfully slow, but you know that's all you've got, so that's just what you have to stick to.

We turned right on to Isabella-Walker Pass Road, shortly beyond the town of Indian Wells. This began a stretch of road that didn't have a very good aura around it. There was something just not right about this one. It felt like riding through a scene out of a scary movie, though I'm not sure why. For whatever reason it felt creepy, with random houses and ranches out here. The rest of the time the road ran through shallow valleys and alongside riverbanks, and then through towns and villages that seemed okay, but again, I didn't feel like stopping, imagining a pickup truck full of hillbillies to start trailing me at any time. Strange how the mind works like that, it all quite irrational really.

I was thankful then when the road turned into a canyon, the tarmac becoming like a set of rapids that you might ride down on a rubber tube, gushing from left to right, such was the way in which the road rolled with the contours of the valley floor. It was beautiful riding, perfect on this bike, because the corners were at times tight, the road narrow, allowing me to scoot on through like a child along a helter-skelter, about to pop out at the end, into a large splash pool.

Instead I splashed down in Bakersfield, a large town I'd much rather have avoided had I known what was coming. Traffic, lots of traffic, with that infernal satnav system (retrieved from the bag) not able to decipher interstates and jam-packed three-lane highways, which is where I ended up.

At such times I would gun the throttle, perhaps seeing a GPS-verified reading of 45mph, little more than that. It wasn't good for me or the engine, but when you have a wave of traffic ploughing up behind, you have little choice but to do all you can to get out of its way.

I braced myself for impact as I felt the 'whoosh' of a car careering from behind, swinging right across the tail light and being so close as to almost graze the right pannier rack, then careering across the crud at the side of the road and swinging back in front of me. I don't know what the guy was thinking, but I could have killed him that day, as he hadn't been that far from killing me.

These final stages of an adventure do seem to be the most perilous. It is during this time that you seem inclined to take more risks, to carry on riding where normally you would stop and think things through. I suspect it's because when you have the finishing line in sight you are so desperate to get there that all sense and sensibility goes out the window. You just want to get there, before it slips away.

Upon sight of an exit road I took it, breathing a sigh of relief as I was finally able to shut off the throttle and return to normal cruising pace. From here I headed west, not entirely sure where I was (much like that first day through New Jersey), finding myself in a world of farmed orchards, the road flanked either side by fields of planted trees, and with the onset of evening I wondered if I should try to find a spot to camp among them. But there were so many farm workers driving along in pickup trucks, heading home for the evening, that the mood just didn't feel right to be trying to find a wild camping spot right now.

I turned on to the Paso Robles Highway, the plantations now gone, the land flat and lifeless, shadows in the dark, a sky turned heavy and bleak. The road crossed over the West Side Freeway. The encroaching darkness was broken by a field of gas stations, motels and fast food diners. It looked to be the place where truckers would stop for the night, and so the roads around this little grid were riddled with heavy traffic. I found it to be an awkward moment; the thought of stopping and finding a cheap motel amongst the madness, or riding on into the darkness that lay west?

I pulled into several motel yards, only to be dissuaded by the sight of burly truckers leaning against the railings, smoking cigarettes outside their rooms. I didn't think I quite fitted in around these parts, deciding instead to ride on.

The road led me through a landscape of nodding oil pumpjacks, their silhouettes picked out by the faint orange glow lingering at the pit of the sky. It was an incredibly moody, apocalyptic sight; this field of nodding donkeys extracting oil from the earth as though it were a scene from a *Terminator* movie, after the machines had taken over the world. It reminded me of parts of Kansas, which at times had been an endless horizon of wind turbines, spinning hypnotically for as far as the eye could see. The road now was long, dark and straight. I was glad to be wearing the fluorescent postal jacket, as the rear light on the bike was still terrible, and the traffic from behind still dense. It was foolish to keep on riding, but clearly, I was a fool.

I reached Paso Robles at around 10pm. It is a town roughly forty miles inland from the Pacific Coast. I pulled into the town's McDonald's, deciding I was in serious need of respite from the road, as I was tired now, and on edge from not finding a place to sleep. I sat in a seat by the window, a life-sized Ronald McDonald on a bench beside me. I waved and said hello. The clown said nothing back, he just carried on smiling with his thick red lips and stripy tights.

The young man mopping the floor chatted with me. We talked about the area and how the town seemed to be growing at an alarming rate, thanks to migrant South and Central Americans arriving to work in the agricultural industry. He also told me that crystal meth use was becoming a large and persistent problem (meth on the west coast, crack cocaine on the east). This surprised me, as it seemed to be a nice town, immune to that sort of thing. I later learnt that Fresno, a city one hundred miles to the north of here, has the highest meth addiction rate in the country.

Hearing such things was very sad, and also hard to understand being someone who has never had any interest in drugs. Yet at the same time I had to concede that we all have different vices. My vices were these adventures, running across the world on a motorbike, and that wasn't always healthy for me either. People around me told me that I should quit, get clean, lead a normal life. But what did they know? How could they say if it was good for me or not? I knew that I needed it in order to try and cure my own unhappiness. Maybe it was the source of my unhappiness and I just couldn't see that. But I knew deep down I needed to keep on doing it, for now at least, because that's just what I felt I needed to stay alive. It was my drug, my fix. So who was I to judge the people who shoot up their arms to enjoy similar respite from a world they can't deal with? Who are any of us to judge?

Around midnight I walked back out into the sodium light. The city was dead, just me and the McDonald's parking lot, even the clown was sleeping. I strapped on the old helmet, threw a leg over the battered old bitch, slipped my hands into the well-worn gardening gloves, making sure the trusty sunglasses were safe in the tank bag as I wouldn't be needing them at this moment in time but couldn't bear the thought of losing them, not now, not having carried them all this way.

I rode to the gas station on the other side of the junction as it was still open, the forecourt empty, just a lone man in the cashier's desk, who darted out at the sight of the bike. He was excited to hear about my trip, and keen to hear just how this old bike had managed to bring me this far.

Enquiring about a place to sleep, the man told me how beneath the bridge, just across the way, was a shallow valley where homeless people slept. A woman walking past with a pushchair vouched for this (it was far too late to be out with a baby), saying she'd slept there a few nights in the past, but just to be careful as the police regularly go down there to move people on. I told them that I would go and take a look for myself, riding off in that direction, but instead of heeding their advice, I took the road out of town instead, as being just forty miles shy of the coast, all I wanted to do was see it, no matter how late it was when I made it there.

Unsurprisingly, I was the only person on the road this late night, winding out the throttle as the air continued to turn colder and damper the closer to the ocean I got. It was an exciting feeling; everything finally coming to a head. Less than two months before being in a world of confusion and self-inflicted pain; hurting myself, hurting others as an unfortunate consequence of that – which is by far the worst part of it all – to being out here, in California, the journey across America almost over.

And then there it was, the Pacific Ocean, our arrival point being the seaside town of Cambria, one hundred miles north of Los Angeles, 225 miles south of San Francisco. I didn't dance, nor cheer, just exhaled, a long exhale, and perhaps my shoulders sagged as well; the heat would certainly have come off the throttle and I would have said something profound, such as, 'Well Dorothy, we've made it. We've made it across America. I think we did okay.' And then I would have patted her on the tank and carried on riding.

***

The plan now was to find somewhere to rest for the few remaining hours of night, then hightail it up the coast at sunrise, to make it to San Francisco and Oakland in time to give that talk I'd been booked to do that very evening.

I considered a campsite in Cambria, even sitting by the entrance at 2am, wondering if I should sneak in, and then out the following morning without having to pay; that age-old dilemma of karma. I sat there trying to decide what to do for almost half an hour, taking a pee in the bushes and generally coming to terms with the reality of being able to hear the Pacific Ocean in the background. A long boat ride west from here and we'd be back in Australia, having gone all the way around the world.

I would not have anticipated any of this that day I rode out of Sydney. I didn't even know if I'd make it to the end of that first day, or even out of Australia. And yet here I was, nineteen countries later, on the other side of the planet.

In the end I slept in a lay-by, little more than a stone's throw from the beach, beneath a 'No Camping' sign. I didn't put the tent up, simply lay the sleeping bag on the ground, tucked myself and the bike away in a bush as best I could, so to be out of sight, and attempted to sleep this cold moist night, waking up to find my sleeping bag soaking from the moisture that had been whipped up from the sea. But what a sensation to wake to the sound of the waves, pounding against the rocks, just over the other side of the fence.

***

The journey now would take me all the way up the Pacific Coast Highway, or Route 1 as it's also known, a legendary road built not that many decades ago. Previously to access these remote corners of the coastline you would have had to have taken a boat. Then the road came, connecting Los Angeles with San Francisco, the tarmac clinging on to the sides of the cliffs, snaking in and out of coves, running across bridges and along the edge of thick lush forests.

I passed through Big Sur this morning; a well-known surfing community found on Route 1, famous for the artists and writers it has attracted over the years. Jack Kerouac, Hunter S Thompson and Henry Miller all had retreats out here. They'd come to write in cabins in the wood, a small community forming over the years, the place with no real centre to it. Instead, a scattering of businesses can be seen dotted along the road side, with signs for isolated guesthouses and hidden-away campsites. I stopped at a rustic cafe for coffee and a pain au chocolat. The atmosphere out here was just serene.

Beyond that the wind really began to pick up. As the bike had so little power it almost literally brought me to a standstill, making the queue of traffic behind grow longer with every mile, which in turn made me rage and scream at the wind with such venom that I felt like my head was going to explode.

It would have been different had it been a tail-wind. That would have been joyous, like a helping hand pushing you from the rear, increasing our speed and having our kite fly right up into the sky. Instead, I was down to twenty miles per hour, frothing wildly at the mouth, worried any moment that my head might blow off and be cast out to sea. It felt like I was in a battle with nature; and at her I would scream.

The afternoon that followed was equally miserable. Not just the wind, but after a while (somewhere around Monterey) the single lane nirvana of Route 1 was replaced by the hell of a three-lane highway, and no matter how hard I looked for alternatives, there didn't seem to be any escape from that.

It was made more complicated by the fact that I wasn't heading to San Francisco itself, but the neighbouring city of Oakland, as that's where the bike club was based. There is a bridge connecting the two cities, but as the bridge is almost three miles long and classed as an interstate, I wouldn't be able to take the quieter coastal road to San Francisco before crossing the bridge to Oakland. Instead I would have to ride up through the heavily populated cities of Salinas, Gilroy, Morgan Hill and San Hose.

Heading slightly inland, the landscape now was one of agriculture and crops, with fields of strawberries and greenhouses being picked and tendered by what looked to be a roaring influx of South and Central American workers. The roads would run alongside these fields of activity, before dipping in and out of towns and villages. I didn't really know where I was, and the satnav proved strangely useless. Instead I just followed my nose, guided by the position of the sun once more, finding myself on a narrow, winding road that I wouldn't be able to find again, even if my life depended on it.

Soon I was back in the throng of the agricultural industry, featuring a roaring flow of heavy traffic and trucks. Once more I was a sitting duck, and the bike, unsurprisingly by this point, was beginning to feel a little out of sorts. I believe it was the heat of Death Valley that had done it. She made noises, and the power just wasn't there. It led to a sense of fear, as I just didn't want to break down out here. Fear turned to panic. Panic turned to dread. Then came another one of those surreal encounters of the road. Another one of Denise's fairies perhaps.

Riding along the edge of these strawberry plantations, approaching a right hand corner on a quiet country road, somewhere south of San Jose, I noticed two bikes parked up in the shade. As I drew closer it revealed itself to be the oddest juxtaposition of mismatched worlds I'd encountered for quite some time. In this world of South American strawberry pickers, I'd stumbled upon a pair of white middle-aged men, on brand-new BMW motorbikes, by the side of the road, in the oddest of locations – on the outside of a corner, standing in the grass – drinking cans of Coca Cola. I flew right by them, before turning around and coming to a stop.

At first they thought I was an alien crash landing from space, such was my tale of recklessness. They were somehow bowled over and in disbelief at the distance Dorothy had travelled. It took a while to convince them that I wasn't having them on.

The two men worked locally, owned their own businesses, rode brand-new bikes, wore top quality clothing and, perhaps, were out here trying to snatch a little bit of peace and quiet from their wives. They asked where I was heading. I told them Oakland, and to that they sucked their teeth and shuffled their feet. 'That place is bad,' they said. I said that was alright, it couldn't be as bad as Detroit and Chicago. They told me of the best way to get there without going on major roads, but it was one of those convoluted sets of directions that go in one ear and out the other.

I told them about the problems I was having with the bike, and how at tick-over she was beginning to sound like an old diesel tractor. I fired her into life. They said she sounded alright. This puzzled me – were my ears and my mind deceiving me? I didn't think so. And the gradual power loss was real. I could feel that. Yet to now have two random men I'd just met by the roadside tell me she sounded okay and that I should just keep on riding (though not necessarily to Oakland!), took my nerves out of the day and allowed me to carry on my way a little more relaxed than I had been up until meeting these men, whose names I can't for the life of me remember.

Shortly after I began my passage through San Jose. It was traffic light after traffic light, picking a way through this endless sprawl of suburbia. I would have given anything to have been back in Death Valley right now. Instead, I was sat at red traffic lights, surrounded by big SUVs and pickup trucks, feeling conspicuous, especially in some of the rougher neighbourhoods I passed through. At times like these I really wish I'd been on a regular motorcycle, looking like a regular chap, without a target on the side of my helmet and a pair of gardening gloves on my hands.

At least in America I think you can get away with putting your head down and minding your own business. Try looking like this in downtown Nottingham, Manchester, Birmingham or London and perhaps you'll receive more negative attention, yet thinking about it, me and the two New Zealanders, Rob and Greg, had been just fine riding through London, even around Buckingham Palace and through Leicester Square. Maybe half the problem is wondering too much what other people are thinking, instead of sitting there at the lights, minding your own business.

Finally, on the eve of that long, long, 16-hour riding day, I made my final approach to Oakland. Granted, it did seem a little rougher than some of the other parts I'd passed through that day, yet nowhere near as bad as the parts of Detroit or Chicago I'd been witness to. It actually seemed like quite a decent place, and I certainly saw plenty of it, mistaking the street I was supposed to have arrived on with one on the opposite side of the city, meaning that I had to cross it at breakneck speed in order to make the presentation in time.

A fellow biker helped me find my way; a black guy who complained how the police kept pulling him over and giving him a hard time, though admitted he had no insurance and his licence had been revoked, so I guess he brought that bad luck on himself.

It did still feel weird though to be in one of these big American cities. They do have an atmosphere about them; intense, moody, dramatic. You feel like you're in a movie. You feel that none of this is real. This is Hollywood, especially when you see one of the police cars or fire trucks, because you've seen them on the silver screen, and now you're here, sat beside them at the traffic lights. At times it was all so very surreal.

Finally I found myself beneath the underpass, near a railroad, on the dark side of the city. It was a place of dim street lights, tyre depots and high mesh fences topped with razor wire. There was a roadblock, forcing me to take a detour around the block, following the line on the map on the satnav as it lead me to a point which just didn't seem plausible. It was fixated with a spot in the midst of a square of industrial buildings, finally finding the entrance to a shadowy run-down estate, the scene, surely, of a potential homicide.

It was now completely dark, crawling up this alley, not certain what we were going to encounter: henchman, our own brutal murder? But no, it was the sight of a dozen or so high-end motorbikes, all lined up outside the Oakland clubhouse door, which was just an old wooden building. 'This must be it,' I thought, parking up at the end of the row, taking off my helmet and walking through the door. Little did I know the day was only just beginning.

Chapter Seventeen
San Francisco

I'd walked into a room of older men, all wearing orange duffel coats with Oakland Motorcycle Club embroidered on the back. I was nervous at the sight of them; a room full of angry white men, as Vermin might have called them. Fortunately Suzanne was there, the lady who'd invited me to give the presentation in the first place. While the chairman went through the club's formalities, Suzanne led me to the back of what was effectively a big scouts' hut, with a bar and a kitchen at the rear, where a plate of food they'd been saving me was heated up, and a fresh cup of coffee made. I wolfed it down, feeling quite nervous, knowing I would soon have to speak in front of all those duffel-coated men, when really, I just wanted to go to bed.

Finally came the time to introduce me to the fifty or so people sat in a square of chairs, many of the men with their arms folded, my stage right in the middle of them. But first impressions can be deceiving, because they were a great bunch, immediately voting to allow Dorothy to be the first bike allowed into the clubhouse, so that I could have her taking centre stage for my talk. We wheeled her in, placing a cloth beneath the engine to catch any dripping oil.

I began telling my story of how I came to be there, in their clubhouse that evening. How, starting in Australia, one day I decided that rather than fly home to England, I would ride home instead. And so began a 23,000-mile journey across the world, leaving after only two days of planning, in only the clothes that I had, not sure if I had enough money, not even sure which way I was going to go. But knowing full well that I was going to give it a damn good go.

I talked to them about Indonesia and what that was like. I explained the process of putting the bike on a plane to get it over Burma, and then the carnage and chaos of India, the surprising delight of Pakistan, and then what a rush it had been coming across Kazakhstan, Russia, Ukraine and Poland with the engine oil bolt held in by a toothbrush, and a real panic as to whether we were going to make it or not.

I skipped briefly over the three years that followed before explaining how finally one day I snapped, riding the same bike down to Heathrow airport, putting her on a plane to New York and landing with no real plan other than to get back on the horse and start riding again. I told them about Chicago and Detroit, how slightly disappointed I'd been by Route 66 and how Kansas had been a weird old place, which they laughed at, because everyone says that about Kansas. Poor Kansas.

I shared my joy of Colorado and the Rockies, telling them how I'd had to push the old bike up and over the mountains, then down through Utah and Nevada to see the Grand Canyon and Monument Valley. I told them of my failed attempt at climbing Zion, mentioned Las Vegas briefly, before Death Valley – my favourite place – and how the last two days, from there to here, had been moronic and destitute in trying to get here in time. I made apology for my lateness, talking for a good hour or more until finally they decided it time to shut me up, at which point I received a warm round of applause, which was nice.

Kindly they said they'd have a whip around for me, to thank me for coming, and having collected over $300 in dollar notes, the club chairman said they'd double it, and so I got handed what amounted to around $650!

I told them I didn't think they realised this, but that amount was almost equal to my entire budget for coming across the States, and so it meant a great deal to me. After that I was almost lost for words, because these were just strangers, and they didn't have to have given me a dime.

Stranger still, in the audience that night was a member of the San Francisco Motorcycle Club, who invited me to give a talk the next night at their clubhouse, which I did, and because there's a friendly rivalry between the two clubs, they too handed around a collection bucket at the end, being instructed that they had to beat the $650 I got from Oakland. And they did beat it, by about twenty dollars. This meant that having crossed America on bits of fluff and cheap McDonald's burgers, I now had over $1,300 in cash in my pockets, much of it one dollar bills, fives and tens, so my pockets were practically bulging with folded money. I felt like a pimp.

The cash injection was certainly handy, as I'd just missed my return flight out of New York (I'd booked it as a return rather than as a single), and had no other means of getting home. This money would pay for a ticket to get me there. How things have a strange way of working out in the end.

***

During this time in San Francisco I was staying at the house of a man named Pete, the nicest of guys who had attended the first presentation in Oakland, who had himself ridden around the world on a motorbike a few years prior. Pete had invited me to stay well before I arrived in San Francisco, with it comforting to know that I had his place as a base. Pete lived not far from the Oakland clubhouse, in a wooden house on a pleasant street, with a garage in which he kept his collection of motorcycles. He owned as many as six in total, most of them of a vintage age, with bags of character and stories to tell.

In Pete's garage I changed the oil on my bike and fitted a new back tyre. I still wasn't sure what I was doing, or where I was going to go from here. I'd arrived in San Francisco, not giving any thought to what would happen next, and so took a few days to think about it. Alaska by now was well out of the question. Too late in the season to even think about it. Though I knew that already.

I had thought about leaving the bike in Pete's garage, or at another address in San Francisco, flying home and maybe coming back next year to do some more. But for whatever reason that just didn't feel right. It didn't quite feel that my journey was over, or that I'd reached a suitable conclusion to this leg of it. I felt restless and anxious. Try as I might I just couldn't stand still. The road still beckoned. And from the north it called.

Lisa, the girl I'd met at the top of Angels Landing in Zion, told me that if I was ever passing through Seattle then I was to stop and say hello. We'd got on well, keeping in touch via email whenever I could get online. I liked her. And I did want to see her again, perhaps part of the process of moving on.

I looked at the map and calculated that it was over 900 miles to her door; straight up the west coast, ride out of the city and just keep going, don't stop until you get there. I buzzed at the thought of this; the sense of excitement that swells at the beginning of any new adventure. And once again, I had nowhere to be, no house, no job, no home; just a tired old motorbike, and enough cash in my pocket to take me to Lisa's door. I just needed to get Dorothy patched up first.

With the help of the satnav I found a decent mechanic right in the heart of San Francisco, deciding to take my chances on the interstate bridge connecting it with Oakland, the distance between getting on and getting off some four miles, which were a little hairy to say the least, but it saved me a massive detour around the bay, and definitely got the adrenaline going; four lanes of heavy traffic, with no breakdown lane or hard shoulder to ride in.

Having taken a ride around San Francisco – stopping off at Pier 39, riding down the twisting Lombard Street and staring out at Alcatraz – I eventually found the bike shop down a narrow side street, where I parked up and headed inside.

'Sounds like piston slap,' said one of the mechanics as they all gathered outside to figure out what was wrong with the bike.

I asked what that was.

'It's when the piston's not firing straight in the barrel and so you're getting this rocking motion, a vibration, which will only get worse.'

I asked what the solution would be and they said a new piston and rebore.

I asked how long she might go on the one she'd got.

'Not sure,' they said. 'Could go for a long while yet, or it could go tomorrow.'

They asked where I was heading.

'Seattle,' I said.

They scratched their heads; 'Yeah, she should make it.'

And that was good enough for me.

***

Outside the bike shop I struck up conversation with a lady by the name of Patricia, who was riding a bicycle as her motorbike was broken and the garage was trying to fix it. She was there to see how they were getting on.

Patricia was an interesting sort, a little kooky, but very interesting to talk to. Not long after saying goodbye our paths crossed once more at a set of traffic lights in the centre of San Francisco. Given the fate of such a thing, we decided to grab a coffee together, parking up our bikes and heading into a trendy cafe that happened to be around the corner from where lines of homeless people were waiting to check in to a homeless shelter for the night.

I'd read somewhere how back in the sixties and seventies the mayor of San Francisco had promoted the city as a safe haven for those wishing to escape their current predicaments in other parts of America, and so flooded in the people who couldn't necessarily take care of themselves. This legacy is thought to be what makes San Francisco a magnet for homeless people to this day, with far more here in this city than anywhere else I'd ever seen. It was quite shocking, and a situation impossible to ignore. But if anything I'd begun to understand it now. America is the freest nation on earth; the freedom to completely succeed, or equally, the freedom to absolutely fail.

It was over coffee that Patricia told me an unusual story, one that made a great deal of sense to me. It was about how one day she had found a massive block of grey polystyrene down on the beach, describing it as something you could barely hold it was so large.

Despite this, Patricia decided to take it home with her, and for the next two years carried it around with her wherever she went. She took it to work, to restaurants, to the theatre; she literally took this giant piece of grey polystyrene everywhere, even strapping it to the back of her bicycle and carting it around the city.

She called it an art experiment, hoping to gauge the reaction of the people who saw her with it. She wondered what questions people would ask, and what they would say. This went on for two years, with Patricia telling me how she was unable to leave the house without it, eventually reaching a point where the lump of grey polystyrene had become such a burden to carry yet something she just couldn't dispose of, as much as she hated having that burden.

As I sat and listened I couldn't help but identify with this, and how one single inanimate object and your devotion/commitment to it can start to dominate your life and demand a certain obligation to it, at the expense of almost everything else. I'd certainly been the same with my motorbike, feeling a strange obligation to not leave it in the shed to fester any longer, as though I had to bring her here and do this, for her sake, as much as for mine.

For Patricia, her freedom came one night in a bar when, with her back turned, a girl ran inside, grabbed the polystyrene block and ran outside with it, jumping on the back of a motorbike and speeding off, never to be seen again. After the initial shock, Patricia described a moment of massive relief, almost as though she could get on with her life again, because while she could never have given up the polystyrene voluntarily, to have it stolen, with that decision made for her, meant that she was finally free of her obligation.

Perhaps this is no different from relationships, friendships or jobs that have run their cause, but you just can't bear to be the one to end it all, because then it will be you who gets haunted by the possibility of regret. And so we might stick them out and put up with them, in the deep-down hope of being sacked, or dumped, or cut adrift. Weak and indecisive? Perhaps. Or maybe a simple case of not really knowing what you want in life, and letting time slip through your fingers while trying to figure things out.

In my case, whether I liked it or not, I was still chased by the regret of how this journey had all panned out. I was on this adventure, but I still missed the woman I loved. And no number of miles would ever compensate for that; just that sense of needing to drag yourself forward, drag yourself out of it, with her shadow behind you at all times, pursuing you like clouds across a desert. But damn it Nathan, move on.

***

Having stayed a few more days in San Francisco, in a hostel overlooking the Golden Gate Bridge – paying for it with my new-found money – I was finally ready to hit the road again, those 900 miles ahead of me with someone I wanted to see at the end of them. It's amazing how focused and determined you are when you have a mission such as this ahead of you, with a clear goal and purpose. The simple task of sitting in the saddle and doing what you do best: riding a motorbike a bloody long way.

Having crossed the gorgeous San Francisco Bay and ridden up the hillside to take a picture overlooking it, the first day was spent gripped to the coastline, circling in and out of the coves and through the pretty fishing villages north of the city. Progress was slow; the road so tight and twisty. I remember it cold and windy as well, though that didn't dampen the enthusiasm of the tourists taking to the beaches of these northern shores. You could say it was utopia out here. The waves, the beach, the white wooden houses, the coffee shops and the cafés; a real surfer's paradise.

I met other bikers, some surprised by my ability to keep up with them. They were on proper bikes, and could travel much faster than me, but they would stop far more often, for cigarettes and coffee, and in that time I would catch them up and dawdle by, either stopping to chat or beeping and waving as I went. The tortoise overtaking the hare.

What I noticed as I pushed on the next day was how the towns changed the further north you went. Out of San Francisco, the communities were scenic and pleasant. Gradually they became more run-down and grubby. More people would be wandering aimlessly, either out of work or just fooling around.

I was told how cannabis is legal up here, and it did seem as though people who liked to indulge in that had migrated north, to the small towns on the coast, where perhaps they could be left to their own devices. I read how the biggest town up here, Eureka, has serious problems with meth users, resulting in a serious number of crimes and burglaries (perhaps all vices aren't equal after all).

It was in Eureka, during that second day on the road, that I met another man by the name of John. This one was parked beside me at the local McDonald's and stepped out of his truck to ask about the bike I was riding on. He unnerved me at first, looking as unwell as he did. He was lent on a stick, his hair falling out in patches, and his eyes wearing a strange dull sheen. He looked in a very bad way.

His story was one of sadness, telling me how he'd served in the Vietnam War, becoming a truck driver when it was all over, having a terrible accident in his truck, shattering his back and being on medication that he believed had made his teeth fall out and his appearance look like it did now.

He told me how he lived up in the hills with a friend, trying to get his life straight. He said he'd come to live up here as weed was the best and most natural remedy for the pain; anything to get off the medication. His issue was with the pharmaceutical companies and the drugs he'd taken and how addicted to them he'd become. He saw America as now being slave to the corporation, it ruining the country, and the people within it. He had a passion for what was happening in Iraq and Afghanistan; the shame he felt, the future he saw for his country.

Before departing, John said something that really resonated with me, about the power of the subconscious, and how it dictates everything we do in life. He said that there is no point in fighting it, that it is happening and making decisions at a level that we can't even comprehend, and that perhaps our internal anguish is most felt when we try to fight it and impose our conscious thought upon it. Deep down we always know what's best, and we should trust it more.

I often wondered how I ended up riding out of Sydney on a motorbike that day, and I suppose this made sense of it; deep down I must have wanted it to happen, over and above anything else (such as finding a way to stay), and so conspired to make the motorbike trip happen, whether I was consciously aware of this at the time or not. I say this because at times I felt guilty about riding out of Sydney that day and was perhaps looking for a little peace in what John was saying. I found some (or at least found some salvation), with it good to have met him this day.

***

I rode well into darkness those first and second nights, not the wisest thing to have done, but I was on a mission and had so much energy to dispel. It was perhaps 9pm when I finally decided to pull off the road at the end of this second day of riding up to Seattle, turning into the carpark of the La Kris motel in the small and pleasant coastal town of Bandon, eighty miles or so over the border into Oregon.

It wasn't a big motel, perhaps only ten rooms, with me able to park my bike right outside. Having unloaded all my gear and taking a shower, I watched *Batman Returns* on DVD, before falling to sleep in a king-sized bed, waking the next morning and continuing to push north, in the direction of Seattle, along that stunning Oregon coastline.

The atmosphere reminded me most of Colorado. California had seemed a little pretentious and trendy, whereas Oregon had an honest and earthy feel about it, the people more calm and relaxed, serving great clam chowder from their restaurants, with the stretches of road between the towns dominated by breathtaking views of the ocean, and meandering through giant redwood trees.

It was a shame that I was in such a hurry to get to Seattle, doing these great distances of some 400 miles a day, as to have taken my time and enjoyed this coastline would have been sublime. But my soul said ride so that's what I was doing.

One thing that struck me was how many cyclists there were coming down from the north. Some alone, others in groups, the road relatively quiet, though steep in places, with plenty of campsites dotted along it, making the route ideal for cycle tourists of all abilities. I also spotted a few hitchhikers out here as well, something I'd not seen on my entire trip across the States, suggesting how outdated it is; but here in Oregon it still went on.

Midway through the third day I arrived in the town of Astoria, at the mouth of a bay, with a huge and impressive bridge built across the estuary. The town was where the iconic eighties movie *The Goonies* was filmed. I double checked this with the attendant in the gas station, who confirmed that it was indeed the town, and asked if I was going to go up and see the Goonies house. I asked if he was serious and if you could genuinely go up and see it. He told me to go inside and ask the lady on the counter for directions.

The lady drew me a map – a treasure map – with the house only a few miles down the road, through the main town, then up on the hill, overlooking the bay and the buildings. The town looked as though it still belonged in the eighties as I rode through it, with antique shops and rustic cafés, a million miles away from the big cities I'd passed through on this adventure. Five minutes after being given directions in the gas

211

station, I was stood on the very same spot that Chunk was seen doing his Truffle Shuffle.

The current owner was outside sanding wood, and more than happy to have me come up and take some photographs, his only plea for visitors to park at the bottom of the drive and walk up, as he shares the drive with three or four other houses and from what I gathered their owners had kicked up a bit of a fuss.

The man told me that as many as 10,000 people a year come to see the house, which by the way is now known as 'Goon Docks' (as I'd ridden up the coast, I had tried to spot the rock formation that One-Eyed Willy's pirate ship breaks free of at the end, but had been unable to pinpoint it. Apparently I'd passed it somewhere along the way).

By this time it was late in the afternoon. Seattle was still 270 kilometres, 170 miles, or over five hours of riding away. I wouldn't get there until at least ten in the evening, maybe even later, as the route I was taking into the city – to avoid the interstates – would involve catching a ferry across Puget Sound, the ferries only sailing every hour and a half. The last one was beyond midnight. In hindsight I should have just stopped in Astoria for the night and had a look around, but inside my body was churning, it just wanted to keep on moving, and so to have found a place to stay would only have left me restless.

Mist descended. The road appeared to skirt around swamps and the marshland of the tidal waters. At one point the road directed me on to the main highway that I had to ride for twenty miles before I could get off and continue along more of the back roads. Dusk faded to darkness as I rode along it. I had my high-vis postal jacket on, and I was glad I did, as when I finally pulled off the highway, stopping in the first town to check my rear spokes were still tight, an angry driver in a pickup truck shouted at me for not having a rear light.

He said he'd seen me on the highway, but only at the last minute, having to swerve around me in order to avoid rear-ending me. He couldn't believe someone would be riding without any lights on. Neither could I.

Clearly at some point the rear bulb had blown again, Lord knows when. I could have been riding the last few nights without a light, lucky not to have been flattened.

The man's name was Lewis and after his initial agitation he calmed down, helping me to find a replacement bulb in the supermarket over the road. He was a big walrus of a man, with a thick grey moustache and broad shoulders. Lewis was a biker too, the owner of a Harley Davidson and a boat he took his children and grandchildren sailing on. He seemed to lead a happy life, and asked if I could take a picture of him sat on Dorothy, using the camera on his phone, to show to his kids when he got home.

Lewis paid for the replacement bulbs and wouldn't take any money for them. He was just glad to have helped me on my way, though it did make me wonder why no one had flashed or signalled to me that I had no rear light before that point. It would have been nice if they had.

These were dark roads I was riding now, and with the fear of the bulb blowing again I would turn around every few minutes to check the rear light was still illuminated. When traffic came up behind I would pull over and let it pass. I shouldn't have been on the road at all. But there was no stopping me now. I was closing in on Seattle and just wanted to see Lisa again.

Finally, I reached the port in Bremerton, hoping to catch one of those ferries that would take me the last short distance across the Puget Sound. This is a vast inlet of water, with Seattle on the other side, the distance way too big to build a bridge. Sadly I'd just missed a ferry and had over an hour to wait for the next one, getting me into Seattle at around 2am. This wasn't ideal, but just one of those things.

The port had a Subway sandwich shop that was still open, so I ate a late-night dinner and used the Wi-Fi to check in with the world and let people back home know I was still alive, surprising them with news that I was not far from Seattle, not San Francisco, where I'd last checked in. In two and a half days I'd ridden over 900 miles.

The ferry arrived and I rode aboard, part of a stream of traffic all desperate to get home that night. The ferry was a decent size with a large passenger lounge upstairs. I sat on a seat with my head and elbows leaning on the table, almost asleep, tired and weary. Very tired, and very weary. What an adventure it had been. From New York to here, with it feeling like it was almost over, just that final distance – once the ferry had crossed the Puget Sound – across Seattle and on to Lisa's door. Not much else to say. Just thank you, to so many things, and people, for helping me make it this far.

The boat docked and off I rode, emerging on the bright streets of Seattle. They were quiet; the occasional car and a zombie-like invasion of homeless people, just there in the gutters (I never did stop seeing and feeling an empathy with them). I relied once more on the satnav, following the arrows as they flashed up on the tank, just as I had done that first night back in New York, some six long weeks ago.

It was around eight miles to the house of the girl that I had met back in Zion, both of us dealing with demons up on Angels Landing that day. From there to here; that sense of excitement of seeing someone again, a person who got under your skin the first time and made you think that just maybe there is life after all this, and love, and everything that comes from that. Maybe it was the start of a new adventure. It was certainly the end of an old one.

Postcards from Alaska

The wild horses near Cortez

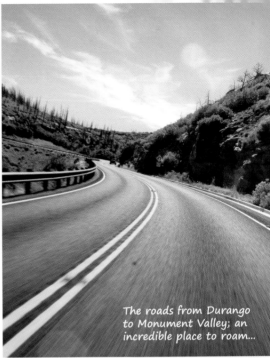

The roads from Durango to Monument Valley; an incredible place to roam...

The bikers and rock formations of Bluff. Mesa Verde (below left).

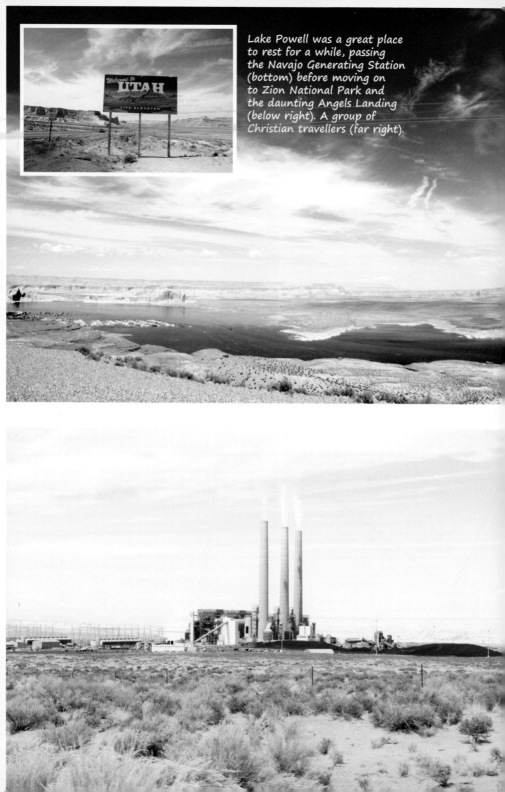

Lake Powell was a great place to rest for a while, passing the Navajo Generating Station (bottom) before moving on to Zion National Park and the daunting Angels Landing (below right). A group of Christian travellers (far right).

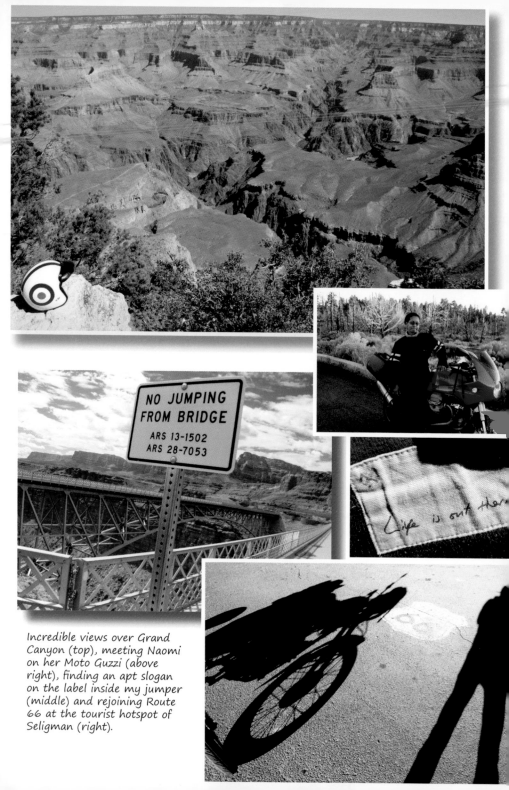

Incredible views over Grand Canyon (top), meeting Naomi on her Moto Guzzi (above right), finding an apt slogan on the label inside my jumper (middle) and rejoining Route 66 at the tourist hotspot of Seligman (right).

NO JUMPING FROM BRIDGE
ARS 13-1502
ARS 28-7053

Life is out there

Sandwich making John of Seligman (above), then Las Vegas and under the shadow of Trump Towers (below).

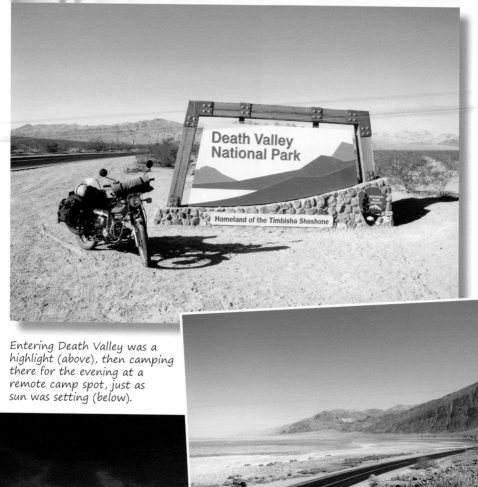

Entering Death Valley was a highlight (above), then camping there for the evening at a remote camp spot, just as sun was setting (below).

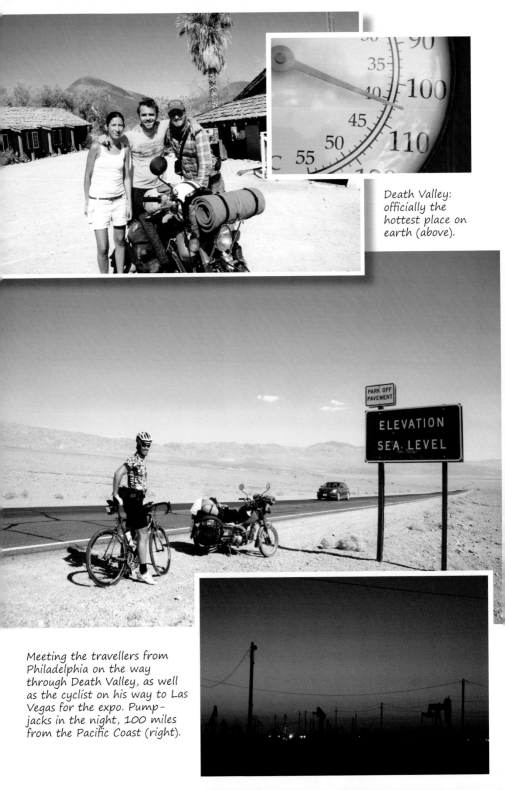

Death Valley:
officially the
hottest place on
earth (above).

Meeting the travellers from
Philadelphia on the way
through Death Valley, as well
as the cyclist on his way to Las
Vegas for the expo. Pump-
jacks in the night, 100 miles
from the Pacific Coast (right).

After 4 weeks and almost 5,000 miles; arriving in San Francis was a great relief; the money given by the bik clubs (top) a great help

Chapter Eighteen
Seattle

I stayed in Seattle with Lisa for two weeks. We went camping to Puget Sound, a peaceful island network to the north of Seattle. It was great to spend some time with her as we had a lot in common and connected in the way that at times two souls do connect. I enjoyed being shown around Seattle, going out for dinner, for walks around the neighbourhood and down by the old market, where the famous 'fish flingers' of Seattle do their trade. I liked Seattle, it was one of the nicest American cities I'd experienced. I left the bike parked out on the street during this time, perhaps a part of me finally wishing she'd be gone when I woke the next morning.

Eventually, I used some of the money donated to me by the San Francisco and Oakland motorcycle clubs to fly myself home to England. I couldn't hide out here in Seattle forever, as much as I might have wanted to. The flight that I finally booked was a return flight, returning to Seattle in six months' time, after winter had passed. In the meantime, I would leave the bike in America, go home to England, see what I found there, then return in the spring to make the final push north to Alaska.

I knew myself well enough now to realise that having set my sights on Alaska, I would have to do it at some point, as I knew the desire wouldn't just go away or expire, and as the bike was already out here it made sense to leave it, go home, then return once the weather was better and my mind was better prepared for it. Besides, I couldn't stay in America as I wouldn't have been allowed to work legally, or stay for longer than three months (and I'd been there almost two months already), due to the nature of the visa I was on.

Lisa took me to the airport. It was perhaps a case of right people, wrong time and I'd learnt not to fight such things as that. I would miss her though, not really wanting to go back to England, as part of me was worried that I would be returning to the darkness that I was in before I left for America. But I knew that I had to go back, as I'd left things in a bit of a mess the day I suddenly took off, and felt I needed to go back and clear that mess up. I just hoped I could make a better job of things than I had done in the past.

The difference this time would be that I was taking with me all the strength and clarity I'd just won on the ride across America. Those times of sleeping rough in dried-up river beds, of arriving at Vermin's house in Colorado Springs and wanting to be done with it all. These were big tests and I'd passed them. I'd survived, and in a way, I'd already won the battle I'd been fighting with myself.

During my time back in England I would leave Dorothy with Jon and Natalie, a couple I'd met on the internet a few years earlier. They'd followed my first trip on Facebook, even buying themselves a Honda CT and naming it Dash, in Dot's honour (Dot and Dash, Morse code, as Natalie worked as a computer technician). Having spotted that I was on my way up to Seattle they'd invited me to drop by and say hi. It was then that I'd asked if there was any chance of leaving my bike in their garage over winter, to which they said it would be no problem at all.

I met Jon and Natalie at a local bar and diner called Cafe Racer, a place where just four short months prior, a gunman – thought to be a disgruntled customer – had entered the premises and shot four people dead, wounding a fifth, and then shooting and killing another person as he car-jacked a vehicle, trying to escape from the police.

It was hard to imagine it happening in such a place. It was an ordinary cafe-come-diner, next door to a music shop, up from a traffic light junction in a pleasant part of Seattle. There is live music and the walls are decorated with the art of local residents, intentionally 'bad' art, just to give the place some character.

It's popular with motorcyclists, as the food is good. For someone to burst in and shoot four random people didn't make any sense, especially as Ian Stawicki, the man responsible, shot and killed himself at the end of it. What a senseless and pointless thing to have done. Why did he just not start, and finish, with himself?

You could join the dots between many things mentioned to this point: the sense of discontent, the prevalence of drugs (prescription or otherwise), the propensity for firearm ownership, the sense of despair you can so easily find in yourself, the rage this can invoke, the desire to unleash that rage, mated to a success-driven society that punishes those at the bottom for not 'trying' harder in life. Add to that a perceived future with no hope, not to mention this human instinct to leave a legacy behind, even if it's a brutal one. Run and jump, or shoot the world to hell? That's not to make excuses, simply suggesting that banning things doesn't necessarily help, not if the problem is more deeply rooted in the minds of those and the societies involved. I'm not even certain that a gun free society would be good for the sense of American liberty. Too many agents there that I'd distrust. Perhaps a new war is looming.

In the recently reopened Cafe Racer, Jon, Natalie and I drank coffee and ate delicious pulled pork sandwiches. We talked for a few hours, about bikes and big trips. They were about to embark on their own big adventure, something they'd never done before; riding a couple of bikes down to Mexico and back. They were nervous and apprehensive, though excited nonetheless. They had two weeks holiday, and they intended to make the most of it. If I'd had any advice it would just have been to enjoy it, and take from it what you need.

After a while we headed over to their house, where they had cleared a space in their garage, beside their own collection of bikes, including a British-made Triumph Bonneville, the bike Natalie was going to use on that journey south in to Mexico. They were certainly a sweet couple, giving me no reservations about leaving with them the bike that had carried me all this way. I was certain it would be as safe here as anywhere else, and the time apart would do both of us some good.

***

Later that week I landed in England and took the long coach ride home to Yorkshire, back to the house with the shed in the garden where the first book was written, it still bearing the scars of the attack by pitchfork. It was strange to be back there, especially after the events of the past two months. Such a long distance travelled with so much having taken place. So many people met. So many thoughts and experiences had. And now I was standing on exactly the same spot as when Rob and Greg had turned up that day, with their postie bikes all the way from New Zealand, their dose of reverse inspiration clearly working.

I definitely felt better in myself now, as though I no longer had that mind of screaming voices, all competing for my attention, all wishing to pull me in different directions, threatening to tear me apart. I also had more direction and purpose in life, combined with an appetite to get my life back on track.

Of all the paths I could have chosen, I was glad that I had chosen the one that I was on. Had I gone with the prescription drugs I imagine I'd still be here, attacking the shed, though probably with less conviction.

A national motorcycle newspaper offered to print some copies of my first book and sell it through their shop, taking a huge weight off my mind as it would bring some much needed money in. I was then invited to sell books on a stand at the big bike festival at the National Exhibition Centre near Birmingham.

I also finally found the focus and decisiveness to move out of the family home (I'd ended up back there when writing that first book), moving to the town of Leamington Spa, in the heart of the Midlands, the nearest town to the university I once studied at. I didn't really know anyone who lived there any more, only a friend named Aide. I moved to Leamington because it gave me clear space, away from family and the majority of my friends. It meant I could concentrate, I could breathe.

I moved into a cheap shared house with rooms for sixteen other people, more like a hostel really, though it didn't require a big deposit and the minimum term was just three months, a commitment even I could deal with. It was cheap, furnished, and had Wi-Fi included. The bathrooms were shared, so too the kitchen and the lounge, but it was close to town, and for the first time in almost four years I finally had my own place, my own set of keys, my own bed, my own desk, and even a little stray black cat that would come and howl outside my window. And because in a strange way it reminded me of myself, I would let it in and feed it, especially during the cold winter months when snow was on the ground.

I found work in a local cardboard box factory, working on the production line, counting the unassembled boxes into bundles of ten or twenty, binding them with strong nylon cord, then stacking them on pallets and sending them down the line. It paid a minimum wage of some £6.50 an hour, with a loud whistle to let you know when your shift started, when you could have a break, and when you could stop for lunch.

It was the antithesis of my life on the road. While I was there, I was completely controlled, and in a way I quite enjoyed it. It took some of the pressure off. I would get up at the same time every day, roll out of bed, put on my scruffy clothes, quick breakfast, rush to work, work hard, get stuff done, then come home and feel that something had been achieved that day. It was the routine that I needed, and the people I worked alongside were a real mix of ages, races and backgrounds. It was racial integration in action; Sikhs working with Poles, working with Brits, working with Muslims. And everyone got on and did their job. It was great.

Some of them, such as Donna, had been there twenty years, working the same machines for all that time. At first I thought it crazy that they could do that. Did they not get bored, did they not wish to move on and see more of the world? But the more I got to know them, the more I realised that they were, for the most part, far more content and happy than I'd ever been. They came to work, did their job, went home, and lived. About my adventures I said little. They made me feel very humble and grateful for what I had seen and done.

I also worked at a supermarket the few days up to and over the 2012 Christmas period. I gathered trolleys in the carpark, collecting them together and pushing them back to their bays after they had been left lying around by lazy customers. Again it was minimum wage, but I loved darting around the carpark on Christmas Eve, everyone in high spirits, wishing each other a Merry Christmas, before loading up their cars and driving home to feed their families over the festive period.

I joined a gym and attempted to get fit; going to boxercise, pilates, even step aerobics, for fitness of course, not to perv on hot girls. But it was good, providing more of that routine I so desperately needed and had been without for so long.

During this time in England I spent as much time as I could with my Nan, visiting on a Sunday and taking her for a ride to the local pub where we'd have a carvery, and then to the garden centre for a coffee. Sometimes we'd load the car up with other old ladies from the warden-controlled flats and head out down memory lane. One lady, Cath, was in her nineties, requesting that we took a particular road one day as it was somewhere along it, 75 years earlier, that she'd done most of her courting. She was almost speechless at the sight of it, as though she'd seen herself again, like a ghost in the rear view mirror.

I find it necessary to spend time with older people. They are great motivators, reminding you of what we all become, and the situation we will all find ourselves in; when we don't have the health to do those things we always wanted to do, and so all that's left is to sit and stew on them, as the long minutes tick by. Far too much time to sit and to think.

I know this is what frustrated my Nan. She'd always been so active, so keen to go and to see things (perhaps it's where I got it from), and now she had to accept that she couldn't do it any more. Only she couldn't accept it. She wanted to fight it, and did fight it, but ultimately it's a battle you can never win. What I take from this is the emphasis to do things now; do things while you still can; even if it's just: 'hello, I'm sorry, I love you.' And we all have someone in our lives we need to say that to every now and again.

The months went by and before long I was facing the prospect of returning to America, and to Dorothy, who'd been waiting patiently in Jon and Natalie's garage for all that time. I'd not bothered to check on her very often. I knew that with them she would be fine and in a way it was a case of out of sight, out of mind. I enjoyed this time apart. Like Patricia and her grey block of polystyrene, these things can be such a burden, and when they're there right in front of you they can taunt you with their fixed stare that is impossible to escape or to avoid. They make you feel guilty for not riding them more.

A month or so before my flight back to America I left the job at the box factory, to begin the task of writing this second book, aiming to have it done before I returned to America, at least the bit from New York to San Francisco. I didn't even get close.

I lay down a rough first draft, sat at my desk with the window ahead offering views over rooftops that I'd drift off and stare at. The hardest thing about writing a book is determining the tone; the way you say things, the mood you evoke. Maybe it's me, and the way my mood fluctuates so wildly at times, making it hard to be consistent, because some days you're up, and some days you're down. But this was nothing compared to what it was like before. I didn't look at ropes or beams. I didn't punch myself in the face. I just got on with it, sat down and wrote.

Finally time came for me to return to America, and complete the push north from Seattle to Alaska. My flight was on the 23rd April 2013. Originally I'd planned on being away forever, or at least with no fixed plan (finances permitting, and they weren't great), but in the weeks preceding the flight I'd been offered a job working on a magazine that specialised in long-distance motorcycle riding, working in their editorial department, finding other people on big trips and making their stories heard in a bi-monthly magazine.

It wasn't the job per se that attracted me, more the sense of security and sustained routine that it would afford me. In summary, it would provide me with the perfect excuse to sit still and stop travelling for a while. And so this trip back to America, to complete the ride up to Alaska, was simply an obligation I felt I needed to fulfil so that I could stop for a while without it being on my mind.

With the job due to start at the beginning of June I would have just over six weeks to complete the journey north. This wasn't very long at all, but having consulted with my dad, it was agreed that for most people wishing for these kind of adventures, there usually is a time frame to work around (like Rob and Greg) – be it family or work commitments – and so it wouldn't do me any harm to have one either. It would just mean I would need to be more focused and hit the ground running when I landed back in Seattle.

From Seattle to Alaska was a distance of only two to three thousand miles – depending on where in Alaska you are heading to – with me having covered six thousand miles, in six weeks, on that original trip across America. So time, really, wouldn't be too much of a problem (or so I hoped). The only issue would be getting me and the bike home at the end of it, though that would be something to worry about at a later date. Let's get there first...

I do wish to state that living like this does take it out of you. This calamitous nature, this life of having no plan, simply feeling the way the wind is blowing and going along with that. I suppose in a way I was in a state of perpetual panic, circling on the spot, surrounded by a wall of flames, waiting for the right avenue to open up and darting down it before the gap was gone again.

I didn't plan on checking out of my rented room while I was away. Instead I locked the door, put the keys in my pocket, boarded a bus to the airport and got on the plane, relieved to know that in six weeks' time, on my return, I would have a place, and a job, to go back to. And I can't begin to tell you just how much I liked the dynamic of this.

I'd even told my parents this time, with no dramatic mad dash to be on the road, but a bit of time to organise and get together all of the things I thought I might need on this journey to the top of the world.

I watched movies on the flight out there, sitting looking out of the window at the world below, not so scared any more as I knew there was nothing left for me to do but this. And I think I was free of almost all regrets.

I fidgeted in my seat, read the in-flight magazine, listened to the in-flight radio. I was flying via Iceland as this had been the cheapest option. In the hold I had packed my familiar open-faced helmet with the target on the side. So too the orange postal jacket, the welding gloves, the manly Australian boots, the laptop, the camera (a new one for the trip), as well as a host of new things, such as a warm biker's jacket, thick trousers, proper winter gloves and some thermal underwear as it was only just breaking out of winter and into spring.

Seattle was scorching when I landed, in the midst of a heatwave. Lisa picked me up from the airport. It was almost six months since I'd seen her last. By now we were friends, nothing more than that. It was just great to see her again. She was a strong girl, fighting her own fight, and with a heart as big as a bucket. I was glad our paths crossed that day up on Angels Landing. She had been just what I needed. Someone to think about and ride towards, with it now just great to see her again and spend some time in her company.

The following day I caught the bus to Jon and Natalie's house on the northern side of the city. It was good to be back in America. I felt as though I was approaching it with a new set of eyes this time, ones not as critical as they'd been first time around, which is more a reflection of me than it was of America.

***

The bike was just where I left her, in Jon and Natalie's garage, though shuffled around a little, as in the past few days they'd attempted to get her going again. To manage this they'd had to drain the fuel and change the spark plug. She always was a little stubborn after being stationary for such a long period of time. But it was good to see her again, like finding a big part of yourself buried in the back of the garage, or old heirlooms up in the loft. On this occasion I sat in that familiar seat, grabbed those familiar handlebars and took her for a quick spin around the block. She felt small, slow and old. To think I'd ridden all that way on this. To think I was going to ride her some more.

There were two things I wanted to fix before pushing north. Those two things were the spokes in the back wheel, which had relentlessly needed tightening ever since that handful had snapped on the way into Detroit. The second issue to be fixed was the engine and that piston 'slap', diagnosed back in San Francisco. Neither of them were major jobs, but it did scupper the initial plan of going back, getting on the bike and setting off for Alaska.

I pitched my tent on Natalie and Jon's back yard while we went to work fixing up the bike. The house was on the north side of the city, in a quiet suburb, well away from any traffic. Jon fortunately had some time off work – he fixed boats for a living – and so offered to drive me around the bike shops, doing our best to find someone who could help us with the parts we needed. Jon had a fixation for bikini latte, a strange phenomenon, native to Seattle (thankfully), where drive-by coffee huts, located at the side of main roads, feature young female baristas wearing bikinis or skimpy lingerie, and making a lousy over-priced coffee, in exchange for a glimpse of their bust and gusset. I felt dirty and cheated, both at the same time. Jon lapped it up (thankfully not literally).

As for the spokes in that back wheel, having asked around the local bike shops, we were told about a man going by the name of the Wheel

234

Wizard, his premises some forty-five minutes' drive away, on the south side of the city. Jon called the guy and asked him about the wheel, which he said he could fix. We also asked him about the engine, which he agreed would need re-boring and a new piston fitted. He said he could do that as well. Perfect.

We disassembled the bike in Jon's garage and drove down with the engine in a box and the wheel in a plastic bag on the back seat. We passed through the heart of Seattle, a place I was really beginning to grow fond of. The outlying suburbs were for the most part pleasant and leafy. Downtown was full of cool bars and restaurants, the Space Needle overlooking it all, then the famous markets where on a Sunday morning the world really came to life. I liked this north-western part of America in general; people just seemed more relaxed and more open-minded up here.

We found the Wheel Wizard's house out in the southern suburbs; a simple bungalow with a huge workshop built in the yard. The Wizard's real name was Murray, a man in his seventies, if not approaching his eighties. Murray told us how he had served his apprenticeship at Boeing, which is based in Seattle, his job to make the aeroplanes work by operating machines with such accuracy that everything fit just right.

Murray took great pride in his work, caring much about the job in hand and gracing us with cans of Coke as he gave an almost two-hour explanation into various parts of the machining process. He talked us through the milling machine and the drill that would re-bore the cylinder, explaining it in meticulous detail. We'd definitely found the right man for the job. Murray was also a religious man. On the back of his car a bumper sticker read: 'My boss is a Jewish carpenter.' I was more than prepared to put my trust in him getting the bike ready for the journey to Alaska.

Of the wheel he said he'd cut new spokes and laced the wheel in such a way that would make it stronger than it had originally been. He said he would re-bore the barrel to accommodate the one oversize piston and leave it to me to put it back together again, which I felt comfortable doing after the practice I'd had in recent years, rebuilding the bike in the garage with my dad. With that, we left the parts with Murray, returned to the city and hung around for a few days, drinking more bikini latte, waiting for the work to be done.

Murray had done an amazing job when we returned to pick them up. The back wheel looked magnificent and appeared solid enough to take twice the weight of what it previously would; perfect then for the long slog through the wilderness of Canada and Alaska. The re-bore on the barrel looked perfect as well, the measurements being checked twice and Murray giving us instructions on how best to put everything back together, which we managed with no real problems.

Jon predicted she'd start at third kick, and she did, firing into life once more. Sadly the noise that had plagued her all the way from Death Valley was still there, meaning that it probably wasn't the piston after all. It was more likely to be much deeper inside the engine, the bottom end perhaps, which was far beyond my knowledge and budget to investigate. This made me ponder the journey ahead, riding into Alaska on an engine that wasn't running quite right. I suppose it was an increasing lack of confidence I had in her, and I'd never had reason to say that before.

I put some thought into it over the next few days, running the engine in gently on a ride out with Jon and Natalie and the rest of their scooter gang, at least fifty of us in total, tearing through the city, some of the bikers blocking the junctions to allow everyone through, red light or no red light. It made me sweat and feel uneasy. I tried to enjoy myself but this sort of thing wasn't for me. It made me realise that I'm a bit of a lone wolf. I like my own company too much.

Finally, I loaded up the bike and still didn't really know what to do. That engine really bothered me. I thought I'd play it safe and ride down to Las Vegas instead, attend an overland bike show that was happening this coming weekend and then fly myself and the bike home to England straight from there. It would be the easiest and safest option.

But as I rode out of town heading south, getting about seventy miles out of the city, I decided that it just didn't feel right (if Sascha had been here, the fearless guy I met riding the Himalayas, he would undoubtedly have called me 'gay'). So I turned the bike around, rode back to Seattle, camped in Jon and Natalie's garden one last night and made haste towards the border with Canada the following morning. It was just a hundred miles or so to get there, riding through the suburbs, then into rural landscape, before arriving at the border.

I recorded a video diary having just crossed it, completely perplexed at being in Canada. I was confused, and bemused. I was in the twentieth country of my trip, the sun was blazing hot, and the guy at the customs booth had been inquisitive about who I was and where I was going.

'To Alaska,' I told him.

'On that?'

'Yes sir.'

(Shrugs) 'Okay, have a good day.'

The plan now was simple. There wasn't one. Just ride north, and figure it out along the way. It would be a case of riding up through Vancouver, taking the back roads that would lead me through the ski resort of Whistler, then continuing north, towards Dawson Creek, picking up the Alaska Highway from there and then following it all the way through British Columbia, then the Yukon, before crossing the border into Alaska and getting as far north as I could get before needing to go back for the new job, starting now in just four weeks' time.

I didn't know how I would get me or the bike back to England in time. All I knew was that I was now riding to reach the end of the road, because I was tired now, and I think I was just tired of running.

Chapter Nineteen
Canada

I rode first into Vancouver, very much liking the look and feel of the city. The streets were full of life and activity, with it hard to believe just how warm it was; this coastal side of North America was enjoying record temperatures during these early days of May.

My intention wasn't to stay in Vancouver very long, aiming instead for Whistler that night, as the distance from Jon and Natalie's house was just perfect to get me clear out of the gate and a safe distance from the 'turning back' zone. It's a trick of the mind perhaps, something you need to do in order to get yourself clear of your starting point. This being my third big trip on Dorothy, I was quite used to the psychology of it by now.

Having crawled through the city streets, I stopped for a quick look around Stanley Park, a 1,001-acre public site on the far western edge of Vancouver. Before British Columbia was colonised by the British in 1858, the area on which the park was built was used by indigenous people for thousands of years. Now it was completely manicured, peaceful, and being cycled around by tourists and locals on push bikes. I circled the perimeter road myself, before taking Lions Gate Bridge across Vancouver Harbour, landing on the north side of the bay.

I traced the Trans-Canada Highway as it ran west along the coast. As I wasn't permitted to take it, due to the engine, and the speed, I took the suburban roads running parallel instead, passing beautiful sea-view houses that reminded me of those in Sydney, the way they'd sit up high, looking down on the water, with perfect views.

From there the road, and the land, turns ninety degrees, almost like riding around the outside curve of a bent elbow, the road now pointing north, following the edge of an inlet known as Howe Sound, named after Admiral of the Fleet, Earl Howe. Just after the curve the interstate becomes a quieter two-lane highway and I rejoined it, leaving the last traces of suburban Vancouver behind.

I was now riding the Sea-to-Sky Highway, a road infamous for the number of people that have died driving along it. The cause was often the bad weather, the unguarded cliff-top drops, the poor visibility or in some cases, the alcohol consumed. It was only in 2010 as part of the bid for the Winter Games to be held at Whistler that the road was finally improved, and so now, high above the water, snakes a smooth and for the most part dual carriageway road, that on this evening was almost entirely free of traffic.

Some forty miles north of Vancouver I stopped in the town of Squamish. There was a Tim Hortons here which, as anyone who has been to Canada will know, is a native chain of coffee shops, selling a variety of doughnuts, bagels, sandwiches and soups. Think of it as a more rustic version of McDonald's, and from this point on it would serve as my resting place when seeking sanctuary from the road. Once more, I would need to travel on the cheap, with the intention again to camp as much as I could.

Beyond Squamish I spotted my first black bear. It was sitting on the top of a bank beside the road, staring at me as I rode by. I was nervous, my fear stemming from a book I'd read in anticipation of my journey to Alaska. The book was called *Bear Attacks*, and written by a man who had studied bears and their attack patterns for many years. The book gave graphic account of the incidents that have happened, and what became of the people involved in them.

The stories were terrifying, with some victims stumbling across a bear and its cub whilst walking a trail and the mother attacking out of defence for her kin. Not everyone managed to get away. There were other stories of grizzly bears actively hunting people while they've been out camping, dragging them from their tents and tearing out eyeballs and chewing off legs. The advice was not to run, but to stand still, not looking the bear directly in the eye and, if attacked, play dead, which sometimes worked and the bear would eventually wander off, but it didn't always work, and then it would be time to fight back; the advice being to go for the eyes.

What surprised me most was the speed at which bears can run. Apparently, a bear at full speed can reach forty miles per hour (so about as fast as my bike), with their acceleration said to be phenomenal.

In a way I wish I'd never read that book, as all it did was instil a fear in me, and so on passing the bear that evening I was quite concerned about what it might do. I watched it intently as I passed on by, its eyes following me as I did so.

Later that evening, when I arrived in Whistler, I was asked if I'd pulled over to take a photograph of the bear, to which I questioned if they were serious or not, and it seemed as though they were. In reality, the chances of being involved in a bear attack are quite rare, with other vehicles and traffic remaining, as it always does, the biggest danger on the road.

Whistler though was lovely; a purpose-built ski resort and village founded in the 1960s, the hotels and shopping district all clustered at the foot of the slopes, the snow well clear of the streets, but up on the mountainside there was still enough for a few more weeks of skiing. In fact, the resort didn't close until the end of May, such was the snow cover up on the mountain. I had a friend working in Whistler, Milene, who I'd met on previous travels. She was now a manager at a hotel here in the resort and was able to get me a luxury room in a central location for a heavily discounted $40.

It was nice to treat myself, the bike parked below in the underground carpark, whilst I took the time to gather my thoughts before the journey north. I was nervous, as once again it felt as though I was taking a giant leap into the unknown, and while I was better prepared and more experienced now, I still felt uneasy knowing that so much uncertainty lay ahead of me. But nerves I think are good for you. They focus the mind, and must mean that you're doing something that will take you forward in life. They are a good indication of a worthy challenge ahead.

I spent two nights in Whistler, even thinking about heading up on the slopes to do some skiing. Instead, I hung around the town centre, sitting in the sun, meeting Milene and her friends for drinks in the evening. It looked to be a great way of spending a winter for those from Europe and Australia wishing to explore a different part of the world; earning some money and making good friends as they did so. When you look around, there are so many opportunities to work overseas and to travel; to Australia, to Canada. It really isn't so difficult if you're interested in doing it, and who knows to where it might lead.

From Whistler I headed north. It felt strange to be heading north, possibly because I'd spent so many miles of this adventure heading west (all the way from Australia), and now I was pushing towards the summit, along a different trajectory, the sun passing overhead, from right to left, not from behind and to the front. It felt like the temporary scrambling of my internal compass.

Just outside Whistler I stopped to look back at the town, and take a photo of the red bike in front of the crisp blue lake, the snow-topped ski mountains behind it. It was around 7am and still quite chilly. I was wearing all of the clothes I had with me, but knew that soon the day would thaw, and once more the temperatures would soar.

From the shores of the lake, the road began to climb and climb, circling Cayoosh Pass, before reaching a peak of 1,275 metres. Compared to what I'd ridden in India, Pakistan and Colorado, this was of no real altitude, but with the freshly rebuilt engine, and the steepness of the incline, I couldn't help but feel nervous, with little choice but to leave the engine in first gear as this poor old bike – Dorothy – weighed down with all my gear, chugged her way up the mountain, the road running between a towering chasm of pine trees.

Until the 1970s there wasn't even a road running through these parts. Prior to that, the terrain was deemed too steep for the building of such a thing, although when James Duffy, a Royal Engineer, mapped these parts back in 1859, his intention had always been to clear a route through. More than a century later, the road was finally laid.

A lake was named after him, Duffy Lake, the road eventually leading me along its shoreline, my impulse being to stop and savour another early morning moment. I parked the bike down by the water's edge, and what grabbed me most was the way in which the land, the trees and the snow-capped mountains were all reflected in the water, creating a perfect mirror image.

The world too was very quiet out here. There was an occasional passing of a pickup truck or a timber lorry, but nothing else of much distinction. Perhaps it was the scale of the place, as all of a sudden you realise you've entered a grand wilderness, with a road just so happening to be running right through the heart of it. This leads to a tendency towards paranoia, thinking of breakdowns, accidents and bears, and what you would do if any of them happened. Generally, you're best trying not to think of such things.

In the town of Lillooet, some eighty miles to the north-east of Whistler, a man I met at a gas station was kind enough to give me a can of bear spray, something not always easy to buy as there are questions over its legality. The man worked on the land and so carried a few spare cans in his truck. The can he gave me was a few months out of date, though we figured it would still do the job.

Bear spray is like regular Mace, though with greater distance, designed to deter the bear should it look to attack, or come too close for comfort. The book I'd read advised carrying a can of the spray, though you need to be careful when spraying it, especially if the bear is upwind, as the Mace will just blow back at you. Even so, I was grateful to the man for offering it me, tucking it within easy reach inside that same Indian tank bag given to me by Nancy and James all the way back in Manali, now four years and some eighteen thousand miles ago.

I heard from them both sporadically, understanding that after their trip through India on a Royal Enfield together, James had gone to New Zealand on a working holiday visa and enjoyed it so much he'd stayed, becoming a resident having been granted his own New Zealand passport. Nancy, meanwhile, moved back to Germany, writing screenplays for TV shows and generally trying to figure out the meaning of life, and how she best contends with it.

As for Lillooet, I read later how it was once one of the main population centres of the St'at'imc, an indigenous tribe also known as the Lillooet Nation. Lillooet was also at the heart of the Fraser Canyon Gold Rush from 1858 to 1859, when it reckoned to be the largest town west of Chicago and north of San Francisco. Situated on an open plain, enjoying scorching hot days in the summer and bitter cold days in winter, the town was now much quieter. It was difficult to imagine it as a thriving gold rush town. From that to this. It made me think of Detroit and how such places expand and contract, just as Lillooet did, almost a century and a half ago. The rise and fall of towns, and empires, I suppose.

From Lillooet, Highway 99 continues along the valley until it meets the junction with the Cariboo Highway, the main artery road heading north. The road I had taken through Whistler to this point was the scenic route and I was fascinated how the landscape changed so quickly, from the frosty alpine mountains of Whistler and the area around, to this stretch north of Lillooet, which was much more open and barren. It was almost as though I was back in the prairies of Kansas; even the temperature was nice and warm.

The Cariboo Highway led me all the way to Williams Lake, the biggest town in the region. It was founded in 1860 and acted as the meeting point of two roads on the gold rush trail. I did nothing but pass through Williams Lake, stopping only for gas and refreshments.

I talked with two local men at the gas station, one of them warning me

243

about the bears. It seemed that everyone I met wished to warn me about the bears. It was the same script as I'd had back in Australia, though there it was the snakes, the spiders, the crocodiles and the Aboriginals I was to be mindful of. Here it was the bears.

***

I covered a total of 321 miles this day, taking me all the way from Whistler to the town of Quesnel, a place that once claimed to have the largest gold pan in the world, and which now survives on tourism and logging. The town appears from nowhere, you suddenly come upon it as it is camouflaged so successfully by the landscape.

I had a friend living in Quesnel, a lady by the name of Danielle, who had read of my first trip and kept abreast of my movements ever since via Facebook. She taught at the local college and, having seen that I would be passing through her town, had invited me to camp down for the night, which I was grateful for, as it served as another beacon on the horizon to which I could head towards.

Sadly I was a little agitated that night, and the following morning, not proving to be the best of company. I have to concede that the mask does slip at times, and the impatient, tetchy and sometimes morose character comes out. I don't like it when it does that, but I find it increasingly hard to hide and so just have to go with it, and do my best to be pleasant and gracious in the meantime.

I believe this is why I avoided many invitations of accommodation from people online, especially on that initial trip across America, as I just didn't fancy wearing the mask on an evening, even if it meant sleeping in dried-up river beds instead. Perhaps it's a fear of not living up to the expectations people have of us, so avoiding those situations all together. What I mean by that is people probably expect a happy-go-lucky adventurer, and I'm just not always like that and I didn't wish to disappoint them, or spend all evening acting. That trip across America would certainly have been a lot easier had I accepted these invitations.

Danielle rode a bike herself, a much bigger model than mine. She planned on riding it up to Alaska one day. She just needed that final push to get her over that first hurdle. It was then heart-warming to hear a little later that she had in fact done that very thing, not many months after my flying visit. She'd ridden her bike up to Alaska.

It would be unfair to take any credit for that; Danielle was obviously on the cusp of doing it herself. It was just nice to think that the passing through of Dorothy had given her that final nudge, to have seen this tiny little bike and know where it had come from, and know where it was heading to, and to think, 'well, if that can do it, then so can I.'

From here I followed the Cariboo Highway in the direction of Prince George, a town at which I would have a decision to make. To continue north would take me to Dawson Creek and the start of the Alaska Highway. Or I could turn left, taking a slightly longer and more remote route along the Cassiar Highway. That route would involve fewer towns, gas stations and services, but ultimately leads to the same place, rejoining the Alaska Highway up in the Yukon Territory, some 1,000 miles north of here.

At any other time I might have considered the more remote option, but I think now, with the bike as old as she was, and not running as well as she could (though thankfully still running), I considered it more sensible to take the more populated route, in case things went wrong and I needed some help along the way. Besides, to ride the Alaska Highway had a certain appeal about it, and just felt instinctively that it was the right path to take.

That day riding out from Quesnel I vividly remember going through everything that had brought me to this point, almost as though my past was laid out in front of me as I rode along. From travelling to Australia on a working holiday visa all those years ago, meeting a girl at speed dating, coming home, going back, trying to make it work for nine months, failing, getting on my bike and riding home, realising what I'd lost, missing it dearly, writing that first book, becoming chained to the past, finding myself on a downward spiral, not knowing how to get back up, crying, punching, wrecking, until Rob and Greg turned up; back on the bike, to New York City, across the guts of America, to San Francisco, Seattle, back on my feet, home to England, job, stability, time to breathe, then back to Seattle, to complete this, to complete this six-year episode of my life. And now I was here; slowly working my way up to Alaska.

Chapter Twenty
The Alaska Highway

Having stayed the night in a dingy cabin behind the gas station at Mackenzie Junction, travelling north-east along the John Hart Highway, I finally landed in Dawson Creek, a frontier town sadly not the same place as the TV show of the same name. It still felt like an important place to be arriving at, the town marking the official start of the Alaska Highway; the main artery that runs through the rest of Canada and up into Alaska.

In its early days the town was nothing more than a small farming community in the centre of these windy northern plains. It grew in 1932 when the Northern Alberta Railway was extended, then exploded in 1942 when it was suddenly decided that a road connecting Alaska with the rest of the United States was needed to counteract a potential strike on the state by the Japanese in the midst of the Second World War.

Without a road, America wouldn't be able to send supplies and equipment up to Alaska, and so, in just nine short months and using a workforce of around 11,000 military troops (a third of which were African American), a road from here in Dawson Creek to Fairbanks in Alaska was built, work commencing on the 8th March 1942.

The road eventually totalled a distance of 1,700 miles, built at an average of six miles per day, and cut through the savage wilderness of Canada and Alaska. The men had to fight against the frost, the terrain and the wildlife, with the road completed on the 20th November 1942. It was a staggering achievement of engineering and manpower, with Dawson Creek the supply town into which everything was initially sent: men, machinery and equipment, with some of the men deciding to stay there once the road was completed.

The main industries now are tourism, oil and gas, agriculture and retail. At the height of the summer season it is the place where convoys of motorhomes gather, before making the long slog north. This being so early in the season I would thankfully be missing the stampede, much preferring that the roads would be quiet, and lonely, and that I would have them largely to myself. It all added to the sense of adventure.

One of the reasons so many gather here in Dawson Creek and head north together is for a greater sense of safety. I'd even heard that some Americans won't travel to Alaska as they aren't permitted to carry their guns through Canada, and don't wish to travel through this wilderness unarmed. To think that Gary, the 77-year-old cyclist I met back on the shores of Lake Erie, came though here on a pushbike and lived to tell the tale.

In Dawson Creek I stayed at Mile 0 Campsite, a site on the edge of the town, the zero representing our position at the start of the Alaska Highway. There weren't many others camped here. In fact, I'd heard that many of the tourist facilities north weren't even open yet, due to the late breaking of spring and it being so early in the season. There were mixed reports on this, though I was sure it was going to be okay.

Two of the few other travellers on the campsite were Jack and Renee, a retired couple (though they didn't look so old) from Wisconsin, travelling up to Alaska to work on a campsite just outside of Anchorage. They had sold their house and bought a huge motorhome, which they were now travelling and living in. It was a fabulous thing, with enough space in the rear for Jack's Harley Davidson, with a ramp so that he could ride the bike right up into the back of the motorhome.

The bike was a classically styled Harley Davidson, with a huge white fairing and a custom paint job; the panels painted white with the image of a bear sprayed on the front fender, and a barbed wire motif wrapping around the rest of the panel work. It was a nod to Jack's past as an unsavoury character: part of biker gangs, involved in violence and other unpleasant things, then finding religion and becoming a different man; a better man as he saw it.

He was certainly imposing; tall and stocky, with a thick moustache and beard, as well as a pair of fists you wouldn't wish to be on the end of. Yet at the same time he was such a gentle soul, who I think had finally found some peace in life. We talked in great depth about many things, the pair of us almost welling up at times, such was the connection.

It was exciting to hear of their plans to spend the summer up in Alaska working on the campground in exchange for free board, before returning home in the winter and then planning on doing it again the year after, and the year after that. The world was their oyster now, and with the motorhome they lived like turtles, with their home on their backs. There was talk of me putting the bike in the back of the motorhome and riding up with them to Anchorage, but as always it would have felt like cheating, as enjoyable as it would undoubtedly have been.

In preparation for the journey north I picked up a cheap pair of Wellington boots from the Walmart at the far end of town, along with a five-litre fuel can just in case the distances between gas stations were too far for what I could carry in the tanks. I also picked up waterproof fishing gloves in case of relentless rain, a survival blanket for the cold, spare oil, and some Tupperware boxes to keep all my electronic gear dry, as those Indian panniers were far from waterproof, especially with the number of tears in them now.

Otherwise, I just spent a few days hanging around the town, taking the bike down to the Alaska Highway sign to have a photograph with it, eating breakfast in a local diner where the chatty waitress would go around the tables endlessly re-filling coffee cups, like they do in the movies; the type of place locals dine every morning before heading off to work in their pickup trucks.

In another cafe I met a local girl named Andi, who gave me a walking tour of the town one evening, the pair of us walking for miles, from one end of town to the other. Andi was only nineteen years of age but she had a wise head on her shoulders and a strength about her personality that made me think she'll go far, and do well in life.

Andi was of First Nation descent, and we talked briefly about how that was, and how she saw the world, and what she'd encountered. Of course, the past always plays a part in the present, with it impossible to forget that her ancestors were here first, and the gold prospectors and other settlers came second. Attempts at reconciliation have recently been made. This to me is a good sign of man; that we can be unjust, and take what we like, but over time recognise our failures in doing that, and go some way to making amends, even if the clock can never be turned back completely. It's a start at least.

***

Finally came time to load up and head out of town, riding north along the Alaska Highway. I was daunted by the prospect of this. It felt like stepping on to a trail that you knew would take you through a very cold and lonely place. I believe that's why I stayed those few extra days. I was simply letting the pressure build until I could hold it back no longer, letting the inevitable explosion propel me out of town and along the first few miles of the road, like a rocket that had been lit by its own impatience at wishing to reach the sky.

Jack and Renee had left an hour or so earlier, the suggestion being that I go and see them on their campsite up in Anchorage, some 1,500 miles to the north of Dawson Creek, when I finally landed. I expected such a distance to take me no more than five days, as with nothing much to detour for, and no real attractions or distractions along the way, I would be able to cover a decent number of miles everyday, much as I'd done on the route through the Australian Outback; just keep heading for the horizon and count the miles as you go.

A short distance out of Dawson Creek I took a quick detour on to an old stretch of the original Alaska Highway (the route of the road has evolved over the years), in order to ride across the Kiskatinaw Bridge; one of the last remaining curved wooden bridges in the world. Built in 1942 and taking nine months to complete, it's also one of the longest, at 531 feet. The bridge was finally made redundant in 1978, when its weight limit of 25 tonnes was deemed insubstantial. The road was diverted a different way, and a new bridge was built.

The Kiskatinaw Bridge was a sight to behold, the way it organically emerged from one bank of this gentle valley – a white water river at the bottom – and across, in an arching manner, to the other side. Built out of wood, you're able to look over the side at all the girders and legs that hold it up from the valley floor. I didn't linger long, just time to take some photographs and savour the moment, remaining alert as I was still paranoid about bears, half expecting one to jump out of the bushes at any moment. Stupid really; bears can't cross bridges, can they?

What I remember most about this day, apart from the bridge, was the rain. It was relentless. For hour upon hour I was riding into it, with all of my waterproof clothing on, and because my helmet was open-faced, I still wore the handkerchief across my face, it bogging with water and proving almost impossible to breathe through at times, the material suctioned against my lips and my nose. I would like to say it was unpleasant, this long day in the cold rain, but somehow I enjoyed it; one of those masochistic battles with the road, a case of putting your head down and ploughing on through.

There is something masochistic about these endeavours. They have to be hard or there wouldn't be a point in doing them. And if they become too easy then you do what you can – perhaps subconsciously – to make them hard again. Perhaps they are instead intended as periods of self

251

punishment and self flagellation. This is the point that some people find difficult to understand, questioning why you would do such a thing. But I think sometimes you need that test, and that process to go through. The harder a journey is, the more you seem to get out of it.

***

I arrived that evening in the town of Fort Nelson (named after British naval hero Horatio Nelson and founded in 1805 as a fur trading post), having covered some 282 miles that day. I was cold and wet, looking for somewhere to sleep and being directed to a campsite at the top end of town. I was the only person in a tent; the others that night were all in motorhomes.

The campsite had a restaurant made out of old wooden beams, the inside like a nineteenth century saloon. For dinner I ordered poutine, a traditional Canadian dish consisting of chips, with chicken, smothered under a blanket of curdled cheese. It tasted worse than it sounds. I ate half of it, and saved the rest for breakfast.

It was cold in the tent that night. I slept in most of my clothes. The bike was parked close by outside, the Wellington boots upturned over the top of the wing mirrors to allow the water to drain out. I threw the tarpaulin over the bike to keep the sheepskin seat cover dry (the same one that I'd had since Caboolture), waking the next morning, crawling out into the cold air and warming myself with a coffee bought from the restaurant, while finishing the leftovers of last night's poutine.

The wilderness really set in from here on in. It was unimaginable to think what it must have been like back when they were carving out the road through this once uncharted wilderness. The rise and fall of the terrain, the wildlife, the mountains, the snow and the ice. Then the years that followed, the road improved but still not paved, people driving along this route in their 1970s cars and trucks. What an adventure that must have been; no mobile phones or sophisticated 4x4s. I gathered there were more gas stations and roadhouses back then, some of them visibly closed by the roadside now, slowly decomposing as nature retook its land. It was the same atmosphere as crossing the Australian Outback, another place I'd so dearly loved passing through.

Sixty miles out of Fort Nelson the road steadily climbs out of the valley you previously entered, rising to a point where a big gravel clearing has been made, with a wooden platform offering incredible views of the Muskwa River Valley below.

It was a spectacular sight, with a carpet of dark green fir trees in the foreground, only recently starting to take on some colour following a cold and brutal winter. Beyond that snow appears on the ground as the terrain on the other side of the valley increases in altitude, forming a crescendo of jagged mountains, met bluntly by a puffy grey and cloudy sky, the type you might see if snow loomed heavy in the air.

I shared this magical sight with several people who stopped that morning to see it for themselves: a couple in a car, pulling a massive trailer, relocating up to Alaska with all of their belongings; then another man travelling solo in an old German car.

This man was tall, wearing blue jeans, a checkered flannel shirt and a thick grey beard, easily in his seventies and with a very calm and easy-going manner about him. He told me how he lived in a cabin in the woods, deep in the heart of Alaska, and was now driving down to Seattle to visit his children, and their children.

He told me a story about a bear he encountered outside his cabin recently, it coming too close for comfort. The man went inside to get his rifle, the bear charged as he emerged, and the man brought it down with a single shot between the eyes. I stood and listened to the story, spellbound. It was a tale from a way of life that would sound so alien to most people, but one that had a certain appeal to it. I could have seen myself living up here for a while.

I think it's the vastness of it all; a real sense of entering the last frontier of man, a kinetic energy about everything you encounter and see, almost as though all those nice houses and cars, and everything you've worked for in your life, count for nothing up here, because it's just you, stood face to face with nature. And there's a certain enchantment in that. Alaska really does seem like the last bastion of the nomad, a place for those desperately scrambling to get away from the world.

Not many miles further along the road you come to Tetsa River Lodge, a place that promises the best cinnamon buns in the land. Sadly, the baker was just about to head out in his truck, meaning there were no buns to be bought. The lodge was just like so many rest stops up here: an old wooden building with a diner inside, some with a petrol pump outside, and a series of outhouses for chopped logs and machinery. Then nothing for another fifty miles.

The next one was Toad River Lodge, the ceiling of which was decorated with thousands of trucker hats, an age-old tradition it seems, started way back in sixties when the first trucker nailed his hat to the ceiling. I chatted with the waitress having downed a couple of hot coffees. She was a young Filipino girl, here to work for a few years before being granted full work rights to stay in America.

Much like the two guys back in the Midwest town of Carlinville (on the approach to St. Louis), I couldn't imagine what a culture shock that must have been; from South East Asia to the top end of Canada. Yet she seemed happy here, even staying through the brutal winter months, when there would have been such long periods of heavy snow and darkness, with few different faces passing through.

I continued on through what felt like an endless gorge, the road winding its way along the base of it, hugging a wall of loose rock and shale. There was a purple hue about the landscape, the trees without their fir appearing almost skeletal, and the countryside barren and bleak. There was an infrequent amount of traffic travelling in either direction, just the odd logging and pickup truck, still the endless need to keep one eye on the rear view mirror, just to be certain of there being no vehicles sneaking up from behind.

No matter how remote the terrain is, you never totally disconnect from the task at hand; you're always alert, always ready and reactive to the environment. You have to be, because it's just you up here; no backup, no mobile phone, no breakdown cover or local hospital. You can't afford to have an accident. And, touch wood, I hadn't had any of a serious nature so far, only those buses I'd found myself sandwiched between back in Indonesia. That had been a close call, but since then I had survived relatively unscathed.

The engine felt tired now. The bike felt old and weary, despite the new piston fitted back in Seattle. Poor old Dorothy. In a way, I think she was trying to relay messages to me. If she could talk I imagine she would have said, 'I've almost had enough now, when can we go home?' And I would have said, 'soon Dorothy, soon…'

The road fed me around a beautiful frozen lake, the edges of which were only just beginning to thaw. I stopped briefly to take a photograph. I reasoned that it would be nice to have someone standing next to me to share the moment, ordering a couple of hot chocolates at the next rest stop, going through the photographs taken, laughing about what we saw, and what we'd encountered. It made me wonder sometimes what I was gaining from all this, coming up here alone. But then I remembered; I was trying to find the end of the road, as elusive as that had been proving. It felt as though I was on my way to finding it. I just didn't know where it was just yet.

A pack of wild buffalo greeted me up ahead. They were mammoth things, with thick shabby brown coats, long curling horns and huge humps of fat behind their necks. I wasn't sure if they were dangerous or not. I'd heard moose could be, attacking for no reason and a more real and present danger than bears. Buffalo, however, I just wasn't sure and so rode forward with caution. A motorhome approached from the opposite direction, gently passing the herd. I used that as protection on one side, keeping an eye on the buffalo less than ten feet to my right, nodding at the occupants of the motorhome, and relieved to see the buffalo remain docile in my rear view mirror.

A little later I raced one, the beast initially over the other side of the roadside barrier, then hopping over it as I passed, so that it was now galloping right behind me along the road, thankfully not at a pace I couldn't outrun. I think it was just playing a game of chase, as I was with the rainbows that rose above me that afternoon, getting caught in rain showers that plagued the day. But everything was so crisp and blue, with thick green forest all around – a blanket of wilderness that I was slowly making my way through. Quite simply, it was brilliant out here.

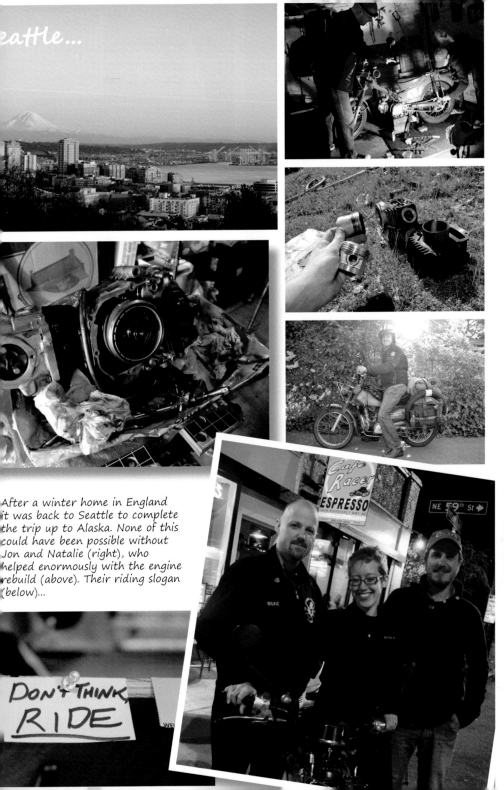

...eattle...

After a winter home in England it was back to Seattle to complete the trip up to Alaska. None of this could have been possible without Jon and Natalie (right), who helped enormously with the engine rebuild (above). Their riding slogan (below)...

DON'T THINK, RIDE

Dawson Creek 48
Fort St John 126
Whitehorse 1526

Despite my early May departure, the
weather was good as I passed into
Canada, travelling up into British
Columbia. Staying in a roadside
guest house (right). The stunning
Duffy Lake (top). Whistler Lake (left).

Dawson Creek signalled
start of Alaska Highway
(left), meeting Jack and
Renee (below) at the
campsite, before pushing
on into the Yukon (right
Sign Post Forest at
Watson Lake (below righ
Putine (mid right) and o
Kiskatinaw Bridge (belov

Growing colder the further north, with lakes still frozen (left) and deep snow on the ground (below). Seth passing on his bike (far left), before meeting him and Calvin at the Teslin roadhouse (left). Crossing the border into Alaska (bottom).

Arriving in Skagway felt like the end of the road, spending a week here, hanging out with Sean (below) and Seth (beneath), before catching the four day inland ferry (bottom) all the way back down to near Seattle and returning home. Journey across the world finally over.

Chapter Twenty One
The Yukon

I arrived that night in the town of Watson Lake, finding it to be a drab little place: one long wide street with a couple of motels and businesses on either side. I wouldn't have stopped here had it not been for the onset of nightfall. There was an RV park at the top end of town, operated by a man originally from Scotland who was not at all pleasant, not initially in any case, being quite blunt about the lack of anywhere else to camp in town.

He told me that to stay at his place I'd have to pay for a pitch on one of his powered motorhome sites. I asked if he'd do me a discount as I only had a one-man tent, but he wouldn't; those were just the rules. Reluctantly I took it, mainly because it had been a long day and I just needed somewhere to settle down for the night and I didn't much fancy bedding down with the bears, the moose and the buffalo.

My tent was set up against a bank of snow. I charged my laptop in the laundry area, sitting in the warmth for a while, before heading over the road to the gas station, only to find it attended by an Englishman out here working for the season. He told me about the problem with drugs and alcohol in the town, a consequence he assumed of the long dark winters, where people need something to turn to. And that's what they tend to turn to, causing massive social implications with no cure yet to be found.

Two other motorcyclists pulled up at the gas station as I paid for my evening snack of peppered beef jerky; a substance I was increasingly beginning to survive on out here. As both riders were on enduro bikes I thought I would introduce myself, and let them know about the campsite I was staying on, in case they needed somewhere to stay for the night. In response, one of them seemed to scowl at me, and then they just went about their business as though I wasn't even there. I caught that their accents were from overseas, I wasn't sure where, though I certainly didn't get a good vibe from them, so I left them to it and wandered up the road to check out Sign Post Forest.

This is Watson Lake's premier tourist attraction, and can be found on the roundabout at the top end of town. It is a strange phenomenon that started way back in 1942, when an American GI working on the Alaska Highway nailed up a sign with his name, the date, and his hometown on it. From there the trend spread, with there now thought to be as many as 80,000 signs, plaques and licence plates nailed to a forest of totem poles, set up in various expanding circles.

It really was an incredible sight, walking through the 'forest,' reading the various messages and memos left by people who had passed through these parts over the last seventy years. Some just carried names and a date, others messages to loved ones, and even long deceased cats. Some messages were scratched into frying pans, written on planks of wood or any writable surface they could find. It made me wonder if the original GI was still alive, and if he'd been back to witness the phenomenon he'd unwittingly started. What a legacy that man had left, without even intending to do such a thing.

Having ridden west out of Watson Lake the following morning, it wasn't long before I was passing the junction where the Cassiar Highway joins the Alaska Highway. The Cassiar is the road I could have taken out of Prince George, a thousand miles ago. What many people do if they're on a return trip to Alaska, is take the Alaska Highway up and the Cassiar Highway back down, or vice versa, just to give them a change of scenery. I was glad I'd stuck to the main route. It was wild enough as it was, with just enough homesteads and stop-off towns to keep you company along the way.

This day was usual. Riding, eating, gas station and riding. I was heading to Alaska, and that's all that I had to do. I was overtaken at one point by another motorcyclist, riding a big Kawasaki trail bike. I waved to the rider as he passed and he waved back, fist pumping the air, his wild hair escaping the back of his helmet and a face of pure thrill. He and his bike slowly faded into nothing as they rocketed along the road, making me wonder who he was and where he was heading to. Another case of sonder perhaps, and much more friendly than the two bikers from the night before.

Some 162 miles out of Watson Lake the road began to descend into the wide expanse of a valley, a great river running through the heart of it. Spanning the river was a sturdy metal bridge, of great length, green in colour, and no doubt surfaced with the same metal grids that covered all the bridges up here. I assume they are to prevent icing, but on a motorbike they are a nightmare to ride across as your front wheel skips and meanders from one groove of the metal grid to the next, making it hard to ride in a straight line.

Before riding down to the bridge I sat up on the rise, a gravel pull-off giving views of the river basin below, with an information board explaining that the small hamlet of buildings on the far side of the riverbank was the community of Teslin, an ancient Indian Reserve – home of the Tlingit First Nation – and a trading post established way back in 1903. You could see why they would build a trading post here; on a bend in the river, shadowed by the mountains around, perfect for hunting and trapping, which apparently is still done by members of the Tlingit First Nation who still live out here.

I stood on a rock to take better pictures of the view before me, starting to feel a real chill in the air now, the temperature certainly dropping in the 1,500 miles I'd been riding since leaving Seattle. I was now in the Yukon

Territory, having crossed the border between here and British Columbia not far out of Watson Lake.

The Yukon is the smallest of Canada's three federal territories, with Whitehorse the territorial capital and Yukon's only city. Long before the arrival of Europeans, central and northern Yukon was populated by First Nations people. Coastal and inland First Nations had extensive trading networks. European incursions into the area only began early in the 19th century with the fur trade, followed by missionaries and the Western Union Telegraph Expedition. By the 1870s and 1880s gold miners began to arrive. The territory's population of 33,000 live in an area the size of Sweden, making it barely populated at all.

I rode down towards the community of Teslin, across the bridge of doom, wobbling and weaving along that metal grid, ready to stick a leg out should I need to. A homestead had been built on the other side of the river, offering a pod of petrol pumps, a small museum and a busy little diner. It was only 2pm and the perfect spot for a rest break after a full morning on the road. Filling up with gas, I met a man with a van load of motorcycles heading down to America, who was kind enough to buy me a coffee having heard all about where this little red bike had come from. He seemed enthralled, having owned a bike like this during his childhood. It gave him the chance to reminisce.

Inside the homestead I also met Calvin, a 24 year old from Tennessee, riding down from Alaska on a KLR650, the same sort of bike that had passed me earlier in the day. Calvin was a handsome chap, square jaw, southern drawl, and as polite as they come.

He had ridden up to Alaska at the end of the previous year, leaving his bike there while he went home and worked on his family's farm in Tennessee. He'd recently returned to Alaska, collected his bike, and was now heading back south, towards Seattle, where he planned on loading the bike on to a cargo boat and sailing it west to Russia. From there he would ride across Russia, also through Mongolia, heading in the direction of Europe.

We spent an age talking about his trip and the time frame he had, which wasn't so long, but he was certainly making the most of the time that he did have. I gave him my email address and told him that if he ever needed anything in England, or just wanted to drop by, that I should be back by the time he makes it there.

Odd to see how the world is connected in that sense; how Calvin can be going around it in one direction, while I go back in the other, and a little later we both end up at the same spot; making you realise just how small the world is, or at least how interconnected and accessible most parts of it are.

It was here that I also met Seth, who turned out to be the guy that overtook me earlier in the day, 'yopping' and hollering as he did so. Off the bike, Seth was a tall and strapping twenty-something; long, curly hair with plenty of volume, kept beneath a dusty old train driver's hat. He also wore a set of old dusty dungarees and had the appearance of a beatnik vagabond, the type that might previously have hitched a ride across America on the rail carts.

He too was from the south, or at least sounded like he was, a real long drawl and a carefree manner. Seth was just one of those people who commands the attention of any room he enters, explaining how he was heading up to Alaska to work on a fishing boat for the summer and planning on sleeping on the beach in a tent the whole time. He was something of a hippy and a nomad at heart, but in many ways all three of us were that day; me, Seth and Calvin, sat around the table drinking hot coffee in this pleasant Yukon community of Teslin.

We talked about my trip, and their trips, and about life on the road, and what had brought us here. The hours flew by, we got through some coffee, everyone trying and failing to flirt with the waitress, who was attractive and didn't she know it. We finally all conceded that none of us wished to ride any further that day and that maybe we should just set up camp in Teslin. Calvin and Seth had both wild camped through much of Alaska and the Yukon, just heading off into the forest and pitching a tent.

With all the talk of bears it was not something I'd ever thought of doing, and I admired their recklessness greatly.

It was suggested that we all go off and wild camp this night, but with a campsite behind the homestead, with views across a frozen lake, I talked them into camping there instead, ten dollars covering the lot of us.

I suppose I was at the opposite end of my adventure to what they were. They were on the leading edge of it, their hearts and souls full of fuel, so camping wild was very much a part of their spirit, whereas I felt like I was nearing the end of my adventure and didn't need the wilderness quite so much, hence why I was happy to stay on a campsite. Besides, I was a little older than they were, and a great deal wearier.

We set up our tents as close to the lake as we could get them, only a low timber fence and a short stretch of soggy marshland and we could have been swimming, though with the mist descending and the light leaving the sky, it would have been a very cold swim. It was at this point that two more bikes arrived, the pair of them pulling into the campsite and heading over in our direction. I recognised them from the night before; the two unfriendly guys who had scowled at me at the gas station.

They turned out to be Israeli soldiers, on leave from the army and spending their extended break on a motorcycle trip around Alaska. They joined us in putting up their tents down by the lake. I wasn't so keen to have them join us at first, but what can you say? Half the problem was my own prejudice. I'd encountered Israeli travellers before, mainly up in the north of India, where many of them seem to head having completed their two years of compulsory military training, which to me seemed to make them militant, and exclusionary, never really mingling with anyone else.

It turned out to be a great evening. The Israeli soldiers, whose names I now don't remember, had bought a huge fresh salmon from a fisherman earlier in the day, wrapped in paper, storing it in one of their pannier sacks. They also carried broccoli, sweet potatoes, ranch dressing, and a whole assortment of spices in a rack, all in their motorcycle panniers. They were kind enough to share their food, and having cooked it over a roaring log fire we all sat down with plates of grub much better than any I'd eaten in a long time.

I got the impression that they didn't think much of me either, not at first in any case. At times they came across as quite intimidating, and dismissive of me travelling on the shit bike that I was. They would joke and laugh about me in Hebrew, and I didn't like the vibe very much. Finally they asked where I'd come from on it, and when I told them Australia they didn't believe me. But when I finally managed to convince them it was true, they discovered a new-found respect for me, and just wanted to hear how I'd done it. Strange how they had no time for me until that point.

In return, they told stories of how, during their time in the army, they'd been sent to guard the border with Palestine after people had tried to sneak through it the previous nights. The following night the soldiers claimed they were ready for them, gloating that they'd gunned down and killed the people who'd tried to come through. For me, living a life relatively free of violence, it was like hearing a story about a different world, one that I couldn't comprehend, despite my journey across half of it.

It reminded me of something the assistant in the army surplus store, back in Seattle, had told me when I was picking up supplies for this journey north. He'd said to me, following a quip I made about the necessity of war for keeping his shop well stocked, that, 'You can't have peace without war', or, 'Without war, you can't have peace.' One of the two…

His comment stopped me in my tracks and had me question whether what he said was true or not. And I couldn't help but conclude that maybe it was, as perverse as that might sound. To enjoy peace, we must have war. I'd be less inclined to agree with him were it not for the fact that, despite knowing how awful wars are, we still seem to engage in them, and find appetite for them, whether they be wars on a national scale, or even those we encounter in relationships, or in our own heads. Without war things would be stable, and I don't think that is man's inherent state. We seem to crave change and forward motion, and forward motion seems to bring about conflict, and so we pit ourselves against one another (or against ourselves). There is also good money to be made from war, whether it be at national or corporate level, or at the army surplus store selling cast-offs. That's not to say I agree with any of this. It's more just what I've come to accept, though not readily.

The following morning we all crawled out of our sleeping bags and lazily got up and packed. There didn't seem any urgency to this day, no desire to take off in any direction. Coffee helped perk us up, and by 11am we were all set to hit the road, apart from the two Israeli chaps, who were going to stay an extra day and chill out in Teslin. Calvin was heading south, in the direction of Seattle, whereas Seth and I were heading north, in the direction of Alaska.

It had been a great experience meeting them all that evening, making me question the way I'd been travelling the last 33,000 miles, and wondering if perhaps I ought to slow down a bit, and do things in a more relaxed manner, as they were doing. I'd raced across the world, desperate to either go, or to get there. Now I saw how others travelled, and I quite liked the look of it.

As it was, Seth and I decided to ride together for a while, perhaps as far as Skagway, some 150 miles to the west. It was like riding with Vermin all over again, expecting him to get fed up after five minutes and come racing past telling me he'll see me when I eventually get there. But in fairness to Seth, he rode alongside for a good few hours, travelling at less than thirty miles per hour for long periods of time, simply because of the wind and the inclines that really pushed us back.

It was great to have some company on the road though; to have someone in your rear view mirror to point things out to, or to pull over and chat to when you want to find a hot coffee. Equally, someone else in the frame to photograph, instead of just taking pictures of you and the bike, which I often tended to do.

Seth did finally get fed up, and about seventy miles out of Skagway pulled over to tell me he would go ahead and see me at the destination some time later that evening. I said that was absolutely fine, it allowing

272

me to relax a little, as ultimately I do tend to grow quite tense if I feel that I am holding someone up. I watched as the black dot of Seth and his bike grew smaller and smaller, before disappearing from sight all together. Back alone, in this vast empty wilderness.

I was tired and weary now, running on fumes, running on empty. I'd thought much about where this journey might end and whether or not I'd make it up to Anchorage or to Prudhoe Bay at the very top of Alaska. Part of me thought that I should, given that I was already up this way, and the other part of me couldn't give a damn, because I was fast approaching the point where I finally felt that I'd ridden far enough, and to ride any further would only have been to say that I had done. It was a conundrum that was beginning to plague my thoughts as I rode.

I hit a junction where the Alaska Highway carries straight ahead and the road to Skagway veers off to the left, along Tagish Road, with Skagway some fifty miles at the end of it. To carry on going straight would take me to the town of Whitehorse, but for whatever reason I felt that left to Skagway was the right way to go, perhaps for no other reason than to catch up with Seth again.

The road now wound through the forest. I remember it being beautifully surfaced, and sheltered from the wind. After a decent distance you cross a river, passing through the community of Tagish, where summer businesses were starting to prepare for the onslaught of visitors from the south; a few restaurants, a bed and breakfast, and a campsite.

A little further along I arrived at the slightly bigger community town of Carcross, or Caribou Crossing as it was originally known. The town was once a fishing and hunting camp for Inland Tlingit and Tagish people, until the Klondike Gold Rush of the late nineteenth century changed the face of it, and the name of it, forever.

The town was now a haven for tourists out of Skagway, ferried out on buses to have a look around the replica buildings of the past. What a strange development the town had seen; from First Nation land, to be claimed by gold prospectors, and now to be swamped by the trade of tourism, the gold now being brought *to* the town in the form of tourist buses, rather than taken *away* from it in wagons.

I ran into Seth here, grabbing a coffee and a cake with him from the local German bakery. The ladies in there made a real fuss of us. I guess we were a novelty act, two desperadoes on motorbikes, in tatty old clothes and a reckless abandon. Normally the bakery would be busy with tourists on organised tours, but this was mid-afternoon, and so most of them would have been back on their tourist coaches, returning to Skagway. We met a nomadic traveller here, pedalling on a bicycle from town to town, everything he owned in bags and boxes on the bike, a bit like the gold prospector I met back in Pahrump. I felt for the man. It looked like he needed some help, though he probably would say the same about us.

***

Seth rode off once more into the distance, it now just 65 miles to Skagway. I'll never forget that afternoon of riding. It's fair to say both me and Dorothy were knackered. She felt tired and fatigued, barely able to haul us up these hills, and I'd long since stopped getting off and pushing. The wind was at our face, the rocks were to our right, and the vast expanse of those icy cold lakes dominated the views to the left. Then the road would climb and climb, snow by the roadside thickening, almost floor to ceiling high in some places. Fortunately it was dry and cold, a blue sky horizon, then the Canadian border post, surprisingly unattended, meaning that we could ride into the no-man's-land between Canada and America without anyone even stopping us.

To say that Skagway is in Alaska is something of a technicality, because when you look on the map it looks more likely to be part of Canada, but that's just the way the borders were formed. Still, at the top of the snow-covered pass, in the midst of no-man's-land, you are suddenly greeted by a sign declaring your passage into Alaska. It was a fantastic sight: Alaska, that place I'd half-heartedly set out to conquer when embarking on that trip across America. I knew I'd make it to San Francisco, but I was never quite sure I would make it this far north. But I was here, feeling a huge sigh of relief, and a little bit of weight lifting from my shoulders.

A pair of girls stopped to have their photo taken with the sign. We took one another's pictures and then they left, soon to be replaced by a young chap named Sean. Sean was only in his twenties, driving a battered old Toyota saloon car, loaded to the brim with camping gear, the boot full of dry foods, as that summer he planned on going off-grid, hiking solo into Alaska's various National Parks and heading off *Into The Wild* for a while, which, as anyone who has seen that movie or read the book will know, is a potential pathway to misery and doom.

Sean was up for it through, and in front of that big Alaska sign we both posed, smiling like Cheshire cats. I admired Sean a lot, he was at the foot of a great adventure, and planning on sleeping in his car in Skagway that night, such was his meagre budget.

The border post into America lay not far beyond this. I was asked the usual sequence of questions: who I was, where I was going, when I was going home, and how long I planned on being in America. I told the man that I had to be back in England in two weeks time, that I had a return flight home and that for now I was just heading to Skagway for a look around. He seemed satisfied with this and waved me on my way. From here it was downhill all the way into Skagway, the point at which this adventure finally comes to an end.

Chapter Twenty Two
Skagway

If you look down at your outspread fingers, imagining them to be the land, and the air around them to be the water, then you will find Skagway right in the crease of where two fingers meet. The neighbouring town of Dyea is in the next crease along, but it now lies abandoned, almost vanished without trace, after the deep water port of Skagway became the most prominent town in the area way back at the turn of the twentieth century, back when the Klondike Gold Rush struck, making Dyea redundant.

The area was previously inhabited by the Tlingit people from prehistoric times, living here for thousands of years. Then the Klondike Gold Rush occurred in the late nineteenth century, bringing hordes of prospectors heading to the gold fields another 500 miles to the north. Skagway emerged to supply the rush and served as a drop-off point for steamboats bringing the prospectors up from San Francisco and Seattle. At the height of the gold rush, as many as 1,000 prospectors would pass through the town each week, many of them failing to return, such was the brutal nature of the landscape that faced them. Two books by Jack London, *The Call of the Wild* and *White Fang*, give an insight into this period and are well worth a read.

It was hard to imagine, as I rode into town on this old motorbike, that little more than a hundred years before this was a lawless place, 'little better than hell on earth,' as one person described Skagway at the time. And now, in the space of one long lifetime, it had evolved into a peaceful, quaint, and immensely pretty town, with just 900 people living there year round. A further 900,000 souls visit on day trips every year, with an endless flow of cruise ships docking in the harbour, disembarking their cargo of passengers to spend the day wandering around the shops, or heading off on day excursions, before getting back aboard and sailing off.

I don't know what it was about the town, but when I got here, I felt like I'd made it. I felt like I'd finally 'arrived'. And despite intentions to move on the following day, I instead stayed an entire week, right up to the point at which I needed to leave. The reason I stayed so long is because I felt at peace here, and no longer felt the need to keep running to the next place. I think, finally, I'd exhausted myself of that, and was just content now to enjoy the place the road had brought me to. It almost felt like I'd been riding the last thirty-odd thousand miles solely in search of Skagway, and it was good to have finally made it here.

I stayed at the Alaskan Sojourn Hostel, in actual fact the beautiful home of Janilyn and Gary, which they just happened to have opened up to passing waifs and strays. The wooden house, with a big glass-fronted veranda, stood on a corner, eight blocks back from the harbour, with a big tree in the garden, and a front door that was always open; a system devised so that if you arrived without having made a booking, then you could see if there was a bunk available, put your name down for it, and check in, even if no one else was home. That alone was enough to set it aside as a place you knew you could relax.

Seth was also in town, staying on an old friend's couch, just a few blocks further out than the hostel. He too planned on staying only a few days yet ended up staying for a week as well. It was something to do with the weather further north, which meant that he was in no hurry to get up to his fishing boat duties outside of Anchorage. Instead, the pair of us hung out that week, getting to know the locals, wandering the streets like two weary old amigos from out of town.

It's said that there are two stories in life. The first, a boy leaves his village. And the second, a man walks into town. I guess that's what it felt like for us two wandering hillbillies.

We'd wander down to the docks to watch the cruise liners sail in and out, or we'd go for a beer in a bar called Red Onion, decked out like a saloon you might see in a vintage western movie, the waitresses dressed up in period clothes of petticoats and garters. It was more authentic than it sounds.

Skagway itself still consisted of the same wooden buildings that would have been there from the start, some of them brightly coloured, one of them covered with white sticks, nailed to the building in various patterns. The first three or four blocks back from the harbour were predominately made up of jewellery or gift shops, but after that it was a mix of everything, with some great little cafes and bakeries, and even a shop devoted to Sarah Palin, though sadly I was no longer wearing the bracelet given to me by Jeanie and Gerald, having lost it back in England.

Seth and I somehow found ourselves invited to the free showing for locals of the town's long standing 'Days of 98' musical production. It exists as a nod to the town's past, telling the story of the legendary Soapy Smith, a scoundrel and racketeer who ran the town until he was shot dead in 1898, hence the name of the act. It was a brilliant show, held in the town's old theatre, on chairs that felt like they too dated back a century.

There was one main actor playing Soapy Smith, and three buxom girls playing the whores that were around him at the time. Popcorn was served, and the theatre whooped and cheered.

It was whilst watching the play that we met a team of young people – most of them in their early twenties – who all worked on the White Pass Railway as tour guides and ticket sellers. The train line was originally built to send supplies to the gold fields in the north, but was now used to take passengers from the cruise ships on a day trip to the top of the mountain, and then back down again, at a cost of around $120, something me and Seth could never have afforded.

Having been taken pity on, we were invited to a complimentary ride on the steam train the next day, which proved to be one of the highlights of this entire adventure.

The train line snaked back up the mountain I'd ridden down a few days prior, up towards the border-crossing into Canada, and then back down again. The track passed through numerous dark tunnels, and across rickety old railway bridges made of wood. The snow grew thicker the higher we climbed, the train and all its carriages so long that on the sweeping corners you could look back and see the rear carriage of the train, way off in the distance, steam billowing from the top, and the sound of the whistle ringing out across the valley.

Most people sat inside in the vintage carriages looking out at the views from behind polished glass. Seth and I stood instead out on the deck at the back of the carriage, exposed to the fresh air, able to reach out and touch the snow banks as we passed between them.

Seth had brought a flask of coffee and a bottle of whisky, which he poured into the coffee and drank until he was drunk. This brought him to song, singing old western tunes and ditties at the top of his voice, much to the amusement, or perhaps annoyance, of all those in earshot. Not one for bringing undue attention to myself, I grew embarrassed and in the end had to demand that he calmed down and stopped 'yopping' at the top of his voice. At one point he even got a young Chinese lad 'yopping,' and everyone else who came to the back of the train, he would try to get them to do a 'yop' or a 'yeehaa,' which he performed relentlessly, until the whole mountain shook.

He was such a crazy character, no doubt running from his own demons on that bike of his. He'd previously not ridden a bike; just thinking it would be a good idea and buying one to ride all the way up to Alaska. Later, in town, he stole a tin of sardines from the grocery store, and made a point of making sure I saw him. It was a strange thing to do. And I think he did it because he was trying to push me away, because I liked the guy. We got on well, and I think somewhere, deep down in his subconscious, there was a part of him that just didn't like being liked. But I told him that, and that I wasn't bothered about the stealing of the mackerel, because I really liked Seth, loved him in a way, not in the *Brokeback Mountain* sense, just in my admiration for the way that he was, and I cherished the time I got to spend with him in Skagway. He made Skagway what it was.

I also spent some time with Sean, the guy I'd met back up at the border. He was another nut case, explaining how he'd bought a raft that folded down into a backpack – called a packraft – and that his plan was to hike out into the wilderness for days on end, then find a river, inflate the raft, and float back down to where he'd parked his car. And then move on to the next spot.

I later saw some of his photographs on Facebook; a man on top of a mountain, with the biggest smile I've ever seen on anyone. Then he met a girl, hiking with her for a while, and from what I can gather he really did have the most amazing of summers. I too met someone up here, a girl by the name of Danielle, who worked on the railway line that had taken us to the top of the mountain. It was a pleasant but brief romance of the road. Wave hello, and say goodbye.

Now it was a case of figuring out how to get home to England from here, as I was due back in just over a week to start the job on the magazine. Of course I felt like going AWOL and just not going back, perhaps turning around and riding all the way down to Argentina, as that had been my original plan. But I didn't have the energy or the desire to do that. Or the money. Indeed I was spent, worn out from the road I'd been riding for so long. No, the more time I spent in Skagway, the more I knew that this was as far I was going, and to hell with riding any further.

Besides, to have pushed on to Anchorage, or Fairbanks, or Prudhoe Bay, would involve stepping once again into the real unknown, with no certainty as to what I'd be able to do with the bike, as the quote I'd got for shipping it out of Anchorage had been an incredible three thousand

English pounds, and I couldn't really afford that. Neither could I have brought myself to abandon the bike out here either. It needed to come home with me, for sentiment if nothing else.

That left one main option, and that was to take the four-day ferry from Skagway all the way back down to Seattle, travelling through the inside passage, along the coastline of Alaska, and then Canada, arriving in Seattle, where from there I knew I could quite easily – and much more cheaply – put the bike on a boat back to England and fly there myself. Geographically, it would be going back on myself, but psychologically it would still be moving forward (still running towards the light I suppose), if that makes much sense.

Actually, it was an easier decision to make than I thought it would be. After all, Alaska would still be there next year, and the year after that, and if I'm to do it, I would like to do it properly – learning something from the way Seth, Calvin and the two Israelis travelled – taking it a bit steadier, enjoying it more, exploring it more, and I just didn't have time to do that this time around.

It was then just a case of waiting for the ferry to show up, enjoying the time in Skagway that I was left with; hanging out with Seth and with Sean, even gate crashing a wedding and listening to Gary and Janilyn's son, Lucas, play some amazing self-written songs on guitar. He was a carpenter by trade but pinned to give it all up in search of a career in music. What can you say to that, other than, 'go on, you have to give this a go, you're too good not to.' And I hope by now that he has.

***

There was a ferry sailing on the seventh day of my stay in Skagway, giving me just enough time to travel down the coast, arrive in Seattle, sort out the shipping, and then get myself home in time for the job in England to start. It would be pushing it fine, but it was doable, and I'd realised by now that if you set your sights on something, then somehow, almost without fail, it'll work out in the end.

Strange how the world seems to work like that; with no rhyme or reason, sometimes with just a dash of magic, and those angels and fairies helping you on your way. How many more I'd met on this adventure across America. If life is a fairytale, then these angels and fairies are the characters that guide you on your way, your quest not quite possible without them. And who can say life isn't a fairytale, not when all of us believe in heroes, villains and monsters, at least to some degree.

In my case, I had not rescued the maiden on this mission, but I had slew many dragons, and passed through many enchanted lands, discovering many people afraid of their neighbours, and the village beyond. I had met people who had given me knowledge and gifts, who had pointed me in the right direction and come to my aid when I needed it most.

This is perhaps the same quest as all of us are on in life, with it only the backdrop that changes. Mine had been the road across the world, my transport a motorbike. But the nature of the quest is the same; to find answers and hopefully contentment. We all seem to be in search of those things in one way or another. We are all running towards our own version of the light, however that voyage happens to manifest. I certainly wish you all the very best on your endeavours.

As for the remainder of my voyage, as the ferry gently pulled away from the docks, I stood out on deck and waved Skagway goodbye, certain that I would miss the place, and most of all the people that I'd met there. I remember it to be a beautiful day, with a vibrant blue sky, and it stayed like that for almost the entirety of those four days at sea.

It really was quite astounding, cruising south, along the coast of Alaska, with the mainland to the left, and a chain of islands to the right, guarding you from the open waters of the ocean. Occasionally we'd stop at towns to pick up other passengers, even Juneau, the capital of Alaska, which can't be accessed by land, only by the sea, these ferries the lifeblood of the state.

The best time was at night, when you could sit at the front of the boat, looking out of the windows ahead to where the full moon hung in the sky, chasing it through the night, it casting reflective glows across the water, often as still as a lake. The lights would be dimmed. Other passengers might be sitting nearby, but everyone would be silent, the faint sound of the engine, the faint sense of movement, the lot of us just staring out at the moon and the endless water ahead. And then in the morning the sun would rise, and out on deck we would all gather again, looking out at this enchanting snow-capped land.

I could have slept out on deck, on the sun loungers provided. This is a popular option for those on a tight budget, as the ferry itself wasn't cheap; the best part of a thousand dollars. Instead, I booked a tiny cabin, paying another few hundred dollars (credit card, overdraft, by this time I just didn't care) for the privilege of being able to shut the door behind me, lie on the bed, read a book, have a nap. It was just what I needed having spent so long exposed on the road. All the while Dorothy languished in the hold beneath me, strapped down beside the cars and the lorries, those old Indian pannier sacks hinting at quite a story to be told.

***

I disembarked in Bellingham, ninety miles to the north of Seattle, as this was the closest place to the city you could get off. Also disembarking was a lady in her seventies, about to ride a converted Harley Davidson – now with three wheels – on what she planned to be a three-month tour of the United States. This lady made me think of Gary, the Old Minister, Snow Cat and all the other adventurers of senior years, still out there, doing their thing, not allowing old age to stop them. What a brave thing to be doing, and I wished her well as we went our separate ways.

From Bellingham I rode south along the coast, taking my time, in no rush to get there, winding through pretty little villages and along the water's edge. It was strange now not to be heading towards Alaska. At times I wondered if I'd done the right thing by not pushing on to

Anchorage or to Prudhoe Bay, but as I now know only too well, it's far harder to stop than it is to carry on. And it was time to stop. My whole body ached for it.

In Seattle I called round to see Jon and Natalie, who kindly offered to let me camp in their garden for a few days. Without Jon and Natalie, I don't know if this adventure would even have been possible. It was them who provided the base I needed to get this off the ground and I owe them both tremendously.

As for getting the bike back to England, I contacted Giles, the man who had organised the flying of the bike from London to New York in the first place. He told me it would be much cheaper to send it by boat, so that's what we agreed, it looking likely to cost around £900 by the time I was done. My dad kindly offered to help me out with this one, as I think secretly he was as attached to Dorothy as I was, and he certainly wouldn't have wanted me leaving her there either.

She sure did have an adventure in store; being picked up by a courier van, driven down to LA, loaded on to a boat, sailed down the Pacific Coast until she reached the Panama Canal, through that, and then across the Atlantic Ocean, arriving in England in an anticipated eight to ten weeks time. I on the other hand needed to fly home, leaving the bike in the capable hands of Jon and Natalie, who made sure she got picked up by the delivery guy sometime during the next few days.

As my return flight was out of Anchorage (that's where I thought I'd end up when I booked it) ironically I needed to fly up there first, then catch the plane that would take me home to England, via Iceland, meaning that it was a bit of slog getting home that day.

It was a strange sensation flying back to England, back to my flat, back to my stray cat, back to the end of an adventure. Thankfully it had all fallen into place, and whilst Alaska wasn't quite the euphoric victory I thought it would be, it had done what it needed to do. It had ticked that box, crossed it off the list, which meant that I could go home without anything on the list for a while. I could then stand still for a bit, which I did, starting that job and getting stuck straight into it, putting together a magazine about bikes and people who are leaving their own comfort zones.

Dorothy turned up a few months later. I went to collect her from the docks to the east of London, finding her in a warehouse much like the one I'd left her in all the way back in Indonesia, when trying to get her across to Malaysia.

I look at her and wonder if she has any adventures left in her, and I'm not so sure she has. Then I look at me, and ask, do I have any adventures left in me? And again, I'm not so sure I have. This journey from Sydney to Alaska, a distance of almost 35,000 miles, at an average speed of 37mph, had certainly opened my eyes to the world, and to my own reflection in it. Though in a way, I'd only just scratched the surface, there still so much to see and to learn, though perhaps just not for the time being at least.

Have I stopped running? I guess that is the key question. And the answer to that is probably no. All I've done is learnt how to control that running, and be in charge of it, and run only when the time is right. I certainly have no regrets now, not really. Things have worked out the way they have for the best. Mandy seems happy, and I'm getting there, certainly not punching myself in the face or attacking wooden sheds with pitchforks. Though that darkness will always be a part of me. It's what propels me. And in the future, I'm probably going to be needing that again. In the meantime thanks for riding with me. See you on the road.